"Clearly written and technically sound, this text should be a staple for researchers and methodologists alike. Not only is the text an excellent resource for understanding propensity score analysis, but the author has recognized the messiness of real data, and helps the reader understand and appropriately address issues such as missing data and complex samples. This is extremely refreshing."— **Debbie Hahs-Vaughn, University of Central Florida**

"This book provides an overview of propensity score analysis. The author's introduction situates propensity score analysis within Rubin's Causal Model and Campbell's Framework. This text will be good for the advanced user with previous knowledge of the R language, complex survey design, and missing data."— **S. Jeanne Horst, James Madison University**

"This book provides an excellent definition of propensity scores and the sequential steps required in its application."— **Mansoor A. F. Kazi, University at Albany**

"It is a well-crafted practical book on propensity score methods and features the free software R. I believe many students will like it."— **Wei Pan, Duke University**

"With the use of examples consisting of real survey data, *Practical Propensity Score Methods Using R* provides a wide range of detailed information on how to reduce bias in research studies that seek to test treatment effects in situations where random assignment was not implemented."— **Jason Popan, University of Texas-Pan American**

"This book offers a comprehensive, accessible, and timely treatment of propensity score analysis and its application for estimating treatment effects from observational data with varying levels of complexity. Both novice and advanced users of this methodology will appreciate the breadth and depth of the practical knowledge that Walter Leite offers, and the useful examples he provides."—**Itzhak Yanovitzky, Rutgers University**

Practical Propensity Score Methods Using R

For Cassandra, Thomas, and Jonas

SAGE was founded in 1965 by Sara Miller McCune to support the dissemination of usable knowledge by publishing innovative and high-quality research and teaching content. Today, we publish over 900 journals, including those of more than 400 learned societies, more than 800 new books per year, and a growing range of library products including archives, data, case studies, reports, and video. SAGE remains majority-owned by our founder, and after Sara's lifetime will become owned by a charitable trust that secures our continued independence.

Los Angeles | London | New Delhi | Singapore | Washington DC | Melbourne

Practical Propensity Score Methods Using R

Walter Leite

University of Florida

Los Angeles | London | New Delhi
Singapore | Washington DC | Melbourne

FOR INFORMATION:

SAGE Publications, Inc.
2455 Teller Road
Thousand Oaks, California 91320
E-mail: order@sagepub.com

SAGE Publications Ltd.
1 Oliver's Yard
55 City Road
London, EC1Y 1SP
United Kingdom

SAGE Publications India Pvt. Ltd.
B 1/I 1 Mohan Cooperative Industrial Area
Mathura Road, New Delhi 110 044
India

SAGE Publications Asia-Pacific Pte. Ltd.
3 Church Street
#10-04 Samsung Hub
Singapore 049483

Printed in the United States of America

ISBN 978-1-4522-8888-8

Acquisitions Editor: Helen Salmon
Editorial Assistant: Chelsea Pearson
eLearning Editor: John Scappini
Production Editor: Kelly DeRosa
Copy Editor: Gillian Dickens
Typesetter: C&M Digitals (P) Ltd.
Proofreader: Scott Oney
Indexer: Will Ragsdale
Cover Designer: Anupama Krishnan
Marketing Manager: Susannah Goldes

This book is printed on acid-free paper.

16 17 18 19 20 10 9 8 7 6 5 4 3 2 1

• Contents •

Preface   xi

Acknowledgments   xv

About the Author   xvii

Chapter 1. Overview of Propensity Score Analysis   1

Learning Objectives   1

1.1 Introduction   1

1.2 Rubin's Causal Model   2

    1.2.1 Potential Outcomes   3

    1.2.2 Types of Treatment Effects   3

    1.2.3 Assumptions   4

1.3 Campbell's Framework   4

1.4 Propensity Scores   5

1.5 Description of Example   6

1.6 Steps of Propensity Score Analysis   6

    1.6.1 Data Preparation   7

    1.6.2 Propensity Score Estimation   8

    1.6.3 Propensity Score Method Implementation   8

    1.6.4 Covariate Balance Evaluation   9

    1.6.5 Treatment Effect Estimation   11

    1.6.6 Sensitivity Analysis   11

1.7 Propensity Score Analysis With Complex Survey Data   12

1.8 Resources for Learning R   14

    1.8.1 R Packages for Propensity Score Analysis   15

1.9 Conclusion   16

Study Questions   16

Chapter 2. Propensity Score Estimation   19

Learning Objectives   19

2.1 Introduction   19

2.2 Description of Example   20

2.3 Selection of Covariates   21

2.4 Dealing With Missing Data   25

2.5 Methods for Propensity Score Estimation   30
   2.5.1 Logistic Regression   31
   2.5.2 Recursive Partitioning Algorithms   34
   2.5.3 Generalized Boosted Modeling   38
2.6 Evaluation of Common Support   41
2.7 Conclusion   44
Study Questions   46

Chapter 3. Propensity Score Weighting   47

Learning Objectives   47
3.1 Introduction   47
3.2 Description of Example   48
3.3 Calculation of Weights   49
3.4 Covariate Balance Check   53
3.5 Estimation of Treatment Effects With Propensity Score Weighting   56
3.6 Propensity Score Weighting With Multiple Imputed Data Sets   60
3.7 Doubly Robust Estimation of Treatment Effect With
   Propensity Score Weighting   62
3.8 Sensitivity Analysis   63
3.9 Conclusion   66
Study Questions   68

Chapter 4. Propensity Score Stratification   69

Learning Objectives   69
4.1 Introduction   69
4.2 Description of Example   70
4.3 Propensity Score Estimation   71
4.4 Propensity Score Stratification   74
   4.4.1 Covariate Balance Evaluation   76
   4.4.2 Estimation of Treatment Effects   77
4.5 Marginal Mean Weighting Through Stratification   79
   4.5.1 Covariate Balance Evaluation   82
   4.5.2 Estimation of Treatment Effect   83
   4.5.3 Doubly Robust Estimation With MMWS   84
4.6 Conclusion   85
Study Questions   85

Chapter 5. Propensity Score Matching   87

Learning Objectives   87
5.1 Introduction   87
5.2 Description of Example   88

5.3 Propensity Score Estimation   88

5.4 Propensity Score Matching Algorithms   90
    5.4.1 Greedy Matching   90
    5.4.2 Genetic Matching   93
    5.4.3 Optimal Matching   95
    5.4.4 Full Matching   96

5.5 Evaluation of Covariate Balance   96

5.6 Estimation of Treatment Effects   99

5.7 Sensitivity Analysis   105

5.8 Conclusion   107

Study Questions   108

Chapter 6. Propensity Score Methods for Multiple Treatments   **111**

Learning Objectives   111

6.1 Introduction   111

6.2 Description of Example   112

6.3 Estimation of Generalized Propensity Scores With Multinomial Logistic Regression   113

6.4 Estimation of Generalized Propensity Scores With Data Mining Methods   116

6.5 Propensity Score Weighting for Multiple Treatments   118
    6.5.1 Covariate Balance With Weights From Multinomial Logistic Regression   120
    6.5.2 Covariate Balance With Weights From Generalized Boosted Modeling   121
    6.5.3 Marginal Mean Weighting Through Stratification for Multiple Treatment Versions   122

6.6 Estimation of Treatment Effect of Multiple Treatments   125

6.7 Conclusion   128

Study Questions   129

Chapter 7. Propensity Score Methods for Continuous Treatment Doses   131

Learning Objectives   131

7.1 Introduction   131

7.2 Description of Example   132

7.3 Generalized Propensity Scores   132
    7.3.1 Dose Response Function   137

7.4 Inverse Probability Weighting   140
    7.4.1 Estimation of the Average Treatment Effect   141

7.5 Conclusion   143

Study Questions   144

Chapter 8. Propensity Score Analysis With Structural Equation Models   145

Learning Objectives   145

8.1 Introduction   145

8.2 Description of Example   147

8.3 Latent Confounding Variables   147

8.4 Estimation of Propensity Scores   152

8.5 Propensity Score Methods   153

8.6 Treatment Effect Estimation With Multiple-Group Structural Equation Models   156

8.7 Treatment Effect Estimation With Multiple-Indicator and Multiple-Causes Models   158

8.8 Conclusion   161

Study Questions   162

Chapter 9. Weighting Methods for Time-Varying Treatments   163

Learning Objectives   163

9.1 Introduction   163

9.2 Description of Example   164

9.3 Inverse Probability of Treatment Weights   165

9.4 Stabilized Inverse Probability of Treatment Weights   167

9.5 Evaluation of Covariate Balance   169

9.6 Estimation of Treatment Effects   170

   9.6.1 *Weighted Regression With Cluster-Robust Standard Errors*   170

   9.6.2 *Generalized Estimating Equations*   172

9.7 Conclusion   174

Study Questions   175

Chapter 10. Propensity Score Methods With Multilevel Data   177

Learning Objectives   177

10.1 Introduction   177

10.2 Description of Example   179

10.3 Estimation of Propensity Scores With Multilevel Data   179

   10.3.1 *Multilevel Logistic Regression*   180

   10.3.2 *Logistic Regression With Fixed Cluster Effects*   182

10.4 Propensity Score Weighting   184

10.5 Treatment Effect Estimation   186

10.6 Conclusion   189

Study Questions   190

References   191

Index   201

• Preface •

This book focuses on propensity score methods for estimating the effects of treatments, programs, or conditions with research designs in which random assignment is not undertaken. These designs are very common in the social sciences, so it is critical for graduate students and researchers to obtain familiarity with propensity score analysis. This book is intended as a tutorial in which realistic examples are used to guide the student through the multiple steps of propensity score analysis. The R statistical software was chosen to demonstrate the implementation of propensity score methods such as matching, stratification, and weighting, because it is very popular worldwide, and it is the software that is updated with the most recent statistical research at the fastest rate. In fact, it is quite common for researchers to propose a new statistical method and present an R package to implement it simultaneously. Therefore, the R statistical software is ideal for an area of very active research such as propensity score analysis. The book's purpose is to enable graduate students and researchers to adequately implement propensity score analysis methods using the R software to obtain publishable results. The reason for the choice of realistic examples in the book is that if students can understand the complexities of the example, they are also ready to tackle their own data set and publish their research. The goals of the book are the following: (1) familiarize readers with the theory supporting each propensity score analysis method, (2) provide readers with the steps necessary to implement propensity score analysis methods, and (3) provide readers with guidelines to choose among methods and an understanding of the advantages and limitations of each method.

The book is situated within the fields of analysis of observational data and quasi-experimental design. It is intended as a core text in courses about quasi-experimental analysis, propensity score analysis, causal analysis, and observational data analysis. Because these courses are usually the third or fourth course within a graduate-level quantitative training sequence in the social sciences, this book assumes familiarity with linear and logistic regression. It could also be used as a supplemental text in courses about secondary data analysis, survey data analysis, or an advanced program evaluation course. The book also serves as a main reference on propensity score analysis for researchers and graduate students whose research projects involve estimating the effects of a treatment, program, or condition where individuals were not randomly assigned to participation.

The pedagogical framework is to scaffold learning by breaking the implementation of each propensity score method into steps. Each chapter starts with learning objectives that indicate what the student should be able to do after studying the chapter. Then, the introduction section situates the method being discussed within the field of propensity score analysis. The introduction also explains how the method discussed there connects with methods presented in earlier and later chapters. Next, a realistic example, mostly from nationally representative surveys, is presented with an overview of the research problem and the characteristics of the data. After the example is introduced, each chapter describes the propensity score analysis method that is its focus in steps that are the same as the steps that the graduate student or researcher should follow during analysis. The book shows technical details as close as possible to where their implementation is demonstrated, so that their impact is visible rather than abstract. When the exact best implementation of a certain step is not clear in the literature, the multiple choices available with the advantages and limitations of each choice are presented. This book is focused on guiding the reader through the steps of propensity score analysis by providing sufficient theoretical background for the reader to understand the methodological choices being made at each step and the advantages and disadvantages of competing propensity score methods.

The examples provided are of interest to researchers in the fields of education, sociology, criminology, and management, but they look familiar to researchers in the social sciences in general. Each chapter shows the R code for the analysis and the R output intermixed with explanations of concepts for each analysis step. Lines of R code are presented in *italics,* while R output is shown in boxes with a different font. The functions and arguments necessary to understand each line of code are explained either right before or after the code. Chapter 1 provides an overview of propensity score analysis methods without R code and indicates resources for learning R. Chapters 2 to 10 assume enough familiarity with R to run a regression analysis. Study questions were placed at the end of each chapter, and these can be used for review of concepts and/or for quizzes.

The book's website at **study.sagepub.com/leite** is an essential resource to complement the book, because it contains all the code presented in the book fully commented, as well as alternative implementations for some of the methods shown in the book.

TABLE OF EXAMPLES IN THE BOOK		
Chapter	**Example**	**Source of Data**
1, 2, and 3	Estimate the effect of high school student participation in career academies on future income	Education Longitudinal Study (ELS)
4	Estimate the effect of having full-time security personnel in schools on the use of harsh discipline	School Survey on Crime and Safety (SSOCS)

Chapter	Example	Source of Data
5	Estimate the effect of mothers having a job that provides or subsidizes child care on the length that they breastfeed their children	National Longitudinal Survey of Youth 1979 (NLSY79) and the NLSY79 Children and Youth
6	Estimate the effects of assigning mentors from different areas to new teachers on the probability that they will continue in the teaching profession in the following year	1999–2000 School and Staffing Survey (SASS) and 2000–2001 Teacher Follow-up Survey (TFS)
7	Estimate the effect of school participation in the Algebra Nation virtual learning environment on the mean student scores on Florida's Algebra I End-of-Course (EOC) Assessment	Data collected by the virtual learning environment, public data from the Florida Department of Education
8	Estimate the effect of new teacher participation in a network of teachers on their perception of workload manageability	1999–2000 SASS and 2000–2001 TFS
9	Estimate the effect of self-employment on job satisfaction	NLSY79
10	Estimate the effect of center-based care in kindergarten on child mathematics achievement	Early Childhood Longitudinal Study—Kindergarten Class of 2010–2011 (ECLS-K:2011)

• Acknowledgments •

The author thanks Sungur Gurel, Siirt University, Turkey, for assisting in the execution of some of the examples. SAGE Publishing and the author would like to thank the following reviewers for their contributions:

Debbie L. Hahs-Vaughn, *University of Central Florida*

Larry R. Price, *Texas State University*

Howard T. Everson, *Center for Advanced Study in Education, Graduate School & University Center, City University of New York*

Robert J. Kaminski, *University of South Carolina*

Wei Pan, *Duke University*

Marisa L. Beeble, *Michigan State University, The Sage Colleges*

Alan R. Ellis, *Department of Social Work, North Carolina State University*

Mansoor A. F. Kazi, *School for Social Welfare, University at Albany, The State University of New York*

Jason Popan, *University of Texas–Pan American*

Toshiyuki Yuasa, *University of Houston*

Ally S. Thomas, *University of Pittsburgh*

Itzhak Yanovitzky, *Rutgers University*

• About the Author •

Walter Leite is Associate Professor in the Research and Evaluation Methodology program of the College of Education at University of Florida. His research objectives consist of developing and evaluating statistical methods to strengthen causal inference and understanding of causal mechanisms using nonexperimental data. He addresses obstacles to effective program evaluation with nonexperimental data such as selection bias, measurement error, and attrition bias. His specific methodological interests are propensity score analysis methods, structural equation modeling, and multilevel modeling. He investigates innovative applications of these methods to educational research and program evaluation with large data sets from state departments of education, nationally representative educational surveys, and massive data sets from virtual learning environments.

Overview of Propensity Score Analysis

Learning Objectives

- Describe the advantages of propensity score methods for reducing bias in treatment effect estimates from observational studies.

- Present Rubin's causal model and its assumptions.

- Enumerate and overview the steps of propensity score analysis.

- Describe the characteristics of data from complex surveys and their relevance to propensity score analysis.

- Enumerate resources for learning the R programming language and software.

- Identify major resources available in the R software for propensity score analysis.

1.1. Introduction

The objective of this chapter is to provide the common theoretical foundation for all propensity score methods and provide a brief description of each method. It will also introduce the R software, point the readers toward resources for learning the R language, and briefly introduce packages available in R relevant to propensity score analysis.

Propensity score analysis methods aim to reduce bias in treatment effect estimates obtained from observational studies, which are studies estimating treatment effects with research designs that do not have random assignment of participants to conditions. The term *observational studies* as used here includes both studies where there is no random assignment but there is manipulation of conditions and studies that lack both random assignment and manipulation of conditions. Research designs to estimate treatment effects that do not have random assignment to conditions are also referred to as quasi-experimental or nonexperimental designs. In this book, the terms *observational study, quasi-experimental design,* and *nonexperimental design* will be used equivalently. Biased treatment effect estimates may occur due to nonrandom differences between treated and untreated groups with respect to covariates related to the outcome. Propensity scores are probabilities of treatment assignment that, once estimated, can be used in several methods to reduce selection bias. These propensity score methods include many variations of weighting, matching, and stratification. Propensity score methods achieve removal of bias by balancing covariate distributions between treated and untreated groups.

Propensity score analysis methods have become a common choice for estimating treatment effects with nonexperimental data in the social sciences (Thoemmes & Kim, 2011). The use of propensity scores to reduce selection bias in nonexperimental studies was proposed by Rosenbaum and Rubin (1983b) and was connected to earlier work by Rubin (1973) on matching methods for selecting an untreated group that was similar to the treated group with respect to covariates. Propensity scores solve a difficult problem with multivariate matching: If there are many covariates, it is difficult to find an appropriate match for each treatment participant with respect to all covariates. With propensity scores, each individual has a unique score that summarizes the relationship between covariates and the treatment assignment. Rosenbaum and Rubin (1983b) have shown that adjustment for the propensity score is sufficient to remove all bias related to covariates.

Propensity score matching, stratification, and weighting have several advantages over conditioning on covariates. First, they separate the process of reduction of selection bias from the analysis of outcomes. Rubin (2005, 2007) refers to the reduction of selection bias with propensity score methods as the "design" stage of study. This design stage consists of the determination of matched observations, strata, or weights that achieve balance of covariate distributions between treated and untreated groups and should be performed independently and without any knowledge of the outcomes. Second, matching, stratification, and weighting allow for smaller outcome models where fewer parameters are estimated, because covariates are not included in the model unless they are of theoretical interest. Third, because the process of balancing covariates between treated and untreated groups is done independently of the outcome, no assumptions are made about the functional form of the relationship between covariates and the outcome.

1.2. Rubin's Causal Model

Rubin (1974) proposed a framework to understand the problem of causal inference, which has been referred to in the literature as the *potential outcomes framework, counterfactual framework,* or *Rubin's causal model* (Holland, 1986; Shadish, 2010). In this book, the latter term will be used. Rubin's causal model has been very influential across a variety of fields concerned with causal inference, such as statistics, economics, education, psychology, sociology, and epidemiology. Rubin's causal model provides the theoretical justification for estimation of treatment effects based on weighting (see Chapter 3), stratification (see Chapter 4), and matching (see Chapter 5).

1.2.1. Potential Outcomes

In Rubin's causal model, all individuals in the population have potential outcomes associated with the presence of treatment and potential outcomes in the absence of treatment. More specifically, each individual i has a potential outcome Y_i^1 associated with participating in the treatment condition $(Z_i = 1)$ and a potential outcome Y_i^0 if not participating $(Z_i = 0)$. Therefore, the treatment effect for each individual is $\tau_i = Y_i^1 - Y_i^0$. However, the outcomes of the participants are only observed in the presence of the treatment condition; conversely, the outcomes of nonparticipants are only observed in the absence of the treatment. This idea is illustrated in Figure 1.1.

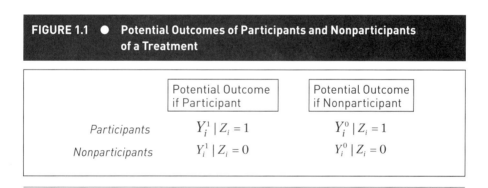

FIGURE 1.1 ● Potential Outcomes of Participants and Nonparticipants of a Treatment

	Potential Outcome if Participant	Potential Outcome if Nonparticipant
Participants	$Y_i^1 \mid Z_i = 1$	$Y_i^0 \mid Z_i = 1$
Nonparticipants	$Y_i^1 \mid Z_i = 0$	$Y_i^0 \mid Z_i = 0$

1.2.2. Types of Treatment Effects

In Figure 1.1, the outcomes $(Y_i^1 \mid Z_i = 1)$ and $(Y_i^0 \mid Z_i = 0)$ are observed, while the outcomes $(Y_i^1 \mid Z_i = 0)$ and $(Y_i^0 \mid Z_i = 1)$ are missing. Based on this framework, different types of treatment effects can be defined: (1) The average treatment effect (ATE) is the difference between the expected values of the potential outcomes of all individuals in the treated and untreated conditions: $ATE = E(Y_i^1) - E(Y_i^0)$. (2) The average treatment effect on the treated (ATT) is the difference between the expected values of the potential outcomes of treated individuals: $ATT = E(Y_i^1 \mid Z_i = 1) - E(Y_i^0 \mid Z_i = 1)$. (3) The average treatment effect on the untreated (ATC) is the difference between the expected values of the potential outcomes of the untreated individuals: $ATC = E(Y_i^1 \mid Z_i = 0) - E(Y_i^0 \mid Z_i = 0)$. The choice between the type of treatment effects should depend on the research question and related literature and also whether assumptions are met for the treatment effect of interest. In experimental designs, the ATE is equal to the ATT and ATC because random assignment of participants to conditions implies that they are exchangeable and therefore $E(Y_i^1 \mid Z_i = 1) = E(Y_i^1 \mid Z_i = 0)$ and $E(Y_i^0 \mid Z_i = 1) = E(Y_i^0 \mid Z_i = 0)$. In nonexperimental designs, the ATE, ATT, and ATC could differ substantially.

1.2.3. Assumptions

Estimating unbiased treatment effects requires the assumption of strong ignorability of treatment assignment, which consists of assuming that the treatment assignment is independent of the potential outcome distributions, given observed covariates X: $(Y^0, Y^1) \perp Z \mid X$ (Rosenbaum & Rubin, 1983b). Obtaining adequate balance of covariate distributions between treated and untreated groups after matching, stratification, and weighting is evidence that strong ignorability of treatment assignment has been achieved given the observed covariates. This assumption also requires that for every value of the covariates X, the probability of treatment assignment is neither 0 nor 1: $0 < p(Z_i 1 \mid X) < 1$.

Estimation of treatment effects under Rubin's causal model also requires the stable unit treatment value assumption (SUTVA), which states that there is a unique value Y_i^t corresponding to unit i and treatment t (Rosenbaum & Rubin, 1983b). This one-to-one correspondence between potential outcome and treatment version has a couple of implications: First, the distribution of potential outcomes for one individual is independent of the potential treatment status of another individual. Second, there are no unrepresented versions of the treatment (Rubin, 1986).

It is common that implementations of propensity score methods either assume full treatment compliance (i.e., adherence) or estimate the effect of offering the treatment regardless of compliance. However, an extension of Rubin's causal model, known as principal stratification, has been proposed to examine treatment effects with partial compliance (Barnard, Frangakis, Hill, & Rubin, 2003; Jin, Barnard, & Rubin, 2010; Jin & Rubin, 2009). No attrition from posttest measurement is also commonly assumed, but methods to deal with attrition through inverse probability weighting (Huber, 2011; Seaman & White, 2013) are similar to inverse probability of treatment weighting discussed in Chapter 3 and can be combined.

1.3. Campbell's Framework

The taxonomy of types of research design validity (i.e., statistical conclusion, internal, construct, and external validity) and associated threats proposed by Campbell and colleagues (Campbell & Stanley, 1966; Cook & Campbell, 1979; Shadish, Cook, & Campbell, 2002) is quite popular in educational and psychological research. Rather than conflicting with Rubin's work, Campbell's framework complements it by offering a broad description of which types of mechanisms (i.e., validity threats) may weaken causal evidence obtained with propensity score methods implemented under Rubin's causal model (Shadish, 2010; West & Thoemmes, 2010). Viewed under Campbell's framework, the methods discussed in this book are primarily concerned with minimizing the influence of selection threats to internal validity, where internal validity is defined as the extent that relationships among variables are causal. External validity, which is the extent that causal relationships identified in a research design generalize to populations and settings, is also discussed in this book, because data from representative samples obtained with complex survey methods are sometimes used for propensity score analysis, and incorporating sampling information into the propensity score analysis assists with obtaining treatment effects that generalize to the sampled population (see Chapter 3). Readers interested in an extensive treatment of Campbell's framework should consult the book by Shadish et al. (2002), and a detailed discussion of its relationship to Rubin's causal model can be found in a special section of the *Psychological Methods* journal (Imbens, 2010; Maxwell, 2010; Rubin, 2010; Shadish, 2010; West & Thoemmes, 2010).

1.4. Propensity Scores

The propensity score is defined as a conditional probability of treatment assignment, given observed covariates (Rosenbaum & Rubin, 1983b): $e(X) = P(Z = 1 \mid X)$. The propensity score reduces all the information in the predictors to one number, which greatly simplifies analysis. The propensity score is a balancing score, because the conditional distribution of covariates given the propensity scores is the same for treated and untreated groups (Rosenbaum & Rubin, 1983b). For example, matching based on multiple covariates to reduce selection bias can be simplified to matching based on the propensity score. Rosenbaum and Rubin (1983b) showed that if treatment selection is strongly ignorable given a set of observed covariates X, then it is also strongly ignorable given the propensity score $e(X)$ that is a function of these covariates. More specifically, Rosenbaum and Rubin proved that if potential outcomes Y^0 and Y^1 are independent of treatment assignment given observed covariates X, they are also independent of treatment assignment given the propensity score $e(X)$, and treatment assignment is independent of covariates given the propensity score:

$$
\begin{aligned}
&if\,(Y^0, Y^1) \perp Z \mid X \ \ then \\
&(Y^0, Y^1) \perp Z \mid e(X) \ and \ Z \perp X \mid e(X)
\end{aligned}
\tag{1.1}
$$

Because the propensity score is a balancing score, the mean difference between treated and untreated outcomes at a specific value of the propensity score is the average treatment effect at that propensity score (Rosenbaum & Rubin, 1983b). From this theorem, and assuming that treatment assignment is strongly ignorable, it follows that matching, weighting, and stratification based on the propensity score can provide unbiased estimates of the treatment effect.

True propensity scores have the balancing property, but they are unknown. They can be estimated by a variety of methods (e.g., logistic regression, random forests), but estimated propensity scores need to be evaluated with respect to whether they actually produce covariate balance. Ho, Imai, King, and Stuart (2007) recommend a pragmatic approach: The estimation of propensity scores should be considered successful if, in combination with a matching, stratification, or weighting strategy, they are able to produce adequate balance of covariate distributions between treated and untreated samples.

1.5. Description of Example

In this chapter, an introduction to propensity score methods is presented in the context of a study of the effect of high school student participation in career academies on future income. This example expands on the study by Rojewski, Lee, and Gemici (2010), who used Education Longitudinal Study (ELS) data and propensity score matching to estimate the effect of career academy participation on student educational aspirations. Career academies are programs within high schools that integrate academic preparation and workplace experiences through a career-focused curriculum (Orr, 2005). Kemple and Willner (2008) reported on an experimental longitudinal study of the effect of career academies in nine urban high schools that followed students from the start of high school until 8 years after their scheduled graduation. Among their results, they found that participation in career academies increased average earnings of participants by $132 per month during the first 4 years and $216 per month in the final 4 years, corresponding to an additional $2,088 in average earnings per year for program participants. In the current chapter, the steps of a propensity score analysis to estimate the effects of participation in career academies on future earnings are demonstrated using survey data from the base year (i.e., 2002) and second follow-up (i.e., 2006) of the ELS (National Center for Education Statistics, 2014). This chapter also describes the characteristics of the sample and data available. This example is also used in Chapter 2 for demonstrating the estimation and evaluation of propensity scores and in Chapter 3 for presenting propensity score weighting.

1.6. Steps of Propensity Score Analysis

The major steps of a propensity score analysis are (1) data preparation, (2) propensity score estimation, (3) propensity score method implementation, (4) covariate balance evaluation, (5) treatment effect estimation, and (6) sensitivity analysis. The following paragraphs present an overview of these steps. Steps 1 and 2 are discussed in detail in Chapter 2. Steps 3 to 6 are presented in the contexts of propensity score weighting in Chapter 3, stratification in Chapter 4, and matching in Chapter 5. The main objectives of each step are presented in Table 1.1.

TABLE 1.1 ● Steps of Propensity Score Analysis		
Step	**Objective**	**Example Procedures**
1. **Data preparation**	Obtain complete data that is ready for analysis	Covariate selection Implementation of missing data methods
2. **Propensity score estimation**	Obtain propensity scores for treated and untreated individuals	Logistic regression Random forests Generalized boosted modeling
3. **Propensity score method implementation**	Implement a strategy to balance treated and untreated covariate distributions using propensity scores	Propensity score matching Propensity score stratification Calculation of propensity score weights
4. **Covariate balance evaluation**	Determine the degree to which balance of covariate distributions between treated and untreated was achieved	Calculation of standardized mean differences Calculation of variance ratios
5. **Treatment effect estimation**	Estimate the treatment effect and its standard error	Weighted mean differences Generalized linear models
6. **Sensitivity analysis**	Determine how strong the effect of an omitted covariate would have to be for the significance test of the treatment effect to change	Rosenbaum's (2002) method Carnegie, Harada, and Hill's (2016) method

1.6.1. Data Preparation

The data preparation step includes examining the data available and how they were obtained, the treated/untreated groups, and the covariates. The sample size available will depend on the definition of the population of interest and the definition of treated and untreated groups. For the career academy example, the population of interest comprises high school students. The data set available from the ELS has 12,554 cases. The treated and untreated groups are determined from the question "Have you ever been in any of the following kinds of courses or programs in high school?" where option k is "Career Academy," from the base year student survey of the ELS. In this data set, there are 995 treated and 11,599 untreated.

Examination of the missing data proportions and missing data patterns, and determining how to deal with missing data, should be part of the data preparation step, and the implementation of missing data methods usually involves multiple steps of the propensity score analysis (see Chapter 2). Selection of covariates consists of identifying variables that are true confounders because they are related to both treatment assignment and the outcome. It is critical to determine that all covariates selected are antecedents of the treatment and not consequences of the treatment. Including covariates that are outcome proxies (Kelcey, 2011a) is particularly important, as well as other variables strongly related to only the outcome because they increase the power to test the treatment effect (Brookhart et al., 2006; Cuong, 2013).

1.6.2. Propensity Score Estimation

Once the data are prepared, estimation of propensity scores (Step 2) can be performed with a variety of methods, such as logistic regression, probit regression, and data mining methods (Setoguchi, Schneeweiss, Brookhart, Glynn, & Cook, 2008; Westreich, Lessler, & Funk, 2010). Several of these methods are demonstrated in Chapter 2 with the estimation of the propensity scores for the career academy example. The selection of covariates for the propensity score model is critical, because the strong ignorability of treatment assignment assumption of propensity score methods requires that there be no omitted confounders. Therefore, researchers should attempt to identify all true confounders, which are covariates that affect the treatment assignment and the outcome. Besides true confounders, the propensity score model can also include predictors of the outcome that are unrelated to treatment assignment, because these covariates will increase power to test the treatment effect. However, the propensity score model should not include covariates that are related to treatment assignment but not the outcome, because doing so would decrease power (Brookhart et al., 2006).

The degree of success of the estimation of propensity scores can only be appropriately understood once evaluation of the area of common support, implementation of the propensity score method of choice, and evaluation of covariate balance are completed. The first diagnostic measure of propensity score estimation is whether the estimation method converged and none of the propensity scores are either 0 or 1. The second diagnostic is a visual examination of the area of common support, which is the region of the distribution of propensity scores where values exist for both treated and untreated cases. A visual evaluation of the area of common support can be performed with histograms, kernel density plots, and box plots of the distributions of propensity scores of treated and untreated groups.

1.6.3. Propensity Score Method Implementation

The most widely used implementations of propensity score methods consist of matching, stratification, and weighting. For propensity score matching, many methods can be used for matching treated and untreated observations. In general, matching methods consist of a matching ratio and a matching algorithm. Matching ratios can be one-to-one, fixed ratio, or variable ratio. Matching algorithms are computational strategies to identify matches. Common matching algorithms are greedy matching, optimal matching (Rosenbaum, 1989), and genetic matching (Sekhon, 2011), and most algorithms can match either with or without replacement. Greedy matching is widely used and includes nearest neighbor matching and caliper matching. The greedy matching algorithm seeks to minimize the distance between each pair but does not minimize the total distance between all matched pairs (Austin, 2011b). For each treated case, nearest neighbor matching finds the untreated case with the smallest difference in propensity scores. Caliper matching enforces a maximum distance within which matches are acceptable, usually in standard deviation units. For example, Rosenbaum and Rubin (1985, p. 37) used a caliper of 0.25 standard deviations aiming to remove at least 90% of bias. Within the caliper of each treated observation, matches are performed by selecting the untreated observation with the closest propensity score.

With optimal matching, treated individuals are matched with untreated individuals by minimizing the total distance between treated and untreated matched pairs (Austin, 2011b) using network flow theory (Hansen, 2007; Rosenbaum, 1989). Optimal matching can be used for one-to-one matching, but it is more commonly used for full matching, which attempts to match all untreated individuals in the data set to a treated counterpart, resulting in no loss of sample size as long as there is an adequate area of common support. Full matching results in the creation of strata where each stratum contains at least one treated individual and at least one untreated individual, minimizing both the within-strata and between-strata propensity score distances (Rosenbaum, 2010). Therefore, full matching can be viewed as a generalization of propensity score stratification where the number of strata is optimized to reduce the distance between treated and untreated individuals, rather than defined a priori.

Propensity score stratification requires defining the number of strata, establishing strata cutoffs based on the distribution of the propensity scores, and creating observation weights based on the number of treated and untreated participants per stratum. Stratification based on propensity scores consists of dividing the sample into strata that are similar with respect to propensity scores. Cochran (1968) showed that stratifying a single covariate into quintiles removes about 90% of selection bias in the treatment effect estimate. Propensity score stratification has become a popular method for adjusting treatment effect estimates for selection bias, and a review of applications of propensity score stratification by Thoemmes and Kim (2011) showed that researchers typically use between 5 and 20 strata, with 5 being the most common choice. With propensity score weighting, as well as with weights based on strata, different formulas for weights are used depending on type of treatment effect (e.g., ATE, ATT) of interest.

1.6.4. Covariate Balance Evaluation

Evaluation of covariate balance is the main measure of success of the propensity score method and entails comparing characteristics of the distribution of treated and untreated after the propensity score method of choice has been applied. Evaluation of covariate balance has been performed by graphical, descriptive, and inferential measures. A graphical balance diagnostic can be performed with empirical QQ-plots for continuous covariates and with bar plots for categorical covariates. Empirical QQ-plots display the quantiles of the treated against those of the untreated group, and having points lined on the 45-degree line indicates adequate covariate balance. Bar plots of the categories of each covariate for treated and untreated groups can be overlapped, and nonoverlapping areas indicate lack of covariate balance.

Standardized mean differences, variance ratios, and mean and maximum distances in empirical QQ-plots have been used to quantify covariate balance. Mean differences can be standardized with pooled standard deviations or the standard deviation of one of the groups. The R packages *MatchIt* and *twang* provide standardized mean differences using the standard deviation of the treated group. A strict criterion for identifying adequate covariate balance based on standardized mean differences is that their absolute value should be below 0.1 standard deviations (Austin, 2011b). A less strict criterion that has been proposed is that the absolute standardized mean differences should be less than 0.25 standard deviations (Stuart, 2010; Stuart & Rubin, 2007). Within the field of educational research, the *What Works Clearinghouse Procedures and Standards Handbook (Version 3.0)* defines baseline covariate balance as adequate without additional covariate adjustment if the absolute standardized mean difference is equal to or lower than 0.05 standard deviations but considers differences between 0.05 and 0.25 standard deviations acceptable if additional regression adjustment for the covariate is performed when estimating treatment effects (U.S. Department of Education, Institute of Education Sciences, & What Works Clearinghouse, 2013). Variance ratio is the ratio of the residual variances of the treated and untreated groups after adjusting for the propensity score. The variance ratio for each covariate is obtained by regressing the covariate on the propensity score, obtaining residuals, and calculating the ratio of the variances of the residuals of treated and untreated groups. A strict criterion for covariate balance based on the variance ratio is that it should be between 0.8 and 1.2 (Rubin, 2001). A less strict criterion is that it should be between 0.5 and 2.0 (Stuart, 2010; Stuart & Rubin, 2007). Covariate balance can be summarized with the mean and maximum differences between the covariate distributions in empirical QQ-plots (Ho et al., 2007).

Inferential measures used for covariate balance evaluation include *t* tests comparing group means, Hotelling's *T* (a multivariate *t* test), and Kolmogorov-Smirnov tests. With inferential measures, obtaining no statistical significance indicates adequate covariate balance. However, inferential measures are not recommended for evaluation of covariate balance, first because covariate balance is a property of the sample, and hypothesis tests refer to the population (Ho et al., 2007). Second, inferential measures depend on sample size, and underpowered tests may fail to indicate substantial covariate unbalance with small samples, and high levels of power may make it hard to achieve balance with very large samples, even if covariate differences between groups are very small.

1.6.5. Treatment Effect Estimation

Once covariate balance is achieved, estimation of treatment effect can be performed with a variety of parametric or nonparametric estimators (Imbens, 2004; Lunceford & Davidian, 2004; Schafer & Kang, 2008), as well as with complex statistical models, such as multilevel models (Leite et al., 2015) and structural equation models (Leite, Sandbach, Jin, MacInnes, & Jackman, 2012). For example, in Chapter 3, the estimation of the ATT of career academy on income 4 years later is demonstrated using weighted mean differences, weighted regression, and regression-adjusted weighted mean differences. The freedom of choice of estimators of the treatment effect comes from the fact that propensity score methods can be viewed as preprocessing methods (Ho et al., 2007) to remove selection bias, and therefore the choice of propensity score method imposes few limitations on the choice of treatment effect estimator.

1.6.6. Sensitivity Analysis

Sensitivity analysis aims to determine how strong the effect of an omitted covariate would have to be for the significance test of the treatment effect to change (Rosenbaum, 2010; Rosenbaum & Rubin, 1983a). Therefore, sensitivity analysis allows the researcher to establish the degree of robustness of treatment effects to hidden bias, which is the part of the selection bias due to omitted confounders. Evaluating sensitivity to hidden bias is important because propensity score methods only remove selection bias due to observed confounders. Although the strong ignorability of treatment assignment assumption is only strictly met if there are no omitted confounders, a sensitivity analysis can show the extent that significance tests for the treatment effect are sensitive to increasing levels of violation of the strong ignorability of treatment assignment assumption. Given that a study of a treatment with a complex selection mechanism may have numerous omitted variables, if a researcher can show that significance tests would not change even with large levels of hidden bias, the confidence on the treatment effect will be substantially strenghtened.

Sensitivity analysis was invented by Cornfield et al. (1959) to determine if the estimated effect of smoking on lung cancer was sensitive to unmeasured factors. Since then, various sensitivity analysis methods have been proposed. Rosenbaum (2002) proposed a sensitivity analysis method for pair matched designs and continuous outcomes based on the Wilcoxon signed-rank test, where different sizes of hidden bias can be used to obtain upper and lower bound p values for the significance test if these levels of hidden bias were present. This process allows the determination of how large the hidden bias would have to be for the effects to become nonsignificant. This method for sensitivity analysis is demonstrated in Chapter 5. The method of sensitivity analysis based on simulation proposed by Carnegie, Harada, and Hill (2016) is demonstrated in Chapter 3. There are several other sensitivity analysis methods not demonstrated in this book, such as those proposed by Brumbach, Hernán, Haneuse, and Robins (2004); Li, Shen, Wu, and Li (2011); and Shen, Li, Li, and Were (2011).

1.7. Propensity Score Analysis With Complex Survey Data

Data used for treatment effect estimation with propensity score methods frequently come from surveys with complex sampling designs. For example, the ELS sample was obtained with a two-stage stratified sampling method where schools were sampled with probability proportional to size (PPS) sampling, and approximately 26 students were selected per school (Ingels et al., 2004). Both school and student samples were stratified, and Asian and Hispanic students were oversampled. This sampling method resulted in ELS data that contain weights, strata id numbers, and cluster id numbers. There are different weight variables available corresponding to different combinations of measurement waves and subjects of interest.

Methods for inference with survey samples can be classified into design based and model based (Heeringa, West, & Berglund, 2010), but combinations of these two approaches are possible (Sterba, 2009; Wu & Kwok, 2012). The design-based approach uses the known probability that a sampling was chosen among all possible samples and makes no assumption about the distributions of the outcomes. Therefore, this approach is sometimes referred to as "nonparametric" or "distribution free" (Heeringa et al., 2010). The model-based approach, on the other hand, relies on assumptions about the distributions of outcomes. For the estimation of the effect of career academy participation on income using ELS data, design-based estimation can be accomplished with the difference between weighted means of treated and untreated groups, with standard error obtained through bootstrapping (Rodgers, 1999). For the same example, model-based estimation can be obtained with maximum-likelihood estimation of a multilevel model (Snijders & Bosker, 2012) with dummy-coded indicators of career academy participation and stratum membership, and random effects of schools, where the treatment effect estimate is the coefficient of the career academy indicator. An example of combining these two approaches is to use pseudo-maximum-likelihood estimation (Asparouhov, 2006; Rabe-Hesketh & Skrondal, 2006) to fit a multilevel model with dummy-coded indicators of career academy participation and random effects of school, using sampling weights to account for stratum oversampling. A detailed example of the use of propensity score analysis with design-based inference is provided in Chapter 3, and an example of propensity analysis with model-based inference and the combination of design-based and model-based inference is provided in Chapter 10.

Design-based inference methods use weights to eliminate bias due to unequal probability of selection, reduce nonresponse error due to unequal response rates, reduce frame error (i.e., unequal coverage of the population by the sampling frame), and improve precision of the estimates through the use of auxiliary information. In a purely model-based inference, rather than using weights, unequal probability of selection and unequal response rates can be accounted for by including covariates in the model that identify the selection and response process. These covariates are typically dummy-coded indicators of membership in groups that were oversampled or had unequal response rates. Also, precision can be improved by including covariates strongly related to the outcome. However, Pfeffermann (1993) showed that using weights is advantageous in model-based inference because weights can protect against nonignorable nonresponse and model misspecification. Furthermore, if covariates related to the sample selection process are used to define weights rather than being included in the model, no assumptions need to be made about the functional form of the relationship between the covariates and the outcome. One undesirable consequence of using sampling weights and/or nonresponse weights is that if the estimate is valid without weights (i.e., the weights are ignorable), the standard errors of the weighted estimates will be larger than of the unweighted estimates.

Weights used in analysis of complex survey data include sampling weights, nonresponse weights, poststratification weights, and raking weights. A raw (or base) sampling weight is the inverse of the probability of selection and sum to the population size. Therefore, raw sampling weights can be interpreted as the number of individuals in the population that each member of the sample is representing. It is recommended that raw sampling weights be scaled into normalized sampling weights, which sum to the sample size, because some estimation software may produce incorrect standard errors (i.e., based on the population size rather than sample size) if raw sampling weights are used. Weights can be normalized by dividing by the mean of the weights. Nonresponse weights are the inverse of survey response probabilities and adjust for unequal response rates. Poststratification and raking weights adjust for differences between population proportions in subgroups and corresponding sample proportions. Final weights that combine sampling weights, nonresponse weights, and poststratification or raking weights (if employed) can be obtained by multiplication and are usually provided in complex survey data sets such as the ELS. Reading the survey's technical manual is strongly recommended because it describes the sampling design, nonresponse adjustments, whether poststratification or raking was used, and how different weights were calculated. Many technical manuals also contain recommendations on how to analyze the data, such as how to compute standard errors that account for the complex survey design.

Using the weights provided with data sets from complex surveys is important in propensity score analysis when the researcher aims to obtain treatment effect estimates that generalize to a population that the complex survey was designed to represent (Dugoff, Schuler, & Stuart, 2014). Furthermore, using the final weights may reduce selection bias by removing observed covariate differences between treated and untreated groups that are either not present in the population or larger than population differences. In other words, the weights provided with the data set may reduce covariate imbalances that are due to sampling bias and nonresponse bias rather than selection bias.

1.8. Resources for Learning R

Before proceeding with learning about propensity score analysis with R in the next chapters of this book, it is strongly recommended that the reader develop some familiarity with the R programming language. R is a powerful computing environment for statistics and has a vibrant community of users and contributors. Information about the most recent version of R, which is available for all major operating systems, can be obtained from the R project website (http://www.r-project.org). The R project website provides access to the Comprehensive R Archive Network (CRAN), which is a network of mirrors around the world providing free downloads of R distributions and contributed packages. The R project website is the natural place to start learning R: It contains the R manuals provided by the R development core team, the *R Journal*, R FAQs, access to mailing lists related to several topics about R, access to search engines about R, links to special interest groups and conferences, information about contributed R packages, and contributed introductions in several languages. From the official documentation, the recommended reading for beginners is "An Introduction to R." The contributed introductions provide many different approaches for learning R, some focused on using R for introductory statistics, while others cater to specific application areas such as econometrics, bioinformatics, and epidemiology. Several books have been published about using the R language, and the R project website provides a partial list of these books with annotations.

Because of the wide adoption of the R language among research statisticians, it is very common that new methods are implemented in R shortly after they have been proposed, and sometimes a method becomes available in R before it is published in peer-reviewed journals. These new methods are implemented in R packages, which are listed in the CRAN mirror websites, but the list of packages can also be accessed from the R graphical user interface (GUI). The CRAN mirror websites also provide "Task Views," which is a list of R packages grouped by topics of interest, such as Bayesian analysis, econometrics, genetics, meta-analysis, psychometrics, and social sciences. In this book, many R packages that are relevant to propensity score analysis will be used. The fact that new methods become quickly available in R is a major advantage over commercial statistical software, but it also comes with some limitations. One major limitation is that the contributed R packages have a very diverse level of documentation, with some packages being extensively documented while others have minimal documentation. It is particularly helpful when an article describing the use of an R package is published in either the *R Journal* or the *Journal of Statistical Software,* which are peer-reviewed publications that enforce standards of quality for how an R package and the methods it implements are presented. In this book, citations are provided for articles that have tutorials on R packages whenever they are used in the chapters' examples. Also, many R package authors write vignettes demonstrating the use of their packages, which are posted in the packages page of the R project website.

Code editors and integrated development environments (IDEs) can facilitate programming in R a great deal. Code editors are sophisticated plain-text editors that typically add color schemes to the code that allow easier reading, among other features. One example of a good code editor for R is Tinn-R (http://www.sciviews.org/Tinn-R). IDEs include the features of a code editor but are also able to run R in the background and manage package installation and associated help files. Some general-purpose IDEs, such as Eclipse, have plugins for the R language. RStudio (http://rstudio.com) is a powerful IDE that was developed specifically for the R language.

The large and enthusiastic R user community has provided excellent online resources for learning R, as well as many mailing lists and forums where users can ask questions and discuss R-related issues. Several general and special interest group mailing lists are provided on the R Project Website. Among other online resources, the Quick-R website (http://www.statmethods.net) stands out as a provider of easy-to-understand information about how to perform a variety of statistical analyses in R. Furthermore, R-bloggers (http://www.r-bloggers.com) is an aggregator of posts about R programming.

1.8.1. R Packages for Propensity Score Analysis

Because propensity score analysis is an active area of research, there are new packages and expansions of existing packages being contributed to the community regularly. Therefore, this book will mostly demonstrate propensity score analyses with well-established R packages. These packages have rich documentation supporting them, in the form of websites, published papers, and tutorials. In this book, the following packages related to propensity score analysis will be extensively used in the examples: *Matching, MatchIt,* and *twang.* The *Matching* (Sekhon, 2011) package implements multivariate and propensity score matching with greedy and genetic algorithms. The *MatchIt* (Ho, Imai, King, & Stuart, 2011) package aggregates functionality from several other R packages, providing access to many methods for propensity score estimation, propensity score matching, and stratification. For example, the *optmatch* (Hansen, 2007) package provides optimal and full matching, but the *MatchIt* package provides user-friendly access to many of the functions of *optmatch.* The *twang* (Ridgeway, McCaffrey, Morral, Burgette, & Griffin, 2013) package focuses on estimating propensity scores with boosted regression trees and propensity score weighting.

The *survey* (Lumley, 2004) package is used in most chapters of this book, because many of the examples use sampling weights, cluster identification, and strata identification variables that resulted from the implementation of a complex survey design such as multistage stratified sampling. Also, because propensity score methods frequently produce weights, such as inverse probability of treatment weights, the R code provided in the examples can be used for propensity score analysis even if sampling weights are not being used. Finally, the data from most examples have missing values, so the *mice* (van Buuren & Oudshoorn, 2000) package is used to implement imputation methods. This is not an exhaustive list of R packages related to propensity score analysis. Also, several other packages are used in this book for example-specific tasks.

1.9. Conclusion

This chapter presented an overview of Rubin's causal model, which provides the underlying framework for propensity score analysis, and an overview of the steps of propensity score analysis. Because the success of propensity score methods depends on achieving adequate covariate balance, it is recommended that variations of the implementation of propensity score methods be compared with respect to covariate balance. It is also common that publications using propensity score analysis to estimate treatment effects report the results of multiple propensity score methods and/or outcome models as a way to indicate whether the estimates obtained were sensitive to the methodological choices made. Because propensity score analysis is a multistep process where several choices are available for each step, it is helpful to provide evidence that results are similar across different methods, and this can be considered a type of sensitivity analysis. Also, it is important to remember that propensity score analysis can only remove bias due to observed confounders, so a sensitivity analysis to determine the extent that conclusions would change if there are omitted confounders can increase confidence in the results.

Study Questions

1. What are the advantages of propensity score methods over conditioning on covariates for reducing bias in treatment effect estimates from observational studies?

2. What is the main advantage of propensity score matching over multivariate matching?

3. What are potential outcomes?

4. What is the difference between the average treatment effect and the average treatment effect on the treated?

5. What is the strong ignorability of treatment assignment assumption?

6. What is the stable unit treatment value assumption?

7. What type of validity in Campbell's framework is strengthened by using propensity score methods?

8. What is a propensity score?

9. What theorem did Rosenbaum and Rubin (1983b) prove to justify the use of propensity scores to remove selection bias rather than conditioning on covariates?

10. What are the steps of propensity score analysis?

11. What are typical tasks involved in the data preparation steps of propensity score analysis?

12. What are true confounders?

13. Besides true confounders, what other type of covariate should be included in the propensity score estimation?

14. What is the area of common support?

15. What is covariate balance evaluation?

16. Which methods can be used for covariate balance evaluation?

17. What are the shortcomings of inferential statistics for covariate balance evaluation?

18. What is the objective of a sensitivity analysis?

19. What is the difference between model-based and design-based inference with complex survey data?

20. What are sampling weights?

21. What are nonresponse weights?

22. What is the importance of accounting for the characteristics of the survey design that generated the data in propensity score analysis?

Propensity Score Estimation

Learning Objectives

- Describe strategies for identification of covariates to include in the propensity score model.

- Distinguish between the roles of true confounders, predictors of treatment assignment, and predictors of the outcome in the propensity score analysis.

- Characterize missing data methods that can be used in propensity score analysis.

- Identify strengths and limitations of logistic regression and data mining methods for estimation of propensity scores.

- Describe the principle of recursive partitioning and its application to propensity score estimation.

- Describe the principle of boosting and its application to propensity score estimation.

2.1. Introduction

This chapter describes the process of data preparation and propensity score estimation, with the choices that have to be made along the process and a comparison of the advantages and disadvantages of each choice. This process is summarized in Table 2.1. This chapter's focus is on propensity scores for a single treatment with a single wave of treatment implementation. Generalized propensity score estimation methods for multiple treatments and continuous treatments are addressed in Chapters 6 and 7, respectively, and propensity score estimation in longitudinal studies with multiple waves of treatment implementation is discussed in Chapter 9.

TABLE 2.1 ● Steps of Data Preparation and Propensity Score Estimation

Step	Description	Example Methods
Selection of covariates	Identify true confounders and predictors of outcome	Include pretest score or outcome proxies
Dealing with missing data	Use available data or impute missing data	Listwise deletion, single imputation, multiple imputation
Propensity score estimation	Estimate predicted probabilities of treatment assignment given covariates	Logistic regression Random forests Generalized boosted modeling
Evaluation of common support	Compare distributions of propensity scores across treated and untreated groups	Histograms Box-and-whiskers plots Kernel density plots

The success of the process of propensity score estimation is typically determined based on three criteria: (a) The propensity score estimation converged, (b) common support is adequate for estimation of the treatment effect of interest, and (c) adequate covariate balance is obtained. Convergence depends on a variety of factors such as the proportion treated; the number, distribution, and colinearity of covariates; and details of the implementation of the estimation method. Adequacy of common support depends on the distribution of propensity scores, the treatment effect of interest (e.g., ATE, ATT), and the propensity score method of choice. Covariate balance can only be evaluated after the propensity score method of choice is implemented and depends on both the propensity scores and the characteristics of the propensity score method. Therefore, it is possible that with the same set of propensity scores, covariate balance is achieved with propensity score weighting (see Chapter 3) but not with stratification (see Chapter 4) or matching (see Chapter 5). In this chapter, covariate balance is not discussed, because it is presented in Chapter 3 for the current example in the context of propensity score weighting.

2.2. Description of Example

In this chapter, the estimation of propensity scores of high school student participation in career academies is demonstrated. This example was introduced in Chapter 1. The data analyzed are from the Education Longitudinal Study (ELS; National Center for Education Statistics, 2014). The data set contains 12,554 cases. The sample was selected with a two-stage stratified sampling method where schools were sampled with probability proportional to size (PPS) sampling, and approximately 26 students were selected per school (Ingels et al., 2004), with oversampling of Asian and Hispanic students. In the base year of the ELS student survey, the survey question "Have you ever been in any of the following kinds of courses or programs in high school?" where option k is "Career Academy," determines treatment participation. Students were in 10th grade in the base year of the study. In total, 995 students (8%) participated in career academy programs, and 11,559 (92%) did not.

2.3. Selection of Covariates

Figure 2.1 shows variables with different relationships with the treatment variable (i.e., an indicator of treatment assignment) and/or the outcome. From the variables depicted, only true confounders and predictors of the outcome should be included in the propensity score model (these variables are indicated with a gray shade in Figure 2.1). A true confounder is a covariate that has a direct effect on the probability of treatment assignment and a direct effect on the outcome. In Figure 2.1, there are arrows from the true confounder to both the treatment indicator and the outcome, showing the direction of the effects. True confounders should always be included in

FIGURE 2.1 ● Relationships Between Covariates, Treatment Assignment, and Outcome, With Gray Boxes Indicating Covariates That Should Be Included in the Propensity Score Model

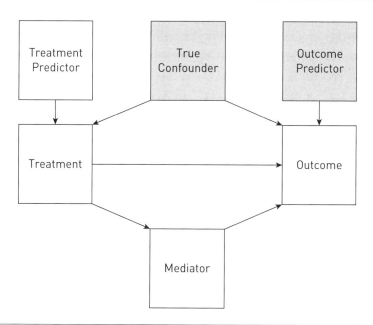

the propensity score model because omitting these variables results in biased treatment effect estimates. Conversely, including true confounders in the propensity score model decreases bias and variance of the treatment effect estimates (Brookhart et al., 2006). Predictors of the outcome, which are unrelated to treatment assignment, should also be included in the propensity score model, because they reduce the variance of treatment effect estimates, although they do not contribute to reduction of bias (Brookhart et al., 2006; Cuong, 2013).

Brookhart et al. (2006) and Cuong (2013) showed that including covariates related to exposure but not the outcome (i.e., the treatment predictor variable in Figure 2.1) in the propensity score model does not decrease bias but increases variance of treatment effect estimates. Including mediators of the relationship between treatment and outcome in the propensity score model should not be done because it will remove part of the treatment effect. Care should be taken in distinguishing between true confounders and mediators, because a certain variable measured before treatment assignment may be a true confounder, but the same variable may be a mediator if measured after treatment assignment. In studies where data on treatment participation and covariates are collected simultaneously, it is sometimes difficult to determine whether covariates influenced treatment assignment or were affected by it.

Rubin (2007, 2008) stressed that, to maintain researcher objectivity in the implementation of propensity score methods and to parallel the design of randomized experiments, the selection of covariates for the propensity score model should be performed without examining the outcome data. Therefore, Steiner, Cook, Shadish, and Clark (2010) suggested the following strategies that do not rely on accessing outcome data to select true confounders and predictors of the outcome for the propensity score model: (1) theoretical analysis of factors influencing the selection mechanism and their relationship with outcomes, (b) pilot study focused on identifying the selection mechanism, and (c) expert reviews and interviews with participants and other persons knowledgeable about the selection process. Some of the strategies used in survey development, such as cognitive interviews (Willis, 1999) and focus groups (Krueger & Casey, 2008), can also be used in investigations of the treatment selection process. For example, Rickles (2011) demonstrated the use of interviews to identify the factors determining selection of students into eighth-grade algebra classes.

Kelcey (2011a) proposed the use of outcome proxies or cross-validation to select true confounders and predictors of the outcome without analyzing the complete outcome data. Examples of outcome proxies are pretest scores at the individual level or pretest aggregated scores at the cluster level (Kelcey, 2011a). The cross-validation approach consists of taking a subsample of the complete data, which is known as a training sample in data mining terminology, to investigate relationships between covariates and both treatment assignment and outcome and select covariates for the propensity score model. With the cross-validation approach, the propensity score analysis is performed with the total sample minus the subsample used to select variables for the propensity score model. Kelsey showed that both the outcome proxy approach and the cross-validation approach work well with large samples.

With small samples, the cross-validation approach is better at bias reduction but leads to lower power to test the treatment, while the outcome proxy approach provides more power but does not reduce bias as much as the cross-validation approach. Although these results are promising, the best process to examine relationships between covariates and outcome proxies or covariates and outcomes in a subsample of the data has not been determined. Kelsey (2011) emphasizes that outcome proxies or cross-validation can be used to augment covariate selection based on theoretical analysis but not as the primary method of covariate selection. Regardless of the combination of methods used to select covariates, it is critical that the reliability of measurement of the covariates be high. Steiner, Cook, and Shadish (2011) showed how reduction of selection bias diminishes as the measurement error in covariates increases. With a large number of covariates, they found that some of the unreliability in covariates can be compensated by high correlations with other covariates, but compensating for all the loss of bias reduction due to an unreliable key covariate by adding other covariates may not be possible.

The list of covariates selected for estimation of the propensity scores of career academy participation is provided in Table 2.2. A total of 16 covariates were selected (12 student level and 4 school level) from the set of 21 covariates selected by Rojewski et al. (2010) in their study of the effect of career academy programs on educational aspirations. From the set of covariates they used, the number of times absent from school, the number of times put on in-school suspension, the number of times suspended, and the mathematics and reading achievement standardized scores were excluded because these variables were measured for the first semester or term of 10th grade and could be mediators of the relationship between participation in a career academy and income rather than confounders. Covariates about students' educational motivation and aspirations in 10th grade were also included. All covariates used in this analysis were taken from the base year data set of the ELS except gender, race, and home language, which were taken from the first follow-up data set but are considered time invariant.

TABLE 2.2 ● Covariates Used for Estimation of Propensity Score of Participation in Career Academy Programs With ELS Data

Variable Name in ELS Data	Variable Description
BYSTLNG2	Sample member's English fluency
byplang	Parent's English fluency
byfcomp	Family composition
bysibstr	In-home sibling structure
bysibhom	Number of in-home siblings

(Continued)

TABLE 2.2 ● (Continued)

Variable Name in ELS Data	Variable Description
bygnstat	Generational status
bypared	Parents' highest level of education
bygpared	Highest reported level of education among parents
BYSES1QU	Quartile coding of SES1 variable
bygrdrpt	Number of grades repeated (K–10)
byhomlit	Home literacy resources
byriskfc	Number of academic risk factors in 10th grade
bystexp	How far in school student thinks will get—composite
F1SEX	Sex—composite
F1RACE	Student's race/ethnicity—composite
F1HOMLNG	Student's native language—composite
BYS26	High school program—student self-report
BYS27D	Education is important to get a job later
BYS27I	Parents expect success in school
BYS28	How much likes school
BYS37	Importance of good grades to student
BYS38C	How often goes to class without homework done
BYS54A	Importance of being successful in line work
BYS54O	Importance of getting good education
BYS57	Plans to continue education after high school
BYS58	Type of school plans to attend
bysctrl	*Type of school currently attending: public, private, other*
byurban	*Urbanicity of school*
byregion	*Geographic region of school*
BY10FLP	*Grade 10 percent of free or reduced lunch students*

Note: Variables in italics are school level, and other variables are student level; variable names starting with BY were measured in the base year (2002) of the Education Longitudinal Study (ELS); variables starting with F1 are composite variables created in 2004 but considered time invariant.

The companion website to this book at **study.sagepub.com/leite** contains the R code used for selecting covariates, identifying and labeling levels of categorical variables, and recoding the many codes used in the ELS to indicate the reasons for missing data into a single missing data code.

2.4. Dealing With Missing Data

Before propensity score estimation, it is very common for researchers to have to deal with missing data. Missing data can be classified as missing completely at random (MCAR), missing at random (MAR), and missing not at random (MNAR; Enders, 2010). Data on a variable are MCAR when the missing patterns are independent of other variables in the design and the observed and unobserved values of the variable itself. MCAR data can be considered a random subsample of the hypothetical complete data. A variable has MAR data when its missing patterns relate to other variables in the data set but not to the variable itself. A variable with MNAR data has missing patterns that depend on the unobserved values of the variable. For example, data are MNAR when individuals with a history of drug use skip a question about drug use in a survey.

Missing data methods can be classified into methods that use available data and imputation methods. Among the methods based on available data, listwise deletion is commonly used and the default of many statistical software programs. It consists of deleting cases with missing values. However, listwise deletion makes the very strong assumption that the data are MCAR, and results in loss of statistical power. In contrast, imputation methods result in no loss of sample size. Mean substitution is the simplest of imputation methods, and it is not recommended because it assumes data are MCAR and leads to loss of variability in the data set. Model-based single-imputation methods such as regression imputation or matching-based single imputation methods such as hot-deck imputation assume that data are MAR but reduce the variability in the data set. Therefore, for statistical analysis with missing outcome data, single imputation is in general not recommended and multiple imputation is a preferable missing data method. However, Stuart (2010) suggested that single imputation is an effective approach to deal with missing covariate data prior to estimation of propensity scores with a model that includes both imputed covariates and missing data indicators. This approach allows for balance to be achieved on both covariates and missing data patterns across treated and untreated groups. In a simulation study, Leite and Aydin (2016) found negligible differences in proportion improvement in covariate balance and bias reduction between single and multiple imputation of MAR data prior to propensity score estimation. Because research on single imputation of missing covariate data for propensity score analysis is incipient, the recommendation of single imputation as a viable alternative to multiple imputation for propensity score estimation should be considered tentative.

Multiple imputation (MI; Rubin, 1987) does not reduce the variability in the data set because it creates sets of imputed data sets with added noise. MI assumes MAR data.

Once multiple imputed data sets are created, the analysis of interest is repeated for each imputed data set and the results are combined. MI can be performed by a variety of implementations, such as joint modeling or chained equations (see Table 2.3). While MI by joint modeling requires the specification of a multivariate distribution for the covariates, MI by chained equations requires only specification of univariate distributions. Given that propensity score models have a large number of covariates with potentially very different distributions, MI by chained equations is a more practical missing data method to implement with propensity score analysis than MI by joint modeling. Research on MI for experimental designs has recommended imputing treated and untreated groups separately, because the missing data mechanism may be different between treated and untreated groups, and imputing the groups separately allows the imputation model to vary across groups (Puma, Olsen, Bell, & Price, 2009). Also, the outcomes should be included in the imputation of the covariates, because omitting the outcome results in the correlations between the covariates and the outcome to be suppressed toward zero (Graham, 2009).

TABLE 2.3 ● Examples of Methods to Handle Missing Data in Covariates		
Method	**Description**	**R Packages**
Listwise deletion	Remove all observations with at least one missing value	*comple.cases* and *na.omit* functions of the *stats* package
Multiple imputation (joint modeling)	Specify multivariate distribution for the missing data, draw imputations from posterior distribution by Markov chain Monte Carlo (MCMC) techniques	*norm* package for continuous covariates *cat* package for categorical covariates *mix* package for continuous and categorical covariates
Multiple imputation (multivariate imputation by chained equations)	Specify multivariate distribution through conditional densities for each variable, draw imputations from the posterior distribution of each variable by MCMC techniques	*mice* package for continuous and categorical covariates
Multiple imputation (expectation maximization with bootstrapping)	Obtain a bootstrapped data set, estimate sufficient statistics with the expectation maximization (EM) algorithm, draw imputations from posterior distribution	*Amelia* package, assumes multivariate normal covariates
Single imputation	Hot-deck imputation, regression imputation, or any method for multiple imputation can be used to obtain a single imputed data set	*HotDeckImputation*, *hot.deck*, *norm*, *cat*, *mix*, *mice*, *Amelia* packages

Research on missing data methods for propensity score estimation has focused mostly on MI. Hill (2004) presented two implementations of MI for propensity score analysis: To implement MI-1, the researcher should obtain multiple imputed data sets, estimate propensity scores for each data set, take the mean of propensity scores for each case to obtain a single vector of propensity scores, and then proceed with the remaining steps of propensity score analysis as discussed in Chapter 1 using a single vector of propensity scores. For MI-2, the researcher obtains multiple imputed data sets and runs the entire propensity score analysis process for each data set, only combining estimates across imputed data sets once multiple treatment effect estimates and standard errors are obtained.

Hill (2004) and Mitra and Reiter (2016) performed simulation studies comparing these two MI strategies: Hill found that MI-1 produced better covariate balance and bias reduction than MI-2, while Mitra and Reiter found that the MI-1 provided greater bias reduction but larger variance than MI-2. However, these studies deal with missing values only in the covariates, but with survey data, there can also be missing values in the treatment indicator and the outcome. One advantage of MI-2 over MI-1 is that it is easier to implement when there are missing values in the covariates, treatment indicator, and the outcome, because results from the multiple imputed data sets are only combined at the end of the outcome analysis. The use of MI-1 when there are missing values in the covariates, treatment indicator, and outcome is somewhat more cumbersome if MI is also being used for the outcome model, because it requires combining propensity scores from imputed data sets to obtain a single vector of propensity scores, using this propensity score vector for propensity score analysis with each imputed data set, and then combining the treatment effect estimates and standard errors. However, MI-1 does have the advantage over MI-2 of allowing for a different missing data method to be used for the outcome.

The following code reads the ELS data set containing the selected covariates, id variables, weights, treatment effect indicator, and the outcome and then calculates the proportion of missing data in each variable and adds dummy missing value indicators to the data set.

```
load(file="ELS_data_example_career_academy.Rdata")

missing.indicator <- data.frame(is.na(ELS.data))

propMissing <- apply(missing.indicator,2,mean)

names(missing.indicator)[propMissing>0] <-

      paste(names(ELS.data)[propMissing>0],"NA",sep="")

ELS.data <- cbind(ELS.data, missing.indicator[,propMissing>0])

print(round(propMissing,3))
```

STRAT_ID	psu	SCH_ID	STU_ID	bystuwt	BYSTLNG2	byplang	byfcomp
0.000	0.000	0.000	0.000	0.000	0.000	0.113	0.000
bysibstr	bysibhom	bygnstat	bypared	bygpared	BYSES1QU	bygrdrpt	byhomlit
0.173	0.180	0.114	0.000	0.212	0.000	0.000	0.123
byriskfc	bystexp	F1SEX	F1RACE	F1HOMLNG	F2BYWT	F2ERN5P2	BYS26
0.198	0.093	0.000	0.000	0.023	0.000	0.007	0.019
BYS27D	BYS27I	BYS28	BYS33K	BYS37	BYS38C	BYS54A	BYS54O
0.007	0.005	0.032	0.000	0.009	0.013	0.028	0.035
BYS57	BYS58	bysctrl	byurban	byregion	BY10FLP		
0.096	0.118	0.000	0.000	0.000	0.078		

The output shown above presents the names of the variables in the data set and the proportion of missing data in each. The variables *STRAT_ID, psu, SCH_ID,* and *STU_ID* are identification numbers for strata, cluster, school, and student, respectively, and the variables *bystuwt* and *F2BYWT* are weights for the base year and second follow-up, respectively. These variables contain no missing data. The indicator of participation in career academy is *BYS33K*. The outcome is *F2ERN5P2,* and 0.7% of its values are missing. The percentage of missing data in the covariates ranges from 0.0% to 21.2%. To improve clarity of the code, the indicator of participation in a career academy is recoded into the variable *treat,* which will be used as the treatment indicator:

ELS.data$treat <- factor(ELS.data$BYS33K)

Several packages in R perform MI, including *Amelia* (Honaker, King, & Blackwell, 2011), *mi* (Su, Gelman, Hill, & Yajima, 2011), and *mice* (van Buuren & Oudshoorn, 2000), each having a unique combination of imputation methods and diagnostic tools. For this example, missing data in the covariates are imputed using the *mice* package. The *mice* package performs multiple imputation by chained equations, which is also known as fully conditional specification or sequential regression multivariate imputation (White, Royston, & Wood, 2011). This is a multivariate method that imputes missing data on a variable-by-variable basis (van Buuren, 2012). Multiple imputation by chained equations does not require specification of a multivariate model for the data because the multivariate distribution is specified through conditional densities for each variable, which are used to sequentially impute variables. Therefore, this method requires the specification of an imputation model for each variable, such as linear regression for continuous variables and logistic regression for dichotomous variables (White et al., 2011). This requirement has the advantage of allowing the conditional model for each variable to be fully under the control of the researcher. The *mice* algorithm begins randomly imputing missing variables for a variable by randomly sampling with replacement from the observed values. Then, the conditional model of choice for the variable is fit to the variable's observed data, and missing values are replaced by simulated draws from the posterior predictive distribution of the variable. This process is repeated for all variables, completing a cycle. This cycle is repeated several times to stabilized results before the desired *m* imputations are obtained by repeating the cycle *m* times (White et al., 2011). An extensive treatment of MI with the *mice* algorithm is provided by van Buuren (2012).

The *for* loop shown below implements multiple imputation of the treatment groups separately, by running the code inside the { } brackets first for *treat = 0* and then for *treat = 1*. The *quickpred* function of the *mice* package is used to create a matrix of zeros and ones where the rows indicate the variables to be imputed and the columns indicate the predictors selected for each variable. This allows the creation of an imputation model for each covariate, where the *mincor=0.1* argument specifies that a predictor is included only if its Pearson correlation with the covariate has an absolute value of at least 0.1, and the *minpuc=0.5* argument specifies that predictors should have at least 50% of usable cases. With the *exclude=c("STU_ID")* argument, the student id variable is excluded.

long.imputation <- c()

for (group in 0:1) {

predictor.selection <- quickpred(subset(ELS.data,treat==group), mincor=0.1,

minpuc=0.5,method='pearson', exclude=c("STU_ID"))

imputation <- mice(subset(ELS.data,treat==group), m=5, method="pmm",

visitSequence="monotone", predictorMatrix = predictor.selection)

long.imputation <- rbind(long.imputation,complete(imputation, action="long"))

}

The *mice* function with the *m=5* argument obtains five multiple imputations by chained equations. The *method="pmm"* argument specifies predictive mean matching (PMM) as the univariate imputation model, while the *visitSequence="monotone"* argument specifies an imputing order from the variable with the least missing data to the variable with the most missing data. The imputed data sets are stored within the *long.imputation* object. The *complete* function of the *mice* package allows extracting imputed data sets in a variety of formats: single imputed data sets, stacked imputed data sets in a long format, and a wide data set with imputed data sets side by side. Here the *action="long"* argument is used to specify that the imputed data sets will be stacked in a long format.

Although a different type of univariate imputation model could have been specified for each variable, in this example, the model specification is simplified by using PMM as the univariate imputation method for all variables. PMM can handle imputing both continuous and categorical variables. PMM is a two-step process that first computes predicted values for the variable being imputed. Then, for each missing value, PMM randomly samples an observed value from a set of candidate donors that have predicted values close to the predicted value of the missing value (van Buuren, 2012). PMM has several advantages: (1) It does not require the specification of an explicit model for the distribution of missing values, (2) it guarantees that imputed values are always within the range of observed values, and (3) it produces imputed missing values with similar distributions as the observed values, which is particularly useful if the observed variable is nonnormally distributed (White et al., 2011).

The following code extracts the first imputed data set from the *long.imputation* object created previously, which contains a total of five imputed data sets. This imputed data set is used later to demonstrate propensity score estimation with a single data set.

imputation1 = subset(long.imputation, subset=.imp==1)

In the next code, the five imputed data sets from the *long.imputation* object are stored into a *list* object named "*allImputations*," created using the *imputationList* function of the *mitools* package (Lumley, 2014). This function is specifically designed to integrate with the *survey* package (Lumley, 2004) for design-based estimation with complex survey data.

library(mitools)

allImputations <- imputationList(list(

  subset(long.imputation, subset=.imp==1),

  subset(long.imputation, subset=.imp==2),

  subset(long.imputation, subset=.imp==3),

  subset(long.imputation, subset=.imp==4),

  subset(long.imputation, subset=.imp==5)))

In the next section, the application of different methods is demonstrated for estimation of propensity scores of participation in career academy programs to the imputed data sets. For each estimation method, the R code is provided for estimation with a single imputed data set and with multiple imputed data sets. The code for a single imputed data set can also be used for data sets without missing data.

2.5. Methods for Propensity Score Estimation

The two broad classes of methods used for propensity score estimation are parametric models and data mining methods. Parametric models include logistic regression, probit regression, and discriminant function analysis. Data mining methods used in propensity score estimation include classification trees, random forests, and generalized boosted regression. From the parametric models, we will only present logistic regression because it is the most popular method to estimate propensity scores and produces propensity scores that are very similar to those obtained with probit regression or discriminant function analysis.

2.5.1. Logistic Regression

Logistic regression is the most commonly used model to estimate propensity scores. This section assumes a working knowledge of logistic regression, and several books on categorical data analysis (e.g., Agresti, 1996, 2002) as well as on regression (e.g., Fox, 2002, 2008) provide introductions. A basic logistic regression model for estimating propensity scores is as follows:

$$\text{logit}(Z_i = 1 \mid X) = \beta_0 + \beta_1 X_{1i} + \dots \beta_k X_k, \tag{2.1}$$

where the logit is the log odds of the probability of receiving treatment:

$$\text{logit}(Z_i = 1 \mid X) = \log \left(\frac{P(Z_i = 1)}{1 - P(Z_i = 1)} \right) \tag{2.2}$$

Covariates X_1 to X_k are either true confounders or predictors of the outcome. This basic model can be made more complex by adding higher order polynomial terms (e.g., X_k^2, X_k^3) and/or interaction terms (e.g., $X_1 X_2$ product). The logistic regression model is estimated with maximum likelihood estimation. The propensity scores are estimated probabilities of treatment assignment given covariates (i.e., $e_i(X) = P(Z_i = 1 \mid X)$), which can be obtained from the estimated logits:

$$e_i(X) = \frac{\exp(\text{logit}(Z_i = 1 \mid X))}{1 + \exp(\text{logit}(Z_i = 1 \mid X))} \tag{2.3}$$

In the next part of the code for the example analysis, a vector containing the name of the covariates is created, which is used for building the propensity score model as well as for assessing covariate balance later. In this vector of covariate names, there are also the names of 12 dummy missing value indicators for variables with more than 5% of missing values. Dummy indicators for covariates with less than 5% missing data were not included to avoid model estimation problems. Another caveat of adding dummy missing value indicators is that two variables may have missing values for very similar sets of cases, and therefore only one dummy indicator should be included. For situations where there are a small number of missing data patterns, dummy pattern indicators may be included in the model instead of missing value indicators. Another alternative is to add a summary of missing data as a covariate, such as the proportion of missing values. For this example, if two dummy missing value indicators have correlations above 0.8, only one of them is added to the propensity score model.[1] The *covariateNames* vector containing names of both covariates and dummy missing value indicators is as follows:

---

[1] More detailed code on how dummy missing value indicators were created is provided on the book's website.

covariateNames <- c("BYSTLNG2", "byplang", "byfcomp", "bysibstr", "bysibhom", "bygnstat",

"bypared", "bygpared", "BYSES1QU", "bygrdrpt", "byhomlit", "byriskfc","bystexp",

"F1SEX", "F1RACE", "F1HOMLNG", "BYS26", "BYS27D", "BYS27I", "BYS28",

"BYS37", "BYS38C", "BYS54A", "BYS54O", "BYS57", "BYS58", "bysctrl", "byurban",

"byregion", "BY10FLP", "bygparedNA" ,"byhomlitNA","bystexpNA" , "BYS26NA",

"BYS33KNA" , "BYS38CNA" , "BYS57NA" , "BYS58NA", "BY10FLPNA",

"byplangNA", "bysibstrNA", "byriskfcNA")

The formula for the propensity score model can be created with the following code:

psFormula <- paste(covariateNames, collapse="+")

psFormula <- formula(paste("treat~",psFormula, sep=""))

print(psFormula)

```
treat ~ BYSTLNG2 + byplang + byfcomp + bysibstr + bysibhom +
    bygnstat + bypared + bygpared + BYSES1QU + bygrdrpt + byhomlit +
    byriskfc + bystexp + F1SEX + F1RACE + F1HOMLNG + BYS26 +
    BYS27D + BYS27I + BYS28 + BYS37 + BYS38C + BYS54A + BYS54O +
    BYS57 + BYS58 + bysctrl + byurban + byregion + BY10FLP +
    bygparedNA + byhomlitNA + bystexpNA + BY10FLPNA + byplangNA +
    bysibstrNA + byriskfcNA + BYS57NA
```

In the R statistical software, the *glm* function can fit logistic regression models, but it is not used for this example because it does not provide estimation for complex survey samples. Instead, the *survey* (Lumley, 2004) package is used, because it provides estimation of logistic regression models with design-based adjustment for the effects of unequal-probability sampling, clustering, and stratification.[2] To prepare for the analysis, the *library* function loads the *survey* package and the *options* function sets the handling of any stratum with a single cluster.[3] Then, the *svydesign* function is used to create the *surveyDesign1* and *surveyDesignAll* objects, for a single imputed data set and all imputed data sets, respectively. The *ids, strata,* and *weights* arguments specify the name of the variables containing cluster ids, strata ids, and sampling weights, respectively. The source of data for the analysis is specified with the *data* argument, and *nest=T* relabels cluster ids to make them nested within strata.

---

[2] Chapter 1 provides an introduction to design-based methods for survey estimation.

[3] Run *help(svyCprod)* in R for more details.

```
library(survey)

options(survey.lonely.psu = "adjust")

surveyDesign1 <- svydesign(ids=~psu, strata=~STRAT_ID, weights=~bystuwt,
                data = imputation1, nest=T)

surveyDesignAll <- svydesign(ids=~psu, strata=~STRAT_ID, weights=~bystuwt,
                data = allImputations, nest=T)
```

The following code uses the *svyglm* function of the *survey* package to fit the logistic regression to a single data set, with design-based adjustment for the sampling design. The *family=quasibinomial* argument specifies a quasi-binomial distribution (Faraway, 2006), rather than the binomial distribution that is typical of logistic regression, because of the presence of sampling weights.

```
psModel1 <- svyglm(psFormula, design=surveyDesign1, family=quasibinomial)
```

In the next step, the estimated propensity scores for a single data set are obtained with the *fitted* function and stored within the variable *pScores:*

```
pScores <- fitted(psModel1)

imputation1$pScores <- pScores
```

In the next code, the logistic regression model is fit to all imputed data sets using the *with* and *svyglm* functions. Then, five vectors of estimated propensity scores are obtained for the five imputed data sets using the *sapply* and *fitted* functions. The *apply* function is used to combine them into a single vector of propensity scores by taking the mean. Finally, the *update* function is used to insert the variable *pScores* containing the single vector of propensity scores into each of the five imputed data sets.

```
psModelAll <- with(surveyDesignAll, svyglm(psFormula, family=quasibinomial))

pScoresAll <- sapply(psModelAll, fitted)

pScores <- apply(pScoresAll,1,mean)

allImputations <- update(allImputations, pScores = pScores)
```

Because the main measure of success of propensity score estimation is the ability of propensity scores to produce adequate covariate balance, a practical model-building strategy is to build the propensity score model with main effects only and then evaluate covariate balance. If covariate balance is not achieved, higher order polynomial terms and interactions are added to the model, and covariate balance is reevaluated.

This process should continue until adequate covariate balance is achieved (Dehejia & Wahba, 1999). However, if a model with main effects is not sufficient for obtaining covariate balance, the researcher could choose to estimate propensity scores with a data mining method instead of logistic regression, because data mining methods based on recursive partitioning automatically detect nonlinear relationships and interactions, as discussed in the next section of this chapter.

Perfect prediction or separation is a problem that may appear in propensity score estimation, especially if a large number of covariates strongly related to treatment assignment are used. When separation occurs, predicted probabilities are 1 for the treated group and 0 for the untreated group. Approaches to prevent this problem include Bayesian logistic regression (Gelman, Jakulin, Pittau, & Su, 2008) implemented in the *bayesglm* function of the *arm* package and the hidden logistic regression model (Rousseeuwa & Christmann, 2003) implemented in the *hlr* package. However, the use of a procedure to prevent separation may not be sufficient to produce useful propensity scores, because distributions of the estimated propensity scores for treated and untreated groups may have inadequate common support (see Section 2.6 for an example of evaluation of common support).

2.5.2. Recursive Partitioning Algorithms

Recursive partitioning applied to propensity score estimation consists of repeatedly splitting the data into groups with similar treatment status based on the categories of a categorical covariate or a cutoff applied to a continuous covariate. While logistic regression requires that interactions and nonlinear relationships are specified in advance of fitting the model, recursive partitioning methods find interactions and nonlinear relationships in a data-driven way (Strobl, Malley, & Tutz, 2009). Another advantage of recursive partitioning algorithms is that they automatically handle missing data in the covariates by using all available cases for each split. Therefore, the use of imputation methods is not needed before estimating propensity scores with recursive partitioning methods.

Classification and regression trees are the simplest recursive partitioning methods. Classification trees predict categorical outcomes, while regression trees predict continuous outcomes. There are several algorithms for classification and regression trees, such as CART, C4.5, CHAID, and GUIDE (Loh, 2011). This section will present the use of classification trees to estimate propensity scores because it is the base of other recursive partitioning methods. However, its use for propensity score estimation is not recommended because the results have a high level of variability with many covariates and frequently produce poor estimates of propensity scores (McCaffrey, Ridgeway, & Morral, 2004). Furthermore, although classification trees are capable of detecting complex interactions between covariates, they do not perform well if the functional form of the relationship between covariates and outcome is linear and additive (Berk, 2006). However, ensemble methods, which combine the results of several classification or regression trees, have been shown to perform well for propensity score estimation and do not suffer from the limitations of classification trees (Lingle, 2011; Watkins et al., 2013; Westreich et al., 2010). Among ensemble methods for propensity score estimation, bagging, random forests, and generalized boosted regression will be demonstrated. Seni and Elder (2010) discuss the advantages of ensemble methods in detail. Loh (2011) provides a succinct description of various data mining methods and some results on studies that compare their performance.

Classification trees applied to propensity score estimation consist of splitting the sample into several nodes (i.e., groups) based on values of predictors that discriminate between treated and untreated groups. Each branch of a classification tree is a split. Figure 2.2 shows an example classification tree created to predict participation in career academy programs. The first split is of the composite categorical variable *F1RACE* into a right node with categories 1, 3, 5, and 6 and a left node with categories 2, 4, and 7. In each iteration of the classification tree algorithm, the responses of a single predictor are split into two nodes that are more homogeneous than the existing node with respect to the outcome variable (Strobl et al., 2009). The following R code uses the *ctree* function of the *party* package to fit a classification tree to the imputed data set and plot the tree. The resulting plot is shown in Figure 2.2.

library(party)

myctree <- ctree(psFormula, data = imputation1)

plot(myctree)

In classification and regression trees, a traditional method to quantify node homogeneity is in terms of impurity $i(\tau)$ at a node τ, which is a nonnegative function of the probability $p(y = 1 \mid \tau)$ (Berk, 2006). Commonly used measures of impurity in classification trees are Bayes error $= \min(p, 1 - p)$, entropy $= [-p \log(p)] - [(1 - p) \log(1 - p)]$, and the Gini index $= p(1 - p)$ (Berk, 2006). Given an existing node, the potential gain in impurity reduction obtained by splitting the node can be quantified as the impurity of the node minus the impurity of the two nodes resulting from its split. The classification tree algorithm calculates this gain for every possible split and selects the split resulting in the largest gain in impuri reduction. Nodes that remain intact once the algorithm is run are terminal nodes. Propensity scores can be obtained as the proportion of treated cases at each terminal node.

For a continuous or ordinal predictor with m values, there are $m - 1$ possible splits, but for categorical variables with k categories, there are $2^{k-1} - 1$ possible splits because the order of categories does not matter. Therefore, the computational demands of splitting categorical predictors are often heavier than splitting continuous or ordinal predictors (Berk, 2006). This process is repeated with additional variables, where selecting the same variable more than once is allowed, until a convergence criterion is reached. However, classification trees tend to overfit the data, producing a tree with many branches that are due to random variation in the data and do not

FIGURE 2.2 ● Classification Tree to Estimate Propensity Score of Career Academy Participation

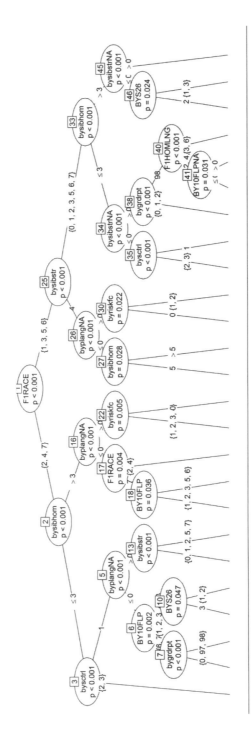

cross-validate to other data sets. To reduce overfitting, the process of "pruning" of branches is usually employed.

Classification tree algorithms can handle missing data in the covariates by using only observed values to select the next variable to split and determining the cutoff values. For cases with missing values, classification into treated and untreated is done based on a surrogate variable that best predicts the value of the variable used for splitting (Strobl et al., 2009). However, classification tree algorithms do not allow missing data in the outcome. Because the data set for the current example has missing values for the indicator of career academy participation, the first imputed data set will be used to demonstrate the classification tree method.

Bagging or bootstrapped aggregation improves upon classification trees by running a large number of trees with bootstrapped samples of the same size of the original sample, taken with replacement. These trees are run using all available variables and without any pruning. Then, the results are combined into a composite tree, which is less affected by random variability in the data than a single tree. The random forests algorithm is similar to bagging, except that only a subset of the complete set of variables is used at each iteration. Consequently, trees have higher variability with random forests than with bagging. Also, because not all variables are taken to build each tree, random forests prevent one variable from dominating another and guarantee that all variables participate in building some trees (Strobl et al., 2009). With bagging or random forests, propensity scores can be obtained by computing the proportion of trees that classified each observation as "treated."

One limitation of recursive partitioning algorithms is that they tend not to perform well when the distribution of the outcome is strongly skewed (Berk, 2006). For propensity score estimation, this problem could manifest if the proportion of treated individuals is small. Another limitation is that recursive partitioning algorithms can artificially prefer numerical variables, variables with more categories, and even variables with more missing data (Strobl et al., 2009), depending on which variable selection and split criteria are used. This problem can be prevented by implementing the random forest algorithm with sampling without replacement (Strobl, Boulesteix, Zeileis, & Hothorn, 2007). The implementation with the R package *party* demonstrated below is designed to prevent this bias. It is important to note that ensemble methods do not produce the same results in two runs of the algorithm, because there is randomness associated with sampling of cases and, in the case of random forests, sampling of variables. The difference between runs of the algorithms can be negligible given an appropriate choice of tuning parameters for the data, but stability of results across different tuning parameters should be examined.

Setting a random seed with *set.seed* before running the algorithms allows for results to be replicated. The *cforest_unbiased* function is used to set options for the random forest, where the *ntree=1000* and *mtry=5* arguments specify that the random forest should have 1,000 trees and five covariates per tree, respectively. The recommended number of covariates per tree for classification trees is the square root of the number of predictors. Given that 30 covariates were used, and $\sqrt{30} \approx 5.48$, the random forest algorithm is implemented selecting five covariates per tree. Setting *mtry = NULL* would run the bagging method rather than random forest, because all covariates would be used for every tree. The *cforest* function is used to run a random forest to estimate propensity scores of participation in career academy programs using a single imputed data set.[4]

set.seed(2014)

mycontrols <- cforest_unbiased(ntree=1000, mtry=5)

mycforest <- cforest(psFormula, data=imputation1, weights = imputation1$bystuwt,

   controls=mycontrols)

The random forest procedure is performed by the *cforest* function using the tuning parameters in the *mycontrols* object, with the propensity score model specified in the formula object *psFormula,* which was described previously. The base year sampling weights *bystuwt* are specified with the *weights* argument and used by the random forest algorithm to sample observations for each bootstrapped sample based on probabilities equal to the weights divided by the mean of the weights. Propensity scores are obtained with the *predict* function, as shown below, which are then organized into the *pScoresRf* variable:

pScoresRf <- predict(mycforest, type="prob")

imputation1$pScoresRf <- matrix(unlist(pScoresRf),,2,byrow=T)[,2]

2.5.3. Generalized Boosted Modeling

Boosting is a general method to improve a weak predictor into a strong predictor by iteratively applying the predictor to the full sample but using an adjustment at each step that improves the quality of prediction (Berk, 2006). Several boosting algorithms, such as AdaBoost, generalized boosted modeling (GBM), and LogitBoost, can be used to improve any predictor, such as classification trees, regression trees, logistic regression, and logistic regression trees. McCaffrey et al. (2004, 2013) proposed and demonstrated combining GBM with logistic regression trees for propensity score estimation, and their method is fully implemented in the R package *twang* (Ridgeway et al., 2013).

This section demonstrates the application of GBM for estimating propensity scores of career academy participation. The GBM implementation proposed by McCaffrey et al. (2004) estimates $\text{logit}(Z_i = 1 \mid X)$, the log odds of treatment assignment, with an iterative process where regression trees are used to obtain an improvement in the

---

[4] Code to run random forests with all imputed data sets is provided on the book's website.

estimate with each new iteration. The starting value of the logit is $\log[\bar{Z}/(1-\bar{Z})]$, where $\bar{Z}$ is the proportion treated. Regression trees are used to model the residuals $Z_i - e_i(X)$, where $e_i(X)$ is the propensity score at each iteration; these scores are then used to update estimates at each terminal node of the tree (McCaffrey et al., 2004). Before updates are added to current estimates, they are shrunken using a shrinkage parameter less than 1, which improves the smoothness of fit.

While node splits in a classification tree are selected to minimize an impurity measure that is a function of the probability of the outcome, the impurity that is minimized in a regression tree is the within-node sum of squared residuals. By combining the results of multiple regression trees across iterations, the GBM algorithm maximizes the logistic log-likelihood. One limitation of boosting algorithms is that there is no defined stopping criterion, so errors decline up to a point and then increase, but there could be multiple inflection points along the process (Berk, 2006). McCaffrey et al. (2004, 2013) recommended using a measure of covariate balance, such as the standardized mean difference between treated and untreated groups, to stop the GBM algorithm the first time that a minimum covariate balance is achieved, but there is no guarantee that better covariate balance would not be achieved if the algorithm runs additional iterations. The following code uses the *ps* function of the package *twang* to estimate propensity scores with the GBM algorithm using one imputed data set.[5]

library(twang)

imputation1$treat <- as.numeric(imputation1$treat==1)

myGBM <- ps(psFormula, data = imputation1, n.trees=10000, interaction.depth=4,

    stop.method=c("es.max"), estimand = "ATT",

    verbose=TRUE, sampw = imputation1$bystuwt)

The second line of code in the block above converts the treatment indicator variable from a factor to a numeric variable with 0 or 1 values, because it is required by the *ps* function. In the code for running the GBM algorithm with the *ps* function shown above, the *n.trees=10000* argument sets the maximum number of iterations, *interaction.depth* = 4 sets the maximum number of allowed splits per tree to four, and *stop.method=c("es.max")* defines the stopping criterion, which is set to the maximum effect size. Thus, after each iteration, the algorithm computes the effect size for each variable as the standardized mean difference between treatment and untreated groups and stores the maximum effect size across variables. Once the maximum number of iterations is reached, the algorithm provides the estimates obtained at the point where the maximum effect size is smallest.

---

[5] Code for using the GBM algorithm with all imputed data sets is provided on the book's website.

For this example, running *summary(myGBM)* shows that estimates were obtained at iteration 1,390, and the smallest value of the maximum effect size is 0.125. Figure 2.3 is obtained with *plot(myGBM, type="b",color=F)* and shows the change in maximum effect size across iterations. If the smallest value of the convergence criterion is obtained close to the maximum number of iterations, the *ps* function issues a warning and suggests increasing the number of iterations.

FIGURE 2.3 ● **Maximum Standardized Mean Differences Between Treated and Untreated Groups for Iterations of the GBM Algorithm**

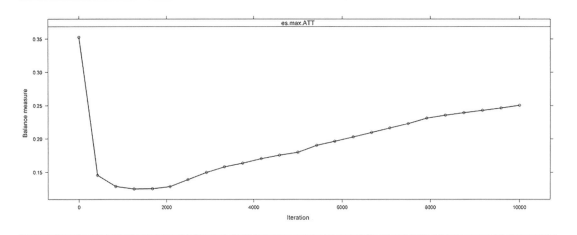

Once the GBM algorithm runs, propensity scores are obtained with the following:

pScoresGBM <- myGBM$ps

Classification trees, random forests, and GBM belong to a class of methods known as data mining, machine learning, or statistical learning, because they do not specify a statistical model in advance that represents a theoretical view of the causal mechanisms that generated the data (Berk, 2006). Many other procedures within this class of methods can be applied to propensity score estimation, so the methods presented in this chapter are a small sample of the possibilities. This is an active area of research, and recent studies have shown that data mining methods may outperform logistic regression for propensity score estimation if the appropriate tuning parameters are used. Emerging research has been identifying suitable tuning parameters of data mining methods for propensity score estimation. There have been few simulation studies comparing data mining algorithms and logistic regression for propensity score estimation. Diamond and Sekhon (2013) compared logistic regression, random forests, and boosted classification trees, finding that either logistic regression or random forests performed best depending on the condition manipulated, but boosted classification trees produced the least reduction of bias. Among the methods not discussed in this chapter, there is existing evidence supporting the application of Bayesian additive regression trees (Hill, Weiss, & Zhai, 2011) and neural networks (Setoguchi et al., 2008) for propensity score estimation.

2.6. Evaluation of Common Support

Propensity score methods require the existence of an adequate area of common support, which is an area of the distribution of propensity scores where values exist for both treated and untreated groups. Having an inadequate area of common support may result in inability to obtain an adequate covariate balance between treated and untreated groups. Furthermore, generalization of the treatment effect cannot be made for those outside of the area of common support. In this section, the common support for the distributions of propensity scores of treated and untreated groups is compared based on visual inspection and descriptive statistics. This examination is sufficient to identify a major lack of common support and is recommended prior to implementation of any propensity score method. However, propensity score methods differ with respect to common support requirements: Propensity score stratification requires that each stratum have at least one treated and one untreated case. Thus, the existence of a stratum with only treated or untreated cases indicates insufficient common support, but large differences in treated and untreated sample sizes within a stratum may also be problematic. Reducing the number of strata may improve common support within each stratum but results in decreased bias removal (see Chapter 4). Propensity score matching of treated observations within calipers requires that there be an untreated observation within the caliper of each treated observation. Therefore, the use of calipers in propensity score matching provides an evaluation and enforcement of common support (see Chapter 5). In contrast with propensity score stratification and matching, propensity score weighting does not have a precise common support requirement and is able to obtain adequate covariate balance even if the distributions of propensity scores show little overlap (Ridgeway et al., 2013). However, poor common support with propensity score weighting may result in many observations with zero weights and some observations with extreme weights, which inflates standard errors of treatment effects estimates and decreases power (see Chapter 3).

Using data from the imputed data set, the common support for propensity scores estimated with different methods is compared using box-and-whiskers plots in Figures 2.4 to 2.6. This is the code for obtaining the box-and-whiskers plot shown in Figure 2.4, with the *bwplot* function of the *lattice* package:

library(lattice)

bwplot(pScores~treat, data = ELS.data.imputed, ylab = "Propensity Scores",

    xlab = "Treatment",auto.key = TRUE)

FIGURE 2.4 ● **Box-and-Whiskers Plot of Propensity Scores of Participation in Career Academy Estimated With Logistic Regression for Treated and Untreated Groups**

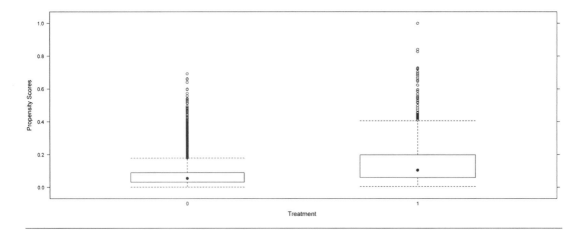

FIGURE 2.5 ● **Box-and-Whiskers Plot of Propensity Scores of Participation in Career Academy Estimated With Random Forests for Treated and Untreated Groups**

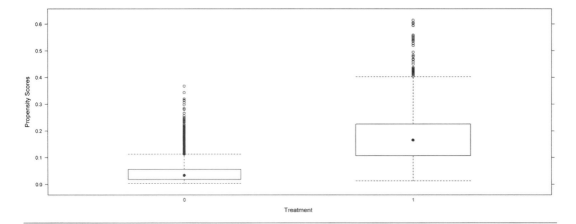

The box-and-whiskers plots indicate that there is some lack of common support for propensity scores estimated with all three methods, but the common support is best with the propensity scores estimated with logistic regression. However, this conclusion is preliminary because the consequences of the observed common support depend on both the type of treatment effect of interest and the propensity score method used and cannot be fully understood until the propensity score method of interest is implemented. It is possible that the degree of lack of common support observed has little impact on covariate balance and treatment effect estimates and standard errors, but it could have the following adverse consequences: With propensity score weighting, there could be inadequate covariate balance and/or inflation of standard errors. With propensity score stratification, strata at the extremes of the propensity score distribution could have only treated or untreated observations, rendering it impossible to estimate treatment effects within these strata. With propensity score matching with a caliper, cases near the extremes of the propensity score distributions could have no case with opposite treatment status within their caliper and therefore would have to be discarded. If matching without a caliper, lack of common support could result in matches of poor quality.

To perform a graphical examination of common support for the propensity scores estimated with logistic regression across five imputed data sets, the lattice package is used to obtain kernel density plots (Figure 2.7) and box-and-whiskers plots (Figure 2.8).[6] These graphs show that the distributions of propensity scores have some lack of common support.

TABLE 2.4 ● Summary of Main Functions Used in This Chapter		
Package	**Function**	**Objective**
mice	*quickpred*	Determine which predictors will be used to impute each covariate
mice	*mice*	Perform multiple imputation by chained equations
mitools	*imputationList*	Create a list of imputed data sets to be used with the *survey* package
survey	*svydesign*	Specify the data set, sampling weights, cluster ids, and strata ids to be used in the analysis
survey	*svyglm*	Fit a logistic regression for estimating propensity scores with complex survey data
survey	*fitted*	Obtain propensity scores estimated with logistic regression
base	*set.seed*	Set random seed to allow replicability of results
party	*ctree*	Run a classification tree to estimate propensity scores
party	*cforest_unbiased*	Set tuning parameters for the random forest algorithm
party	*cforest*	Run random forests to estimate propensity scores
party	*predict*	Obtain propensity scores estimated with random forests
twang	*ps*	Run generalized boosted modeling to estimate propensity scores

[6] The code to obtain these figures is on the book's website.

FIGURE 2.6 ● Box-and-Whiskers Plot of Propensity Scores of Participation in Career Academy Estimated With GBM for Treated and Untreated Groups

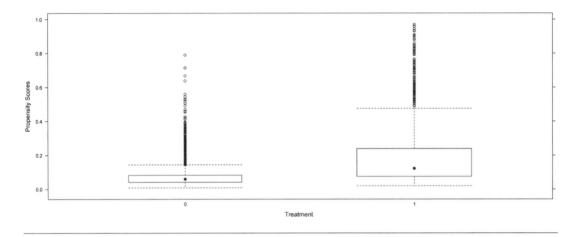

FIGURE 2.7 ● Kernel Density Plots of Propensity Scores Estimated With Logistic Regression From Five Imputed Data Sets

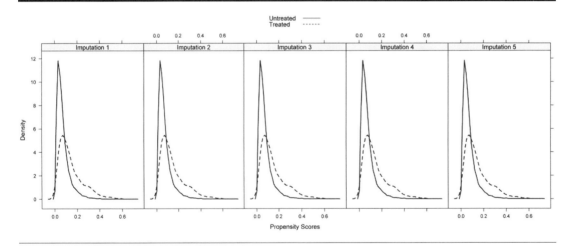

2.7. Conclusion

The example presented in this chapter, as well as other examples in this book, demonstrates that propensity score analysis methods are well suited for large-scale longitudinal surveys, because they measure a large number of covariates potentially related to both

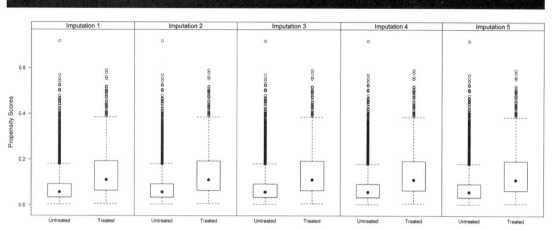

FIGURE 2.8 ● Box-and-Whiskers Plots of Propensity Scores Estimated With Logistic Regression From Five Imputed Data Sets

treatment participation and the outcome. Logistic regression, random forests, and generalized boosted modeling are just a small sample of the several methods that can be used to estimate propensity scores. Although not reviewed in this chapter, Bayesian methods for propensity score estimation (An, 2010; Kaplan & Chen, 2012, 2014; McCandless, Gustafson, Austin, & Levy, 2009) and bootstrap-based propensity score estimation (Bai, 2013) are promising new approaches because they can incorporate the uncertainty of estimated propensity scores into the analysis. Furthermore, the covariate balancing propensity score method (Imai & Ratkovic, 2014) is a promising new approach for estimating propensity scores, because it fits a logistic regression model to the data to predict treatment assignment while maximizing covariate balance with inverse probability of treatment weighting.

Because propensity score methods only remove bias due to observed covariates, the importance of identifying true confounders of the causal relationship between treatment and outcome cannot be overstated. It is recommended that researchers spend time identifying covariates controlled in previous studies, as well as using preliminary quantitative analysis, such as examining relationships between covariates and outcome proxies (Kelcey, 2011a), to identify potential true confounders. The choice of method to estimate propensity scores between many available parametric models and data mining methods is not as important as controlling for the right covariates, because there is evidence that multiple methods to estimate the propensity score (e.g., Setoguchi et al., 2008; Westreich et al., 2010) can provide adequate results with good tuning parameters/specifications, but if an important true confounder is omitted, substantial bias will remain even if covariate balance is achieved. However, tuning a propensity score estimation method to achieve adequate balance of observed covariates may not be a straightforward task if there are many interactions between covariates. Although data mining methods specifically target identification of interactions, tuning parameters for these methods that consistently perform well for propensity score estimation have not been extensively researched. Therefore, it is practical for a researcher to try a single method for estimating propensity scores and, if there are no convergence or common support problems and covariate balance is achieved, to proceed with the remaining steps of the analysis. However, if the researcher's chosen method is not successful, it is helpful to try different propensity score estimation methods.

Study Questions

1. What are the steps of propensity score estimation?

2. How can the success of propensity score estimation be determined?

3. What are true confounders?

4. What is the consequence of including variables that are related to the outcome but not to treatment assignment in the propensity score model?

5. What is the consequence of including variables that are related to the treatment assignment but not to the outcome in the propensity score model?

6. What are three strategies that can be used to select covariates for the propensity score model?

7. Why is it important not to use the outcome data in the process of selecting covariates for the propensity score model?

8. What are two strategies to use multiple imputation to deal with missing data in the propensity score estimation process?

9. Identify three methods that can be used to estimate propensity scores.

10. What is the main challenge for using logistic regression to estimate propensity scores?

11. How do classification trees produce estimates of propensity scores?

12. What are the limitations of classification trees for propensity score estimation?

13. What is the difference between classification trees and bagging?

14. What is the difference between bagging and random forests?

15. What are the advantages of random forests over bagging?

16. How can generalized boosted modeling produce estimates of propensity scores?

17. What is the difficulty of implementing generalized boosting with respect to determining a stop criterion?

18. What stop criterion can be used with generalized boosted modeling in propensity score estimation?

19. What is common support?

20. How can common support be evaluated?

3

Propensity Score Weighting

3.1. Introduction

This chapter addresses the estimation of treatment effects using weights that are derived directly from propensity scores. For estimating the average treatment effect on the treated (ATT), propensity score weighting is commonly referred to in the literature as weighting by the odds (Harder, Stuart, & Anthony, 2010), but for estimating the average treatment effect (ATE), it is known as inverse probability-of-treatment weighting (IPTW; Hernán, Brumback, & Robins, 2000; Robins, Hernán, & Brumback, 2000). However, the use of weights that originated from propensity scores to adjust the distributions of confounding variables so that they are similar for treated and untreated groups is not unique to the propensity weighting techniques discussed in this chapter. As shown in Chapters 4 and 5 of this volume, propensity score stratification and matching can also be used to define observation weights that reduce selection bias. A key difference between propensity score methods that use weights is how coarse the weight is: The propensity score weighting methods discussed in this chapter produce potentially as many different weights as there are observations in the sample. On the other hand, variable ratio greedy matching without replacement (see Chapter 5) can be viewed as a strategy to define weights where treated units receive a weight of 1, matched untreated units receive a weight equal to the inverse of the number of matches, and unmatched units receive a weight of 0. With propensity score stratification (see Chapter 4), weights are calculated for each stratum by treatment condition combination.

The estimation methods with propensity score weights that are presented in this chapter belong to the class of methods for estimation with sampling weights (Heeringa et al., 2010; Kish, 1965; Lohr, 1999). Sampling weights adjust for bias due to oversampling of individuals with certain characteristics so that the weighted sample is representative of the population of interest. Similarly, propensity score weights adjust for overselection of participants with certain characteristics to treated or untreated groups so that the weighted sample represents a pseudo-population where treated and untreated groups have similar covariate distributions. This chapter uses the *survey* package of R (Lumley, 2010) for implementing the demonstration of propensity score weighting. Because of the similarity between estimation with propensity score weights and estimation with sampling weights, this chapter will also demonstrate combining propensity score weights with sampling weights.

3.2. Description of Example

Continuing the analysis steps shown in Chapter 2, this chapter demonstrates propensity score weighting through the estimation of the effect of high school student participation in career academies on future earnings, expanding on the study by Rojewski et al. (2010). The example uses data from the base year (i.e., 2002) and second follow-up (i.e., 2006) of the Education Longitudinal Study (ELS). The base year student survey of the ELS contains the question "Have you ever been in any of the following kinds of courses or programs in high school?" where option *k* is "Career Academy." It is important to qualify that in this example, the treatment effect is estimated without any consideration of the duration of the program, duration of student enrollment, and program quality. Earnings were measured at the second follow-up (variable *F2ERN5P2*) and coded into seven categories in the public data set (earnings in exact dollars are available in the ELS restricted data set) but are treated as continuous and approximately normally distributed in this example analysis.

The ELS sample was obtained with a two-stage stratified sampling method where schools were sampled with probability proportional to size (PPS) sampling, and approximately 26 students were selected per school (Ingels et al., 2004). Both school and student samples were stratified, and Asian and Hispanic students were oversampled. In this example, the clustered nature of data is accounted for using a design-based approach (Heeringa et al., 2010; Lumley, 2010), which provides cluster-robust standard errors, but analysis of multilevel data with a model-based approach is shown in Chapter 10. A brief comparison of design-based and model-based approaches for propensity score analysis of complex survey data is presented in Chapter 1. The estimation of propensity scores for this example with logistic regression, random forests, and generalized boosted modeling (GBM) is presented in Chapter 2.

3.3. Calculation of Weights

In this section, propensity scores estimated with logistic regression as shown in Chapter 2 are used to demonstrate the calculation of propensity score weights. For estimation of the ATT, the weight w_i for each individual is defined as

$$w_i = Z_i + (1 - Z_i) \frac{e_i(X)}{1 - e_i(X)}, \tag{3.1}$$

where Z_i is a treatment indicator assuming values of 1 for the treated and 0 for the untreated, and $e_i(X)$ is the estimated propensity score (Harder et al., 2010). The following code creates the weight variable *weightATT* by using the *ifelse* function to implement the rule that the weight for the ATT is equal to 1 for students who participated in a career academy and the odds of treatment for students who did not participate:

ELS.data.imputed$weightATT <- with(ELS.data.imputed, ifelse(treat==1,
1, pScores/(1-pScores)))

The treatment indicator in the *ELS.data.imputed* data set is the variable *treat,* and the variable *pScores* contains propensity scores estimated with logistic regression. A summary of the ATT weights for treated and untreated groups is obtained with the following:

with(ELS.data.imputed, by(weightATT,treat,summary))

```
treat: 0
      Min.    1st Qu.   Median     Mean    3rd Qu.     Max.
  0.001527  0.032260  0.057220  0.085960  0.099450  2.247000
  -----------------------------------------------------------------
treat: 1
      Min.    1st Qu.   Median    Mean    3rd Qu.     Max.
         1         1         1        1         1         1
```

For each individual, the propensity score weight for estimating the ATE is the inverse of the probability of exposure to the condition the individual was exposed to. Therefore, weights are obtained with the following equation (Stuart, 2010):

$$w_i = \frac{Z_i}{e_i(X)} + \frac{1 - Z_i}{1 - e_i(X)} \tag{3.2}$$

In the following code, the weight variable *weightATE* is created by using the *ifelse* function to obtain the inverse of the propensity score if the student participated in a career academy or the inverse of 1 minus the propensity score if the student did not participate in a career academy:

ELS.data.imputed$weightATE <- with(ELS.data.imputed, ifelse(treat==1,

1/pScores, 1/(1-pScores)))

This code provides a summary of weights for the ATE for participants and nonparticipants of a career academy:

with(ELS.data.imputed, by(weightATE,treat,summary))

```
treat: 0
   Min.    1st Qu.    Median    Mean    3rd Qu.    Max.
   1.002     1.032     1.057    1.086     1.099   3.247
----------------------------------------------------------------
treat: 1
   Min.    1st Qu.    Median    Mean    3rd Qu.     Max.
   1.000     5.036     9.478   14.200    16.640  187.800
```

Propensity score weighting may result in extreme weights, which inflate the standard errors of the treatment estimates (Robins et al., 2000) and may also increase bias (Harder et al., 2010). Extreme weights may be due to model misspecification and/or lack of common support of propensity score distributions. Extreme weights may occur with the weights for the ATE in Equation (3.2) but rarely occur with the weights in Equation (3.1) for the ATT (Harder et al., 2010). For example, the maximum weight for the ATT shown above is 2.24, but the maximum weight for the ATE is 187.8. Individuals with extreme weights for the ATE are those who are either very likely to participate in the treatment given their covariate values but did not or very unlikely to participate but did so. Lee, Lessler, and Stuart (2011) demonstrated that misspecification of the propensity score model tends to increase the occurrence of extreme weights, so attempting to respecify the model or to use a data mining algorithm that automatically searches for interactions and nonlinear terms (see Chapter 2) may reduce extreme weights. An important difficulty with respect to dealing with extreme weights is that there is no precise definition of how large a weight needs to be to have adverse effects. Furthermore, in data sets with sampling weights such as in the example presented here, the final weights used to estimate treatment effects are a product of the propensity score weight and the sampling weight (Hahs-Vaughn & Onwuegbuzie, 2006), and therefore identifying extreme propensity score weights is potentially misleading given that they may be associated with small sampling weights.

Four strategies can be used to deal with extreme weights: (1) respecify the propensity score model to check whether extreme weights are due to model misspecification, (2) change the propensity score method (e.g., marginal mean weighting through stratification [Hong, 2010, 2012] shown in Chapter 4 is unlikely to produce extreme weights), (3) perform weight truncation, and (4) use stabilized weights. Options 3 and 4 are described below.

Some researchers have proposed truncating the distribution of weights at certain percentiles when there are extreme weights. Truncation can be performed by assigning the weight at a cutoff percentile to observations with weights above the cutoff. Lee et al. (2011) found that truncation of weights reduced treatment effect estimate bias and standard errors for propensity scores estimated with logistic regression but not with data mining methods, but there are no guidelines about an adequate level of truncation. On the other hand, Gurel and Leite (2012) found that truncating weights at the 99th percentile decreased bias removal compared with using untruncated weights and that the decrease in bias removal increased as the ratio of treated to untreated became smaller. The following code demonstrates weight truncation. More specifically, it uses the *quantile* function to calculate the weight at the 99th percentile and the *ifelse* function to assign this weight to any student whose weight exceeds the 99th percentile:

ELS.data.imputed$weightATETruncated <- with(ELS.data.imputed,

> *ifelse(weightATE > quantile(weightATE, 0.99),*

> *quantile(weightATE, 0.99),weightATE))*

This code obtains a summary of the truncated weights for career academy and non–career academy students separately:

with(ELS.data.imputed, by(weightATETruncated,treat,summary))

```
treat: 0
   Min.    1st Qu.   Median    Mean   3rd Qu.    Max.
  1.002     1.032    1.057    1.086    1.099    3.247
-----------------------------------------------------------------
treat: 1
   Min.    1st Qu.   Median    Mean   3rd Qu.    Max.
  1.000     5.036    9.478   11.390   16.640   24.760
```

Another option to reduce extreme weights is to use stabilized weights (Robins et al., 2000) for estimating the ATE, which are obtained by multiplying the weights of the treated units by the constant c_1 and the weights of the untreated units by the constant c_0, which are equal to the expected values of being in the treated or untreated group, respectively. These constants can be obtained with the following equations (Harder et al., 2010):

$$c_1 = \frac{\sum_{i=1}^{n_1} e_i(X)}{n_1},$$ (3.3)

$$c_0 = \frac{\sum_{i=1}^{n_0} (1 - e_i(X))}{n_0},$$ (3.4)

where n_1 is the number of treated units and n_0 is the number of untreated units. If the data set has sampling weights w_{si}, then the stabilizing constants are weighted means:

$$c_1 = \frac{\sum_{i=1}^{n_1} w_{si} e_i(X)}{\sum_{i=1}^{n_1} w_{si}},$$ (3.5)

$$c_0 = \frac{\sum_{i=1}^{n_0} w_{si} (1 - e_i(X))}{\sum_{i=1}^{n_0} w_{si}}.$$ (3.6)

The stabilized weights are obtained with

$$w_i = \left(c_1 \times \frac{T_i}{e_i(X)} \right) + \left(c_0 \times \frac{1 - T_i}{1 - e_i(X)} \right).$$ (3.7)

The following code uses the survey package to calculate the weighted means of the propensity scores for obtaining c_1 and the weighted means of 1 minus the propensity scores to obtain c_0. The first line of code uses *ifelse* to create a variable with the propensity score for career academy students and 1 minus the propensity score for non–career academy students. The second line of code uses the *surveyDesign* function to declare that the cluster id variable is *psu*, the strata id variable is *STRAT_ID*, the weight variable is *bystuwt*, and the data set is *ELS.data.imputed*. The third line of code uses *svyby* to calculate the constants c_1 and c_0 with the *svymean* function applied separately for career academy and non–career academy groups.

ELS.data.imputed$C <- with(ELS.data.imputed,ifelse(treat==1,pScores,1-pScores))

surveyDesign <- svydesign(ids=~psu, strata=~STRAT_ID, weights=~bystuwt,

data = ELS.data.imputed, nest=T)

constants <- svyby(~C, by=~treat, design=surveyDesign, FUN=svymean)

With the constants c_1 and c_0 calculated in the previous step, the following code uses *ifelse* to obtain stabilized weights according to Equation (3.7):

ELS.data.imputed$stabilizedWeightATE <- ifelse(ELS.data.imputed$treat==1,

constants[1,2]/ELS.data.imputed$C,

constants[2,2]/ELS.data.imputed$C)

with(ELS.data.imputed, by(stabilizedWeightATE,treat,summary))

```
treat: 0
    Min.   1st Qu.   Median    Mean   3rd Qu.    Max.
  0.1584    0.1632   0.1672   0.1717   0.1738   0.5134
--------------------------------------------------------------
treat: 1
    Min.   1st Qu.   Median    Mean   3rd Qu.    Max.
  0.9202    4.6340   8.7220  13.0700  15.3100  172.8000
```

One limitation of stabilized weights with cross-sectional studies is that the reduction of extreme weights may not be substantial.[1] The maximum stabilized weight is 172.8, which is not very different from the maximum original weight of 187.8.

3.4. Covariate Balance Check

In this section, covariate balance evaluation is performed by comparing the standardized difference between the weighted means of the treated and untreated groups. Covariate balance evaluation is the main indicator of the success of the propensity score analysis. It provides evidence that the distribution of each covariate for treated and untreated individuals is similar, and therefore selection bias due to the covariate has been removed.

For the current example, the propensity score weight is multiplied by the sampling weight to account for the unequal sampling probabilities used to select the sample for the ELS. This step is optional and applies only to propensity score analysis of surveys with sampling weights, if the researcher wants to obtain effects that generalize to the population of the survey (see Chapter 1 for extended discussion). The code to compute the *finalWeightBY* variable, which is the product of the propensity score and sampling weight, is shown as follows:

*ELS.data.imputed$finalWeightBY <- with(ELS.data.imputed, bystuwt*weightATT)*

The *bal.stat* function of the *twang* package (Ridgeway et al., 2013) is useful for covariate balance evaluation. It computes the weighted means for continuous covariates,

---

[1] Chapter 9 discusses weight stabilization for longitudinal studies with time-varying treatments.

weighted proportions for categorical covariates, standard deviations, and standardized mean or proportion differences between treated and untreated groups for each covariate. With the *bal.stat* function, standardized mean or proportion differences are computed using the standard deviation of the treated group rather than the pooled standard deviation. This function also tests the between-group differences for statistical significance, but this is not recommended, as discussed in Chapter 1.

For the remainder of this chapter, the R code presented uses propensity score weights to estimate the ATT, because the code for the ATE is identical. The code to evaluate covariate balance with the *bal.stat* function of the *twang* package is below. This function has a *w.all* argument for the propensity score weights (in this case, the product of propensity score weights and sampling weights) and a *sampw* argument for the sampling weights, which are just used for the baseline covariate balance. If there are no sampling weights, then *sampw=1*.

require(twang)

balanceTable <- bal.stat(ELS.data.imputed, vars= covariateNames,

        treat.var = "treat",

        w.all = ELS.data.imputed$finalWeightBY, get.ks=F,

        sampw = ELS.data.imputed$bystuwt,

        estimand="ATT", multinom=F)

balanceTable <- balanceTable$results

round(balanceTable[c(1:5,28),],3)

	x.mn	tx.sd	ct.mn	ct.sd	std.eff.sz	stat	p
BYSTLNG2:0	0.017	0.131	0.018	0.133	-0.003	0.158	0.944
BYSTLNG2:1	0.009	0.095	0.013	0.113	-0.040	NA	NA
BYSTLNG2:2	0.119	0.323	0.119	0.323	0.000	NA	NA
BYSTLNG2:3	0.033	0.179	0.031	0.174	0.010	NA	NA
BYSTLNG2:4	0.822	0.383	0.819	0.385	0.006	NA	NA
bysibhom	1.914	1.617	1.899	1.625	0.009	0.214	0.831

The *balanceTable* object contains the covariate balance table. Because the table is very large, only results for the five levels of the categorical variable *BYSTLNG2* (English fluency) and the numeric variable *bysibhom* (number of siblings at home) are shown above, rounded to three decimal places. The column *tx.mn* of the balance table contains the weighted means of numeric variables and weighted proportions for levels of categorical variables (i.e., factors in R) of the treatment group; the standard deviations of the treatment group are in the column *tx.sd*; the means/proportions of the untreated group are in the column *ct.mn*; the standard deviations of the untreated group are in the column *ct.sd*; the standardized effect sizes are in the column *std.eff.sz*), which are obtained with (*tx.mn-ct.mn*)/*tx.sd*; the test statistic for group differences (a *t* statistic for numeric variables and a chi-square statistic for factors) are in column *stat*; and the *p* values of the test statistics are in column *p*.

In Chapter 2, propensity score estimation is demonstrated with logistic regression, random forests, and GBM, and for the career academy example, logistic regression provided propensity scores with best common support. In this section, propensity scores obtained with these different methods are compared with respect to covariate balance. Covariate balance is evaluated for 30 covariates and 12 dummy missing data indicators, but because covariate balance is evaluated for each level of categorical covariates, the resulting balance table has 154 rows.

Table 3.1 provides summaries of covariate balance with different propensity estimation methods using weights for the ATT. Absolute standardized effect sizes below 0.1 standard deviations can be considered to indicate adequate covariate balance (Austin, 2011b), but differences below 0.25 standard deviations could be acceptable if additional regression adjustment is performed (see discussion of covariate balance in Chapter 1). Weights from propensity scores estimated with logistic regression provided the best covariate balance among the methods used to estimate propensity scores and met the criteria for adequate balance for all covariates.

TABLE 3.1 ● Summary of Absolute Standardized Effect Sizes With Weights for the ATT

Propensity Score Estimation	Minimum	Mean	Maximum
Logistic regression	0.000	0.010	0.057
Random forest	0.000	0.035	0.157
GBM	0.000	0.033	0.125

Table 3.2 shows covariate balance for estimating the ATE, with weights, truncated weights, and stabilized weights obtained with logistic regression, and weights obtained with random forest and GBM. The maximum standardized mean difference across covariates is similar across methods. None of these methods provided covariate balance below 0.1 for all covariates. It should be emphasized that Tables 3.1 and 3.2 aim to illustrate the process of comparing covariate balance across different methods and do not indicate any advantage of one method over others that generalizes beyond this specific example. A researcher may choose a single method to estimate propensity scores and calculate weights, but if adequate covariate balance is not achieved, it may be helpful to attempt different propensity score methods and compare covariate balance across them. Another option is to proceed with the analysis but to add regression adjustment in the outcome model, as demonstrated later in this chapter.

TABLE 3.2 ● Summary of Absolute Standardized Effect Sizes With Weights for the ATE					
Propensity Score Estimation	Weight Type	Index	Minimum	Mean	Maximum
Logistic regression	IPTW	Effect size	0.000	0.029	0.169
	Truncated IPTW	Effect size	0.000	0.031	0.158
	Stabilized IPTW	Effect size	0.000	0.029	0.185
Random forest	IPTW	Effect size	0.001	0.045	0.167
GBM	IPTW	Effect size	0.000	0.038	0.199

3.5. Estimation of Treatment Effects With Propensity Score Weighting

The outcomes of interest in this example are the individual earnings measured at the second follow-up (variable *F2ERN5P2*) of the ELS. Although the calculation of weights to estimate both the ATT and the ATE is presented earlier in this chapter, only the estimation of the ATT is demonstrated in the remainder of this chapter, because only weights for the ATT provided satisfactory covariate balance for all covariates. Furthermore, the code to estimate the ATE is identical if the appropriate weight is used. The ATT of career academy participation is the difference between the mean earnings of career academy students in the second follow-up of the ELS and the mean earnings they would have obtained if they had not participated in a career academy (see Chapter 1 for details about potential outcomes).

In the following code, the final weight that is used to estimate the ATT is calculated as the product of the propensity score weight and the sampling weight. Sampling weights sum to the population size, so before proceeding with the analysis, the final weights are divided by the mean of weights to make them sum to the sample size, which is a process known as normalization. This is done to make sure standard errors are based on the sample size, not on the population size.

ELS.data.imputed$finalWeight2006 <- with(ELS.data.imputed, bystuwt*weightATT)

ELS.data.imputed$finalWeight2006 <- ELS.data.imputed$finalWeight2006/

mean(ELS.data.imputed$finalWeight2006)

The *survey* package is used to estimate the treatment effect. Before the estimation can be performed, the *surveyDesign2006* object is created with the *svydesign* function to declare the names of the variables that contain cluster ids, strata ids, weights, and the data set:

surveyDesign2006 <- svydesign(ids=~psu, strata=~STRAT_ID,

weights=~finalWeight2006, data = ELS.data.imputed, nest=T)

Methods to obtain standard errors for propensity score weighted estimates include Taylor series linearization and resampling methods such as bootstrapping, jackknife, and balanced repeated replication (see review by Rodgers, 1999). To use resampling methods with the *survey* package, the *surveyDesign2006* object created above should be modified to include weights for each replication. The following code takes the *surveyDesign2006* object and adds weights for 1,000 bootstrapped samples:

surveyDesign2006Boot <- as.svrepdesign(surveyDesign2006, type=c("bootstrap"), replicates=1000)

An estimator of the treatment effect with propensity score weighting is the difference between the weighted means of the outcome for treated and untreated groups (Schafer & Kang, 2008):

$$\Delta = \frac{\sum_{i=1}^{n_1} w_{i1} y_{i1}}{\sum_{i=1}^{n_1} w_{i1}} - \frac{\sum_{i=1}^{n_0} w_{i0} y_{i0}}{\sum_{i=1}^{n_0} w_{i0}}, \tag{3.8}$$

where Δ is the estimated treatment effect, w_{i1} and w_{i0} are weights, and y_{i1} and y_{i0} are outcomes for the treated and untreated groups, respectively. The expression above can produce an estimate of either the ATT or the ATE if the appropriate weights are used. The estimator in Equation (3.8) is implemented with the following code in two steps. First, the *svyby* function is used to apply the *svymean* function separately to career academy and non–career academy students to obtain weighted group means of earnings at the second follow-up:

(weightedMeans <- svyby(formula=~F2ERN5P2,by=~treat,design=surveyDesign2006Boot,

FUN=svymean, covmat=TRUE))

```
     treat      F2ERN5P2           se
0        0      3.355654   0.04206533
1        1      3.644437   0.08424351
```

Calculating the weighted variances for each group is also helpful, so they can be used to obtain standardized effect sizes:

(weightedVars <- svyby(formula=~F2ERN5P2,by=~treat,design=surveyDesign2006Boot,

FUN=svyvar,covmat=TRUE))

```
     treat            V1              se
0        0      4.282430      0.08755116
1        1      4.408251      0.15992330
```

In the following code, the *svycontrast* function is used to calculate the difference between the weighted means, which is the ATT of career academy participation on earnings. The argument *contrasts=c(–1,1)* specifies values that result in the mean of the untreated group to be subtracted from the mean of the treated group. Standard errors of both the group means shown above and the ATT shown below were obtained with bootstrapping with 1,000 replications.

(ATT2006 <- svycontrast(weightedMeans, contrasts=c(–1,1)))

```
              contrast           SE
contrast      0.28878       0.0927
```

In the results shown above, the estimated ATT of participation in a career academy is 0.289 (*SE* = 0.093), and it is statistically significant (*p* < .05). Because the effect estimated is the ATT, the interpretation of these results should be made with respect to the career academy participants only. Therefore, these results show that those who reported participating in a career academy in 2002 had earnings in 2006 that were higher than if they had not participated. Calculating a standardized effect size is helpful for understanding the magnitude of the effect independently of the scale of measurement of earnings. Among several measures of effect size available, the Glass delta will be used in this example. The Glass delta is $(\bar{y}_1 - \bar{y}_0)/sd_0$ where $\bar{y}_1$ is the weighted mean of career academy students, $\bar{y}_0$ is the weighted mean of non–career academy students, and sd_0 is the standard deviation of non–career academy students, which can be obtained by taking the square root of the variance estimate obtained previously. For the current example, Glass delta is $0.289/\sqrt{4.282} = 0.140$ indicating that by participating in a career academy, students had an increase in earnings of 0.140 standard deviations.

The treatment effect can also be estimated with weighted least squares (WLS) estimation of the regression model $y_i = \beta_0 + \beta_1 Z_i + \varepsilon_i$ where β_0 is the weighted mean of the untreated group and β_1 is the treatment effect. This estimator is equivalent to the weighted mean differences in Equation (3.8). However, WLS estimation is designed for weights that are the inverse of residual variances (i.e., precision weights), not sampling weights, so even though estimates will be correct, standard errors will be biased (Heeringa et al., 2010). Unbiased standard errors for estimates of regression models with propensity score weighting can be obtained through Taylor series linearization, which is the default method of the *svyglm* function of the *survey* package, as well as with resampling methods. The code to obtain the treatment effect with a regression model is shown as follows. The model formula using R notation is *F2ERN5P2~treat*. This formula can be expanded to include any covariates and interaction effects of interest.

outcomeModel2006 <- svyglm(F2ERN5P2~treat,surveyDesign2006)

summary(outcomeModel2006)

```
Call:
svyglm(formula = F2ERN5P2 ~ treat, surveyDesign2006)
Survey design:
svydesign(ids = ~psu, strata = ~STRAT_ID, weights = ~finalWeight2006,
  data = ELS.data.imputed, nest = T)
Coefficients:
            Estimate  Std. Error  t value  Pr(>|t|)
(Intercept)  3.35565    0.04079   82.272   < 2e-16 ***
treat1       0.28878    0.09348    3.089   0.00215 **
---
Signif. codes: 0 '***' 0.001 '**' 0.01 '*' 0.05 '.' 0.1 ' ' 1
(Dispersion parameter for gaussian family taken to be 4.343435)
Number of Fisher Scoring iterations: 2
```

The code to estimate the treatment effect with a regression model with standard errors estimated with nonparametric bootstrapping is shown as follows. The only difference between this code and the previous one is that the *surveyDesign2006Boot* object, which contains weights for 1,000 bootstrapped samples, is used instead of *surveyDesign2006*.

outcomeModel2006Boot <- svyglm(F2ERN5P2~treat,surveyDesign2006Boot)

summary(outcomeModel2006Boot)

```
Call:
svyglm(formula = F2ERN5P2 ~ treat, surveyDesign2006Boot)
Survey design:
as.svrepdesign(surveyDesign2006, type = c("bootstrap"), replicates = 1000)
Coefficients:
            Estimate  Std. Error  t value  Pr(>|t|)
(Intercept)  3.35565    0.04207   79.772   < 2e-16 ***
treat1       0.28878    0.09273    3.114   0.00198 **
---
Signif. codes: 0 '***' 0.001 '**' 0.01 '*' 0.05 '.' 0.1 ' ' 1
(Dispersion parameter for gaussian family taken to be 4.343089)
Number of Fisher Scoring iterations: 2
```

It should be noted that the standard errors obtained with Taylor series linearization and bootstrapping methods are very similar. Although the regression model shown above has the treatment effect indicator as the only predictor, it can be expanded to include other covariates, with the advantage that confounding variables of no substantive interest are controlled by weighting instead of being included in the model for the outcome (Joffe, Ten Have, Feldman, & Kimmel, 2004). However, if other covariates are included in the regression model, the regression coefficient of the treatment indicator can only be interpreted as the ATT if covariates are centered on the mean of the treated group and all treatment-by-covariate interactions are included in the model. For estimating the ATE, covariates should be centered on the grand mean, and interactions should also be included (Schafer & Kang, 2008).

3.6. Propensity Score Weighting With Multiple Imputed Data Sets

In Chapter 2, both single imputation and multiple imputation were demonstrated as methods to handle missing data when estimating propensity scores. The R code presented in this chapter so far implements propensity score weighting with a single data set. If the researcher is working with multiple imputed data sets, both the *mice* (van Buuren & Oudshoorn, 2000) and *mitools* (Lumley, 2014) packages have functions that facilitate applying the same methods to multiple imputed data sets. The *mitools* package works together with the *survey* package, so it is particularly useful when the imputed data come from complex survey samples. In the code shown in Chapter 2, the *allImputations* object was created with the *imputationList* function of the *mitools* package to store the multiple imputed data sets. The following code uses the *update* function of the *mitools* package to modify the *allImputations* object by creating a *weightATT* variable with propensity score weights within each imputed data set.

library(mitools)

allImputations <- update(allImputations, weightATT = ifelse(treat==1,

1, pScores/(1-pScores)))

When multiple imputation is used to handle missing data in the covariates, treatment indicator, and outcomes (see additional discussion of missing data in Chapter 2), it is necessary to estimate the treatment effect for each imputed data set and then combine the multiple treatment effect estimates and their variances using Rubin's (1987) rules: The treatment effect estimate is $\Delta = \sum \Delta_m /m$, the mean of the treatment effect estimates Δ_m from the m imputed data sets. The total variance var (Δ) of the treatment effect estimate is a weighted sum of the within-imputation variance and the between-imputation variance. The within-imputation variance is $\text{var}(\Delta)_w = \sum \text{var} (\Delta)_m /m$, the average of the treatment effect variances obtained from the imputed data sets.

The between-imputation variance is var $(\Delta)_B = \Sigma (\Delta_m - \Delta)^2 /(m-1)$, the variance of the treatment effect estimates Δ_m. The total variance is var $(\Delta) = $ var $(\Delta)_w + (1 + (1 + /m))$ var$(\Delta)_B$. The *survey* package can handle estimation using data from multiple imputed data sets prepared with the *imputationList* function of the *mitools* package. With the following code, the final weight is computed within each imputed data set by multiplying the propensity score weight by the sampling weight and then dividing the final weight by its mean:

allImputations <- update(allImputations, finalWeightATT = bystuwt*weightATT)

allImputations <- update(allImputations, finalWeightATT =
finalWeightATT/mean(finalWeightATT))

The next step is to create the *surveyDesign2006MI* object using the *svydesign* function of the *survey* package, which specifies variables related to the sampling design and that the *allImputation* object contains all the imputed data sets:

surveyDesign2006MI <- svydesign(ids=~psu, strata=~STRAT_ID, weights=~finalWeightATT,

data = allImputations, nest=T)

The following code implements the estimation of the treatment effect with each imputed data set using a weighted regression model:

outcomeModel2006MI <- with(surveyDesign2006MI, svyglm(F2ERN5P2~treat))

The function *MIcombine* of the *mitools* package applies Rubin's rules to combine the treatment effect estimates and variances across imputed data sets and also provides the fraction of missing information.

resultsModel2006MI <- MIcombine(outcomeModel2006MI)

summary(resultsModel2006MI)

```
Multiple imputation results:
   with(surveyDesign2006MI, svyglm(F2ERN5P2 ~ treat))
   MIcombine.default(outcomeModel2006MI)
               results          se    (lower      upper) missInfo
 (Intercept) 3.3754822  0.03656966  3.30379330  3.4471711      3 %
 treat1      0.2722613  0.09304645  0.08988992  0.4546328      1 %
```

The ATT of participating in a career academy on income is 0.272 ($SE = 0.093$), which is statistically significant, with a confidence interval of 0.090 to 0.455. For this example, the fraction of missing information for the estimation of the treatment effect is only 1%, and therefore both the final estimate and standard error are very similar to those obtained with a single imputed data set.

3.7. Doubly Robust Estimation of Treatment Effect With Propensity Score Weighting

Doubly robust propensity score methods rely on dual modeling of both the treatment assignment mechanism (i.e., the propensity score model) and the outcome to provide unbiased estimates if either the propensity score model or the outcome model is correct (Imbens & Wooldridge, 2009). The doubly robust estimator demonstrated in this section consists of regression estimation of propensity score weighted means using the propensity score as a covariate (Schafer & Kang, 2008), followed by estimation of the difference between weighted means with Equation (3.8), but several other doubly robust estimators have been proposed (e.g., Bang & Robins, 2005; Kang & Schafer, 2007a). Regression estimation of a population mean or total is used frequently in the survey literature (Lohr, 1999; Lumley, 2010) to capitalize on the relationship between outcomes and covariates and from known population totals for the covariates to reduce bias and increase efficiency of estimates. For application of regression estimation with propensity score weights, separate regressions are fit to the outcomes of treated and untreated individuals:

$$y_{i1} = \beta_{01} + \beta_{11} X_{i1} + \varepsilon_{i1} \tag{3.9}$$

$$y_{i0} = \beta_{00} + \beta_{10} X_{i0} + \varepsilon_{i0} \tag{3.10}$$

Because the predictors are known for the entire sample, the regressions above can be used to obtain predicted values $\hat{y}_{i1}$ and $\hat{y}_{i0}$, in the presence and absence of treatment, respectively, for the entire sample. Therefore, a doubly robust estimate of the ATE can be obtained with Equation (3.8) but with predicted outcomes $\hat{y}_{i1}$ and $\hat{y}_{i0}$ replacing observed outcomes y_{i1} and y_{i0}, respectively (Schafer & Kang, 2008). For the ATT, the predicted outcomes are for the treated observations only, using Equations (3.9) and (3.10). The code to use the *survey* package to obtain a doubly robust regression estimate of the treatment effect with the propensity score as a covariate is shown below. The first step is to use the *subset* function to obtain separate survey design objects for treated and untreated observations. The second step is to fit outcome models with linear, quadratic, and cubic functions of the propensity score for treated and untreated groups using the *svyglm* function. The third step is to use the *predict* function to obtain predicted values of the outcome for propensity scores of the treated group using the outcome models developed in the previous step. In the final step, the differences between predicted outcomes for the treated group in the presence and absence of treatment are calculated and then averaged with the *svycontrast* function to obtain the ATT.

surveyDesign2006T <- subset(surveyDesign2006Boot, treat==1)

surveyDesign2006U <- subset(surveyDesign2006Boot, treat==0)

modelT <- svyglm(F2ERN5P2~pScores+I(pScores^2)+I(pScores^3),surveyDesign2006T)

modelU <- svyglm(F2ERN5P2~pScores+I(pScores^2)+I(pScores^3),surveyDesign2006U)

Yt1 <- predict(modelT,

    newdata=data.frame(pScores=with(ELS.data.imputed,pScores[treat==1])),

    vcov=TRUE, type="response")

Yt0 <- predict(modelU,

    newdata=data.frame(pScores=with(ELS.data.imputed,pScores[treat==1])),

    vcov=TRUE, type="response")

diff <- Yt1 - Yt0

ATT2006DR <- svycontrast(diff, contrasts=rep(1/length(diff),length(diff)))

```
Statistic:
             [,1]
contrast 0.3159268
SE:
           [,1]
[1,] 0.0824568
```

In this example, the doubly robust estimate of the ATT of participating in a career academy on earnings is very similar to the estimates obtained previously with non–doubly robust estimators with either single or multiple imputed data sets. This is a desirable result because it shows that the effect is not sensitive to the specification of the outcome model.

3.8. Sensitivity Analysis

The objective of a sensitivity analysis is to identify how much unmeasured confounding would produce a change in the conclusions of the study. Carnegie, Harada, and Hill (2016) developed a method for sensitivity analysis where the relationships of a single confounding variable U with the treatment Z and outcome Y are manipulated through a simulation to identify how large these relationships need to be for the treatment to become nonsignificant. Their method consists of evaluating changes of the treatment effect and its p value for a set of values of two sensitivity parameters.

More specifically, ζ^Z is a sensitivity parameter quantifying the relationship between U and Z, while ζ^Y quantifies the relationship between U and Y. These sensitivity parameters are shown in Figure 3.1. There are five steps in Carnegie, Harada, and Hill's method:

1. Define sensitivity parameters based on the observed data. Multiple values should be selected for both ζ^Z and ζ^Y, which results in a matrix of combinations of values.

2. For each pair of values of ζ^Z and ζ^Y and the vector of observed values of Y, Z, and X, simulate U from the conditional distribution of U given Y, Z, and X.

3. Fit the outcome model with Z, X, and U as predictors and obtain the treatment effect and its standard error.

4. Repeat Steps 2 and 3 for k iterations with the same pair of sensitivity parameters, and average the treatment effects across iterations. The standard error is obtained by squaring the sum of the within-replication and between-replication variances.

5. Select another pair of sensitivity parameters and repeat Steps 2 to 4.

FIGURE 3.1 ● Sensitivity Parameters for a Single Unmeasured Confounder in Carnegie, Harada, and Hill's (2016) Sensitivity Analysis Method

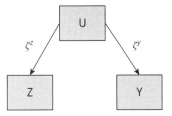

The sensitivity analysis based on a matrix of sensitivity parameters results in a corresponding matrix of treatment effects and standard errors. Examining this matrix allows the identification of which pairs of sensitivity parameters resulted in nonsignificant treatment effects. It is also interesting to examine which pairs of sensitivity parameters resulted in a zero effect. The *treatSens* package (Carnegie, Harada, Dorie, & Hill, 2016) implements the sensitivity analysis. It is able to automatically select sensitivity parameters by identifying which values would make the treatment equal to zero and increase or decrease the sensitivity parameters in steps from these values. In this example, automatic selection of sensitivity parameters is used.

require(treatSens)

sensitivity <- treatSens(formula=F2ERN5P2~treat+pScores+I(pScores^2)+I(pScores^3),

trt.family = binomial(link="probit"), grid.dim = c(5,5), nsim = 20,

data=ELS.data.imputed, weights=ELS.data.imputed$finalWeight2006)

The *formula* argument specifies the outcome model, with the treatment indicator as the first predictor. The same outcome model of the doubly robust analysis presented previously is used. The *trt.family = binomial(link="probit")* argument specifies that the generalized linear model for the treatment assignment used for simulation is a probit regression. The *grid.dim = c(5,5)* argument specifies that a 5×5 matrix of sensitivity parameters should be evaluated. The *nsim = 20* argument specifies that 20 simulated values of U should be generated for each cell of the matrix of sensitivity parameters. The *weights* argument specifies the propensity score weights. The results of the sensitivity analysis obtained with the *summary* function are shown as follows:

summary(sensitivity)

```
Coefficients on U where tau = 0:
      Y       Z
  1.034   2.109
  1.085   0.870
  1.150   0.000
  1.348  -1.610
  1.423  -1.806
  1.897  -2.182
Coefficients on U where significance level 0.05 is lost:
      Y       Z
  0.981   2.109
  0.998   0.870
  1.033   0.000
  1.113  -1.610
  1.423  -2.418
  1.897  -2.574
Estimated treatment effects
          -2.85   -1.61       0    0.87   2.109
  0        0.146   0.146   0.146   0.146   0.146
  0.474    0.423   0.394   0.145  -0.027  -0.124
  0.948    0.696   0.637   0.140  -0.190  -0.389
  1.423    0.939   0.812   0.121  -0.299  -0.640
  1.897    1.201   0.980   0.110  -0.501  -0.907
```

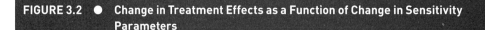

FIGURE 3.2 ● Change in Treatment Effects as a Function of Change in Sensitivity Parameters

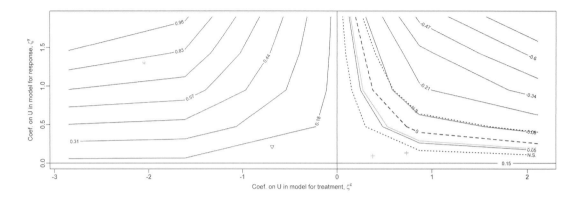

The first part of the results of the sensitivity analysis shows coefficients on U where the treatment effect is zero. These standardized coefficients are large, which leads to the conclusion that an unmeasured confounder with a strong relationship with Z or Y would have to exist for the current effect to become zero if the confounder is included in analysis. The second part of the results shows coefficients on U where statistical significance at alpha = .05 is lost. These coefficients are also large, which shows that there would have to be a strong omitted confounder for the effect to be nonsignificant. Therefore, the results of the sensitivity analysis support the conclusion that the estimated treatment effect is robust to omitted confounders. The last part of the sensitivity analysis output displays a matrix of treatment effects for different values of sensitivity parameters. The *treatSens* package also has a plotting function that is helpful in visualizing the sensitivity analysis results. The code *sensPlot(sensitivity)* produces the graph in Figure 3.2. In this graph, the dotted line indicates a nonsignificant effect and the dashed line indicates a zero effect. It is possible to observe in this graph how the effects change as a function of the sensitivity parameters.

3.9. Conclusion

One of the main advantages of propensity score weighting is that it can be combined with any parametric or nonparametric modeling of outcomes capable of including sampling weights. Inverse probability of treatment weighting, in particular, is widely used in epidemiology with marginal structural models (Bodnar, 2004;

TABLE 3.3 ● Summary of Main Functions Used in This Chapter		
Package	**Function**	**Objective**
base	*ifelse*	Execute a conditional statement to assign weights to treated or untreated groups
base	*by*	Obtain statistics separately for treated and untreated groups
stats	*quantile*	Obtain quantiles
survey	*svydesign*	Describe the data, sampling weights, cluster ids, and strata ids of a survey design
survey	*svyby*	Obtain statistics separately for treated and untreated groups from a complex survey sample
survey	*svyglm*	Fit the outcome model with design-based methods for complex survey samples
survey	*svycontrast*	Estimate differences between means
mitools	*MIcombine*	Combine estimates from multiple imputed data sets
mitools	*update*	Add variables to multiple imputed data sets
treatSens	*treatSens*	Obtain a sensitivity analysis
treatSens	*sensPlot*	Plot the results of the sensitivity analysis

Cole, 2005; Hernán et al., 2000; Petersen, Deeks, Martin, & van der Laan, 2007). From all propensity score methods, propensity score weighting has the most straightforward application to continuous treatments (see Chapter 7) and longitudinal studies of time-varying effects of repeatable treatments (see Chapter 9). Another key advantage of propensity score weighting is that, differently from matching, it does not require that each treated observation has at least one untreated observation within its area of common support. However, a certain degree of common support is needed to achieve adequate covariate balance. Although extreme weights may be a problem when implementing propensity score weighting, there are alternatives to minimize this problem such as truncation and stabilization. However, there has not been a comprehensive evaluation of these strategies in the literature, so if extreme weights are a concern, multiple strategies to address the problem should be compared.

Study Questions

1. What is the difference between propensity score weights and sampling weights?

2. What is the difference between the weights for estimating the ATE and the ATT?

3. What are possible causes of extreme propensity score weights?

4. What are possible consequences of extreme propensity score weights?

5. What are possible methods to deal with extreme weights?

6. What is the difference between propensity score weights and stabilized propensity score weights?

7. How should covariate balance be checked after propensity score weighting?

8. What are two options to estimate the treatment effect with propensity score weighting?

9. How can sampling weights be incorporated into the treatment effect estimation with propensity score weights?

10. Describe two options to obtain standard errors of the estimated treatment effect.

11. What is a doubly robust estimator?

12. How can doubly robust estimation be implemented with propensity score weighting?

4

Propensity Score Stratification

Learning Objectives

- Identify the characteristics of propensity score stratification that separate it from other propensity score methods.

- Describe the strategies to perform propensity score stratification for estimating the ATE and ATT.

- Calculate weights associated with strata.

- Perform a covariate balance check with propensity score stratification.

- Estimate the ATE and ATT with propensity score stratification.

- Estimate the ATE and ATT with doubly robust propensity score stratification.

- Identify the limitations of propensity score stratification and alternatives.

4.1. Introduction

Propensity score stratification or subclassification consists of using the propensity score distribution to divide the sample of treatment participants and nonparticipants into groups that are similar with respect to the distribution of covariates. In essence, propensity score stratification is a method of coarse matching of treated and untreated participants based on propensity scores. The most popular method of propensity score stratification is to divide the sample based on quintiles of the propensity score distribution (Thoemmes & Kim, 2011). This practice originated from seminal works on covariate stratification by Cochran (1968) and propensity score stratification by Rosenbaum and Rubin (1983b, 1984), who proposed that the propensity score can be used as a balancing score instead of covariates, thus solving the dimensionality problem of stratifying by multiple covariates. With propensity score stratification, increasing the number of strata also increases reduction of bias. In a review of applications of propensity score stratification, Thoemmes and Kim (2011) found studies that used between 5 and 20 strata. However, the number of strata is limited by the common support of the propensity score distributions of treated and untreated groups, because each stratum must have at least one treated and one untreated observation.

There are two approaches to using propensity score stratification to estimate treatment effects: (1) pool strata-specific treatment effects and (2) obtain a marginal treatment effect across strata. The first approach was used in the original application of propensity score stratification presented by Rosenbaum and Rubin (1984). The second approach was promoted by Hong (2010, 2012), who refers to it as marginal mean weighting through stratification. In this chapter, the two approaches will be demonstrated.

4.2. Description of Example

The example for this chapter is inspired by a study by Na and Gottfredson (2013), which investigated the effects of having full-time police officers in schools on the incidence of crime, percentage of incidents reported to the police, and percentage of administration of harsh discipline practices, using three waves (i.e., 2003–2004, 2005–2006, and 2007–2008) of restricted-use data from the School Survey on Crime and Safety (SSOCS). The example in this chapter will be based on public use data from the 2007–2008 wave of the SSOCS (Ruddy, Neiman, Hryczaniuk, Thomas, & Parmer, 2010) to demonstrate propensity score stratification for estimating the average treatment effect (ATE) and average treatment effect on the treated (ATT) of having one full-time security employee (i.e., police officer or security guard) in schools on the proportion of harsh discipline measures administered in response to incidents of crime, violence, and insubordination. Because the reported numbers of full-time security personnel in the SSOCS schools vary widely (i.e., mean: 1.40, standard deviation: 5.42), the focus here will be on comparing schools with one full-time security employee and schools without any full-time security staff. Na and Gottfredson found that adding full-time police officers was related to an increase in the incidence of crime related to weapons and drugs, as well as an increase in the percentage reporting nonviolent crimes to police, but was unrelated to the percentage of use of harsh discipline. In addition, they found no interaction effects between use of full-time police offices and the percentages of minority and special education students in the schools on the use of harsh discipline. Na and Gottfredson provide detailed discussion of these results in light of existing theory and previous studies, including the limitation that adding full-time police officers may affect the measurement of school crime.

The 2007–2008 SSOCS was administered to a nationally representative sample of primary, middle, and high schools. Schools were selected for participation using stratified sampling with explicit stratification by instructional level, locale (i.e., city, suburb, town, and rural), and enrollment size. The complete SSOCS data include responses for 2,560 schools, but removing schools with more than one full-time security employee reduced the sample size to 1,786. A variable with case weights is provided with the data set that adjusts for nonresponse bias and differences between population strata sizes and sample strata sizes. Missing data were imputed prior to the data set being made available. The documentation for the public use data (Ruddy et al., 2010) describes how imputation was performed. The public use SSOCS data set provides indicators of which values were imputed, so the analyst can implement other treatments of missing data, such as multiple imputation. For this example, the imputed public use SSOCS data are used in the analysis, but dummy missing value indicators are included as covariates in the propensity score model. A detailed example of dealing with missing data using multiple imputation in propensity score analysis is presented in Chapters 2 and 3.

The treatment for this example is defined as a school having one full-time security employee, which could be a full-time school resource officer (SRO), sworn law enforcement officer, or security guard. Schools that did not employ any security personnel or employed only part-time ones were considered untreated. For this example analysis, there were 1,265 untreated and 521 treated cases.

The outcome in this example analysis is the proportion of application of harsh discipline for use or possession of weapons, explosives, alcohol, or illegal drugs; physical attacks or fights; and insubordination. As in Na and Gottfredson (2013), harsh disciplinary practices were defined as removing students from the school with no additional services for the remainder of the year, transferring to specialized schools, or suspending for at least 5 days. Other disciplinary practices, such as suspension for less than 5 days and retention, were considered nonharsh. The proportion of harsh discipline is calculated from the responses to Item 22 of the SSOCS as the number of times harsh disciplinary practices were used divided by the number of times harsh and nonharsh practices were used. The mean proportion of times harsh discipline practices were used with this sample of schools is 0.25% (unweighted).

4.3. Propensity Score Estimation

This chapter shows the estimation of propensity scores of schools having one security employee using logistic regression, but code for estimation with random forests and generalized boosted modeling is shown on the book's website. The covariates used in the propensity score model included most variables controlled for by Na and Gottfredson (2013) (e.g., categories of total enrollment, percentage of students in special education, percentage of students who are eligible for free or reduced-price lunch, percentage of minority students, average daily attendance, crime level in the school's area, school locale, and grade level), as well as indicators of the security measures used in the school (e.g., use of locks, uniforms, training of teachers, written plans). A total of 63 covariates were selected. Following Stuart's (2010) recommendation for propensity score estimation with single imputed data sets, dummy missing value indicators were added in the propensity score model. The imputation indicators provided with the SSOCS data set for each imputed value are categorical variables with three levels indicating whether the value was not imputed, imputed with exact match, or imputed with a relaxed criterion. These were converted into binary indicators (i.e., imputed or not imputed) and included in the propensity score model for variables with more than 5% of imputed values. If two variables had imputed values for similar sets of cases (i.e., the correlation between their dummy missing value indicators was above 0.8), only one of the indicators was included. This procedure produced four dummy missing indicators, and therefore the propensity score model has 67 predictors. The code to prepare the data set and select covariates for the propensity score model is provided on the book's website. The following code is used to estimate propensity scores of having one full-time security employee with logistic regression using survey weights to adjust for sampling and nonresponse bias. First, the *surveyDesign* object is created with the *svydesign* function to declare that the variable *STRATA* contains the strata id numbers, the variable *FINALWGT* has the weights, and the data set is *SSOCS.data*.

library(survey)

surveyDesign <- svydesign(ids=~0,strata=~STRATA,weights=~FINALWGT,

  data=SSOCS.data)

The logistic regression model is fit using the *svyglm* function. The argument *family= quasibinomial* is needed instead of *family=binomial* for logistic regression because there are sampling weights that cause overdispersion. The *fitted* function is used to extract the propensity scores into the *pScores* variable.

psModel <- svyglm(psFormula, design=surveyDesign, family=quasibinomial)

SSOCS.data$pScores <- fitted(psModel)

by(data=SSOCS.data$pScores, INDICES=SSOCS.data$treat, FUN=summary)

```
SSOCS.data$treat: 0
    Min.  1st Qu.   Median     Mean  3rd Qu.     Max.
0.009175 0.086750 0.172900 0.222800 0.306000 0.942400
-----------------------------------------------------------------
SSOCS.data$treat: 1
   Min.  1st Qu.   Median     Mean  3rd Qu.     Max.
0.02584  0.26470  0.41700  0.43440  0.59730  0.95450
```

The summary shown above indicates that the maximum propensity scores of schools with and without a security employee are similar, which is preliminary evidence of adequate common support. Examination of histograms, kernel density plots, and box-and-whiskers plots of the distributions of propensity scores of treated and untreated groups can be used to provide additional evidence of adequate common support, because they show whether for part of the distribution of the propensity scores of the treated there are also values in the distribution of propensity scores for the untreated. Overlapping histograms to evaluate common support, shown in Figure 4.1, were obtained with the following code:

hist(SSOCS.data$pScores[SSOCS.data$treat=="Untreated"], density = 10, angle = 45,

main="Propensity Scores", xlab="Shaded = Untreated | Gray = Treated")

hist(SSOCS.data$pScores[SSOCS.data$treat=="Treated"], col=gray(0.4,0.25), add=T)

The box-and-whiskers plot shown in Figure 4.2 is obtained using the *bwplot* function of the *lattice* package with

library(lattice)

bwplot(pScores~treat, data = SSOCS.data, ylab = "Propensity Scores", auto.key = TRUE)

The histograms and box-and-whiskers plots provide some indication that common support is adequate but do not show conclusive evidence because propensity score stratification requires that there be at least one treated and one untreated observation within each stratum. A more precise evaluation of common support can be performed after the cases are distributed into strata, as shown in the next section.

FIGURE 4.1 ● Histograms of the Distributions of Propensity Scores of Treated and Untreated Groups

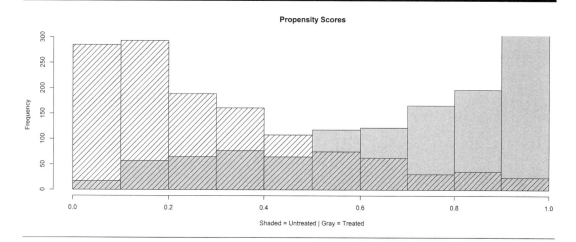

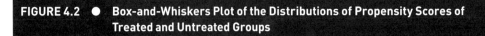

FIGURE 4.2 ● **Box-and-Whiskers Plot of the Distributions of Propensity Scores of Treated and Untreated Groups**

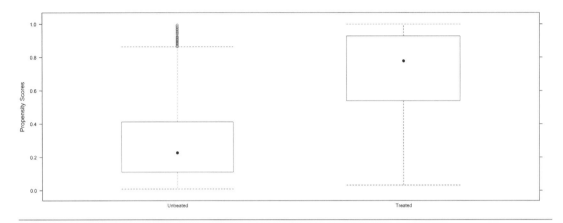

4.4. Propensity Score Stratification

Once propensity scores are estimated, the next step of analysis is to divide the sample into strata based on propensity scores. Strata can be created by converting the propensity score variable into a categorical variable using thresholds defined by quantiles of the propensity score. The most common choice for number of strata is five (Thoemmes & Kim, 2011). The following code used the *cut* function to create five strata of approximately the same size based on the quintiles of the distribution of propensity scores for both treated and untreated groups. The quintiles are obtained with the *quantile* function. The function *levels* is used to assign number labels from 1 to 5 to the strata, and then *xtabs* is used to display strata by treatment counts.

SSOCS.data$subclass <- cut(x=SSOCS.data$pScores,

breaks = quantile(SSOCS.data$pScores,

prob = seq(0, 1, 1/5)),include.lowest=T)

levels(SSOCS.data$subclass) <- 1:length(levels(SSOCS.data$subclass))

xtabs(~treat+subclass,SSOCS.data)

```
       subclass
treat      1      2      3      4      5
    0    340    303    276    209    137
    1     18     54     81    148    220
```

In the cross-classification of treatment group by strata shown above, the total stratum size is approximately the same for all strata. The differences in stratum sizes indicate that the distribution of propensity scores for the treated is negatively skewed, while the distribution for the untreated is positively skewed. Common support is adequate because in all strata, there are some treated and some untreated observations.

If a researcher is interested in estimating the ATT, it may be preferable to stratify based on quintiles of the treated, so that each group has approximately the same number of treated cases, because better covariate balance and power to test the treatment effect may be obtained than when stratification is based on the propensity scores of both groups. The *MatchIt* (Ho et al., 2011) package automates the creation of strata, strata weights, and evaluation of covariate balance. The following code uses the *matchit* function with the arguments *method = "subclass"* and *subclass=5* to divide the cases into five strata. The argument *sub.by = "treat"* specifies that the strata are created based on quintiles of the propensity scores of the treated, rather than the propensity scores of the entire sample. Propensity scores are indicated with *distance = SSOCS.data$pScores*.[1] Then, the *match.data* function creates the *data.stratification* data set containing the original data, strata ids, and weights.

library(MatchIt)

SSOCS.data2<-SSOCS.data[,c("SCHID","treat","percHarsh","pScores",covariateNames)]

stratification <- matchit(psFormula,distance=SSOCS.data$pScores,

      data = SSOCS.data2,

      method = "subclass", sub.by = "treat", subclass=5)

data.stratification <- match.data(stratification)

The following code converts the treatment indicator to a factor with levels *Treated* and *Untreated*, and then *xtabs* displays a cross-classification table of treatment levels by strata.

data.stratification$treat <- factor(data.stratification$treat, levels=c(0,1),

      labels=c("Treated","Untreated"))

xtabs(~treat+subclass, data.stratification)

```
           subclass
treat         1     2     3     4     5
Untreated   796   223   124    72    50
Treated     104   104   105   103   105
```

---

[1] This argument is optional because *matchit* can estimate propensity scores.

It is noticeable in the cross-classification of treatment by strata shown above that the stratification based on the propensity scores of the treated resulted in a similar number of treated units within strata. The differences in number of untreated units across strata indicate that the distribution of propensity scores for the untreated is positively skewed. Also, the cross-classification indicates that there is no common support problem, because there are some untreated units in all of the strata.

4.4.1. Covariate Balance Evaluation

The extent of success of propensity score stratification in reducing selection bias can be evaluated by examining the similarity of distributions of covariates between treated and untreated groups. If the goal is to estimate the treatment effect by pooling stratum-specific treatment effects, covariate balance should be evaluated and achieved within strata. However, if the number of covariates is large, evaluation of covariate balance within strata can become cumbersome. Also, if the sample sizes of treated or untreated groups within strata are small, covariate balance evaluation can become very sensitive to outliers. The *MatchIt* package is used to demonstrate covariate balance evaluation because it provides tables of covariate balance both within strata and across strata. The function *summary* is applied below to extract a covariate balance table from the *stratification* object created earlier.

balance.stratification <- summary(stratification, standardize=T)

The covariate balance table for this example is very large, because there were 67 covariates. To summarize, the following line of code extracts only the standardized mean differences for all strata and then obtains minimums, means, and maximums, which are displayed in Table 4.1.

strataDifferences <- data.frame(balance.stratification$q.table[,3,])

summaryStrataDifferences <- summary(strataDifferences)

TABLE 4.1 ● Summary of Standardized Mean Differences of Covariates Within Each Stratum					
	Stratum				
	1	**2**	**3**	**4**	**5**
Minimum	−0.16787	−0.28865	−0.34637	−0.4921	−0.42214
Mean	0.005179	0.001641	−0.03004	−0.02564	−0.06004
Maximum	0.25173	0.264709	0.39388	0.25578	0.37623

It can be concluded that adequate covariate balance was not achieved within any of the strata, using either the criterion that standardized mean differences should be less than 0.1 to be considered evidence of adequate balance (Austin, 2011b) or the less strict criterion of 0.25 (Stuart, 2010; Stuart & Rubin, 2007). Therefore, treatment effect estimates obtained with these strata will have a substantial amount of bias. This bias could be due to a misspecified propensity score model or could be residual bias due to the limited number of strata and the fact that observations are not optimally allocated to strata to minimize bias. Increasing the number of strata will reduce residual bias, but having a larger number of strata may result in some strata having too few treated or untreated observations, and therefore the estimate of within-stratum group means becomes unreliable. The researcher may investigate the following options to achieve adequate covariate balance: (1) Change the form of the propensity score model or the method to estimate propensity scores; (2) remove within-stratum residual bias by combining stratification with weighting, matching, or direct covariate adjustment with analysis of covariance (ANCOVA; Schafer & Kang, 2008) or regression estimation of group means within strata (Lunceford & Davidian, 2004); and (3) use marginal mean weighting through stratification, which is demonstrated later in this chapter.

4.4.2. Estimation of Treatment Effects

The next step in obtaining a treatment effect is to calculate the stratum weights w_k. For estimating the ATE, the stratum weight is $w_k = n_k/n$, which is the stratum size divided by the total sample size. For estimating the ATT, the stratum weight is $w_k = n_{1k}/n_1$, which is the treated sample size within the stratum divided by the total treated sample size. The stratum weights based on the strata that are obtained by using the quintiles of the treated are shown in Table 4.2.

TABLE 4.2 ● Group Sizes and Weights for Each Stratum						
	Stratum					Group Totals
	1	2	3	4	5	
Untreated	796	223	124	72	50	1,265
Treated	104	104	105	103	105	521
Stratum totals	900	327	229	175	155	1,786
Weight ATE	0.50	0.18	0.13	0.10	0.09	
Weight ATT	0.20	0.20	0.20	0.20	0.20	

Once stratum weights are obtained, it is possible to estimate the treatment effect Δ_k for each stratum k. The simplest estimator of the stratum-specific treatment effect is $\Delta_k = \bar{Y}_{1k} - \bar{Y}_{0k}$, which is the difference between the means of treated and untreated observations within each stratum shown in Table 4.3. The treatment effect Δ for the entire sample can be obtained with a weighted sum of within-stratum treatment effects:

$$\Delta = \sum_{k=1}^{K} w_k \Delta_k \tag{4.1}$$

The standard error of the treatment effect estimate can be obtained with the following formula (Guo & Fraser, 2015):

$$SE(\Delta) = \sqrt{\sum_{k=1}^{K} w_k^2 \, \mathrm{var}(\Delta_k)} \tag{4.2}$$

TABLE 4.3 ● Mean and Standard Error of Proportion Harsh Punishment by Combinations of Treatment Group and Stratum			
Treatment Group	**Stratum**	**Mean Proportion Harsh Punishment**	**Standard Error**
Untreated	1	0.097	0.009
Treated	1	0.114	0.028
Untreated	2	0.202	0.028
Treated	2	0.216	0.033
Untreated	3	0.198	0.027
Treated	3	0.195	0.030
Untreated	4	0.261	0.039
Treated	4	0.343	0.055
Untreated	5	0.336	0.068
Treated	5	0.294	0.031

The first step of the implementation of the estimation method with the *survey* package (Lumley, 2004) is to use the function *svydesign* to specify that the data are in the *data.stratification* object. The argument *strata=~STRATA* specifies the strata id variable provided by the SSOCS data set, not the strata based on the propensity score.

library(survey)

surveyDesign <- svydesign(ids=~0,strata=~STRATA, weights=~FINALWGT, data=data.stratification)

Rather than using Equation (4.2) to obtain standard errors, the following code obtains standard errors through bootstrapping, with 1,000 replicates (Lumley, 2010). The function *as.svrepdesign* adds 1,000 replication weights to the *surveyDesign* created in the previous line of code.

surveyDesignBoot <- as.svrepdesign(surveyDesign, type=c("bootstrap"),replicates=1000)

The following R code uses *svyby* to apply the *svymean* function to estimate the mean proportion of application of harsh discipline separately for schools with and without a security employee within each stratum, taking into consideration the features of the sampling design that generated the data.

subclassMeans <- svyby(formula=~percHarsh, by=~treat+subclass,

design=surveyDesignBoot, FUN=svymean, covmat=TRUE)

To obtain the ATE or ATT by pooling stratum-specific effects, *svycontrast* is used with the weights shown in Table 4.2. For this example, the strata obtained with the quantiles of the propensity scores of the treated are used because the within-stratum group sizes are more balanced than when strata are based on the quintiles of propensity scores for both groups. The ATE and ATT can be estimated by using the weights in Table 4.2 but assigning negative values for the untreated and positive values for the treated. For this example, neither the ATE (0.015, $SE = 0.021$, $p > .05$) nor the ATT (0.013, $SE = 0.025$, $p > .05$) are statistically significant.

(pooledEffects <- svycontrast(subclassMeans, list(

ATE=c(-0.5,0.5,-0.18,0.18,-0.13,0.13,-0.10,0.10,-0.09,0.09),

ATT=c(-0.2,0.2,-0.2,0.2,-0.2,0.2,-0.2,0.2,-0.2,0.2)))))

```
        contrast      SE
ATE     0.014936   0.0205
ATT     0.013313   0.0250
```

4.5. Marginal Mean Weighting Through Stratification

Marginal mean weighting through stratification (MMWS) consists of creating weights based on strata membership that adjust for the difference between the observed proportions of treated and untreated units within strata and the proportions that would be obtained if randomized treatment assignment was used. MMWS is similar to poststratification in survey data analysis because poststratification adjusts for differences between sample proportions within strata and population proportions.

For estimating the ATE with MMWS, the weight w_{sz} for a unit in stratum s and treatment group z is (Hong, 2012)

$$w_{sz} = \frac{n_s \times pr\left(Z = z\right)}{n_{zs}},$$

(4.3)

where n_s is the total number of units in stratum s, $pr\left(Z = z\right)$ is the total proportion of units assigned to group z (i.e., treated or untreated), and n_{zs} is the observed number of units in stratum s and treatment group z. Therefore, the weight is the expected stratum size for group z in a completely randomized experiment divided by observed stratum size. This weight is similar to the poststratification weight, which is the population stratum size divided by the observed stratum size.

The weights for estimating the ATT with MMWS are as follows (Hong, 2010):

$$w_{sz} = Z + \left(1 - Z\right)\frac{n_{1s}pr\left(Z = 0\right)}{n_{0s}pr\left(Z = 1\right)},$$

(4.4)

where Z is 1 for the treated group and 0 for the untreated group, n_{1s} is the number treated, and n_{0s} is the number untreated within stratum s, while $pr\left(Z = 1\right)$ and $pr\left(Z = 0\right)$ are the proportion of treated and proportion of untreated units, respectively.

The weights for MMWS shown in Equations (4.3) and (4.4) for the ATE and ATT, respectively, can be considered coarse, nonparametric versions of the weights shown in Chapter 3, which are computed directly from propensity scores instead of from strata. More specifically, n_s/n_{zs} is the inverse of the proportion treated or untreated per stratum, which is a nonparametric estimate of the inverse probability of treatment shown in Equation (3.2). Also, Equation (4.4) is similar to weighting the untreated units by the odds of treated shown in Equation (3.1), because the term n_{1s}/n_{0s} in Equation (4.4) is the within-stratum ratio of treated to untreated units and therefore is a nonparametric estimate of the odds of treatment within each stratum. Example code for the steps to obtain the weight for estimating the ATT as shown in Equation (4.4) is shown as follows.[2]

1. Create a table with the number of treated cases per stratum.

subclassTreat <- data.frame(table(

> *data.stratification$subclass[data.stratification$treat=="Treated"]))*

names(subclassTreat) <- c("subclass","N.1s")

---

[2] Similar code to obtain the weight for the ATE is shown on the book's website.

2. Create a table with the number of untreated cases per stratum.

subclassUntreat <- data.frame(table(

data.stratification$subclass[data.stratification$treat=="Untreated"]))

names(subclassUntreat) <- c("subclass","N.0s")

3. Merge the tables obtained in Steps 1 and 2.

(table.subclass <- merge(subclassTreat,subclassUntreat))

```
  subclass N.1s N.0s
1        1  104  796
2        2  104  223
3        3  105  124
4        4  103   72
5        5  105   50
```

4. Merge table with data.

data.stratification <- merge(data.stratification,table.subclass)

5. Obtain the marginal proportions of treated and untreated cases.

(prop.treat <- svymean(~treat, surveyDesign))

```
                  mean      SE
treatUntreated  0.81433  0.0105
treatTreated    0.18567  0.0105
```

6. Calculate the weight for the ATT.

data.stratification$mmwsATT <- with(data.stratification,

*ifelse(treat=="Treated", 1, N.1s*prop.treat[1]/N.0s*prop.treat[2]))*

xtabs(~mmwsATT+subclass, data.stratification)

```
                 subclass
mmwsATT              1    2    3    4    5
 0.0197541428603098 796    0    0    0    0
 0.0705125458152764   0  223    0    0    0
 0.128028168444843    0    0  124    0    0
 0.216293090922955    0    0    0   72    0
 0.317509857743211    0    0    0    0   50
 1                  104  104  105  103  105
```

7. Combine marginal mean weight and sampling weight; then normalize final weight.

data.stratification$mmwsATTFinal <-

> *data.stratification$mmwsATT*data.stratification$FINALWGT*

data.stratification$mmwsATTFinal <-

> *data.stratification$mmwsATTFinal/mean(data.stratification$mmwsATTFinal)*

The fact that weights for MMWS are computed from strata rather than directly from propensity scores brings the advantage that MMWS is less likely to produce extreme weights, which can affect the performance of propensity score weighting, as discussed in Chapter 3. Furthermore, MMWS is more robust to misspecifications of the propensity score model than inverse probability of treatment weighting because misspecification to a certain degree may change the propensity scores but not affect strata membership (Hong, 2010). However, MMWS is expected to produce a smaller degree of bias reduction than propensity score weighting because of the coarseness of the weights, but bias reduction is expected to increase as the number of strata increases. On the other hand, increasing the number of strata reduces the number of treated and untreated within strata, which may result in volatile weights and therefore compromising the precision of treatment effect estimates (Hong, 2012).

4.5.1. Covariate Balance Evaluation

Covariate balance evaluation for MMWS can be performed in the same way as with propensity score weighting, shown in Chapter 3. The balance of each covariate across treated and untreated groups is evaluated across strata rather than within each stratum. In the following code, the *twang* package is used to obtain standardized mean differences for all covariates. Because the data have sampling weights, the final weight is the product of the marginal mean weight and the sampling weight. A summary of the covariate balance with MMWS for both the ATT and ATE is shown in Table 4.4, which indicates that covariate balance is very close to the criteria for covariate balance of absolute standardized mean difference below 0.1 (Austin, 2011b). This table also shows which covariates did not meet these criteria for covariate balance. It should be noted that if less strict criteria are used for covariate balance evaluation—namely, absolute standardized differences below 0.25 (Stuart, 2010; Stuart & Rubin, 2007)—then balance is achieved with all covariates.

library(twang)

data.stratification$treat2 <- ifelse(data.stratification$treat == "Treated", 1,0)

balanceTableMMWS <- bal.stat(

data=data.stratification, estimand="ATT", w.all=data.stratification$mmwsATTFinal,
  get.ks=F, vars=covariateNames, treat.var="treat2",
  sampw=data.stratification$FINALWGT, multinom=F)

balanceTableMMWS <- balanceTableMMWS$results[,1:5]

TABLE 4.4 ● Summary of Standardized Effect Sizes With MMWS for the ATT and ATE				
Effect	**Minimum**	**Mean**	**Maximum**	**Unbalanced Covariates (Austin, 2011b, Criteria)**
ATT	−0.120	0.000	0.122	FR_SIZE, C0540
ATE	−0.125	0.006	0.188	C0114, C0158, C0268, C0272, C0274, FR_LVEL, FR_SIZE, C0540, C0542, C0556, IC0542, IC0546, IC0558

4.5.2. Estimation of Treatment Effect

For marginal mean weighting through stratification, the same estimators of treatment effect can be used as with propensity score weighting. Some of these estimators are shown in Chapter 3 and include the difference between weighted means of the treated and untreated groups and a weighted regression of the outcome on the dummy treatment indicator. This example analysis demonstrates estimation of the weighted regression model $y_i = \beta_0 + \beta_1 Z_i + \varepsilon_i$ where β_1 is either the ATT or ATE, depending on which marginal mean weight is used. Standard errors are obtained with bootstrapping. The R code to obtain the ATT estimate is shown below. Table 4.5 provides the estimates of both the ATT and ATE. Neither is statistically significant, indicating that the presence of a full-time security professional does not increase the administration of harsh punishment in schools. This conclusion is tentative given that covariate balance only met with the less strict criterion of absolute standardized differences below 0.25. In the next section, doubly robust estimation is performed to obtain additional correction of bias.

surveyDesignATT <- svydesign(ids=~0,strata=~STRATA, weights=~mmwsATTFinal,
  data=data.stratification)

surveyDesignATT <- as.svrepdesign(surveyDesignATT, type=c("bootstrap"),replicates=1000)

modelATT <- svyglm(percHarsh~treat, surveyDesignATT, family=gaussian())

TABLE 4.5 ● ATT and ATE Estimates With Marginal Mean Weighting Through Stratification			
Effect	**Estimate**	**Standard Error**	***p* Value**
ATT	0.01736	0.02108	.411
ATE	0.018714	0.022797	.412

4.5.3. Doubly Robust Estimation With MMWS

When the treatment effect is estimated with the difference between weighted means of the treated and untreated groups, double robustness can be achieved by using regression estimation to obtain the means of each group (Lunceford & Davidian, 2004). Estimates of the treatment effect obtained with weighted regression using the MMWS can be made doubly robust by adding covariates and/or dummy stratum indicators in the model. The advantage of adding dummy stratum indicators rather than propensity scores is that it allows for nonlinear relationships between propensity scores and the outcome, while adding the propensity score directly would require the inclusion of polynomial terms. Regardless of whether covariates and/or dummy stratum indicators are included in the model, it is critical to also include interactions between these variables and the treatment indicator. It is also necessary to center continuous covariates around the grand mean (for the ATE) or the treated group mean (for the ATT) to ensure that the estimate treatment effect can still be interpreted as the ATE or the ATT (Schafer & Kang, 2008). The following code estimates the ATT with a weighted regression model where dummy stratum indicators as well as the seven covariates that did not meet the strict criterion (Austin, 2011b) for balance are included as predictors, with all two-way interactions. The continuous covariates are centered on the mean of the treated group prior to estimation of the regression model. The doubly robust ATT estimate is –0.024 (SE = 0.061, p = .692).

surveyDesignATT <- update(surveyDesignATT,

    C0540 = C0540 - mean(C0540[treat=="Treated"]),

    C0568 = C0568 - mean(C0568[treat=="Treated"]),

    C0544 = C0544 - mean(C0544[treat=="Treated"]),

    C0558 = C0558 - mean(C0558[treat=="Treated"]))

modelATTDR <- svyglm(percHarsh~

(treat+subclass+FR_SIZE+C0540+C0158+C0166+C0568+C0540+C0544+C0558)^2,
    surveyDesignATT, family=gaussian())

TABLE 4.6 ● Summary of Main Functions Used in This Chapter		
Package	**Function**	**Objective**
base	*cut*	Categorize the propensity scores into strata
MatchIt	*matchit*	Obtain strata based on propensity scores, and evaluate covariate balance
MatchIt	*summary*	Evaluate covariate balance
twang	*bal.stat*	Evaluate covariate balance
survey	*svydesign*	Create a survey object with the data and sampling weights
survey	*as.svrepdesign*	Add weights for bootstrapped samples to a survey object
survey	*svyglm*	Fit the outcome model with weights to estimate the treatment effect
survey	*update*	Add or transform variables within a survey design object

4.6. Conclusion

One major advantage of obtaining a marginal treatment effect across strata over pooling strata-specific treatment effects is that the former requires only marginal covariate balance, while the latter requires covariate balance within each stratum. As demonstrated in this chapter, within-stratum covariate balance is more difficult to obtain because small stratum sizes lead to unreliable within-stratum group means for each covariate. Because propensity score stratification is expected to provide less bias reduction than matching or weighting, it is always advisable to combine propensity score stratification with either another propensity score method or doubly robust estimation.

Study Questions

1. What are two strategies to perform propensity score stratification to estimate the ATE and ATT?

2. What are the steps of propensity score stratification?

3. How are strata obtained?

4. What is an indication of common support problems in propensity score stratification?

5. What is the relationship between the number of strata and bias reduction?

6. How can covariate balance be evaluated with propensity score stratification?

7. What are three strategies that can be used if covariate balance within strata was not achieved?

8. How can treatment effects estimated within each stratum be combined?

9. How is marginal mean weighting similar to poststratification in survey data analysis?

10. What is the interpretation of the numerator of the marginal mean weight through stratification to estimate the ATE?

11. What is the advantage of marginal mean weighting through stratification over inverse probability of treatment weighting?

12. What is the limitation of propensity score stratification methods compared with propensity score weighting methods?

13. What are two options for doubly robust estimation of treatment effects with propensity score stratification?

5

Propensity Score Matching

Learning Objectives

- Describe and compare greedy, genetic, and optimal matching algorithms.

- Characterize the impact of matching with or without replacement on results and analysis choices.

- Compare one-to-one, fixed ratio, variable ratio, and full matching strategies.

- Implement methods to estimate treatment effects with samples obtained with different matching methods.

- Implement methods to estimate standard errors of treatment effects with samples obtained with different matching methods.

- Understand the rationale and implementation of Rosenbaum's sensitivity analysis.

5.1. Introduction

This chapter presents the implementation of different propensity score matching methods, as well as a comparison of methods in terms of covariate balance and bias of treatment effect estimates. Propensity score matching consists of grouping observations with similar values of propensity scores. However, while propensity score weighting (see Chapter 3) and propensity score stratification (see Chapter 4) preserve the original sample size if there is adequate common support, most forms of matching result in the discarding of some observations. The sample size after matching is smallest with one-to-one matching and can vary considerably with variable ratio and full matching strategies. Propensity score matching methods differ in the ratio of treated observations matched to untreated observations, the algorithm used for identifying matches, whether matches are done with or without replacement, and whether matches are based solely on propensity scores or also use values of covariates. This chapter presents an overview of variations of propensity score matching and demonstrates them with an example. Issues specific to matching methods related to the enforcement of common support, covariate balance evaluation, the estimation of treatment effects, and standard errors are also discussed.

5.2. Description of Example

The example for this chapter consists of the estimation of the effect of mothers having a job that provides or subsidizes child care on the length that they breastfeed their children, using data from the National Longitudinal Survey of Youth 1979 (NLSY79) and the NLSY79 Children and Youth. The health and cognitive benefits of breastfeeding on children are well documented (Borra, Iacovou, & Sevilla, 2012; Quigley et al., 2012). Therefore, it is important to understand the factors that lead mothers to initiate and maintain breastfeeding, including job characteristics, because job demands can conflict with breastfeeding efforts. Jacknowitz (2008) examined the effects of mothers having a job that provides or subsidizes child care on whether mothers initiated breastfeeding and on whether they breastfed until the child was 6 months old. Using multiple regression models, she found that mothers who worked for a company that offered child care were more likely to breastfeed to 6 months.

The sample for this example contains 1,209 child records from the NLSY79 Children and Youth data set. The sample is restricted to one child per mother, mothers who had at least one job in the fourth quarter of pregnancy, and mothers who returned to work within 12 weeks of the birth of the child. The NLSY79 data used were restricted to years 1988 to 1994, 1996, 1998, 2000, 2002, 2004, 2006, 2008, and 2010 because responses about the treatment of interest were available for these years. Because the NLSY79 was not designed to be representative of the population of working mothers that is the focus of this example, the NLSY79 sampling weights will not be used in this demonstration (for an example of propensity score analysis with sampling weights, see Chapters 2 and 3).

The outcome variable is the age of the child in weeks when breastfeeding ended. This outcome was taken from the NLSY79 Children and Youth data. The treatment indicator is whether the mother's job provided or subsidized child care and was obtained from the NLSY79. From the data set analyzed, child care was provided or subsidized in 107 (8.85%) of 1,209 cases.

5.3. Propensity Score Estimation

In this example, propensity scores for whether the mother's job provided or subsidized child care are estimated using logistic regression. Covariates for the propensity score model selected for this example include variables hypothesized to be true confounders, because they relate to both the probability of having a job that provides or subsidizes child care and breastfeeding duration (the outcome), as well as predictors of breastfeeding duration, which are included to increase the efficiency of treatment effect estimates. Some examples of covariates are the benefits provided by the mother's current job (i.e., life insurance, dental insurance, profit sharing, retirement, training opportunities), the mother's education level, hours worked per week, and employment sector. The propensity score model also included covariates related to breastfeeding duration controlled by Jacknowitz (2008), such as family size, amount of public assistance received by the family, and whether a cesarean section was performed. A total of 31 covariates were included in the propensity score model. A complete list of covariates used is available in the R code for this chapter on the book's website. A detailed discussion of strategies to select covariates and estimate propensity score models is presented in Chapter 2.

It is advantageous to match on the linear propensity score (i.e., the logit of the propensity score) rather than the propensity score itself, because it avoids compression around 0 and 1 (Diamond & Sekhon, 2013). The linear propensity score is obtained with

$$\log(e_i(X)) = \log\left(\frac{e_i(X)}{1 - e_i(X)}\right), \tag{5.1}$$

where $e_i(X)$ is the estimated propensity score. The following R code shows the use of the *glm* function to fit a logistic regression model to the data,[1] and then linear propensity scores are obtained according to Equation (5.1).

psModel <- glm(psFormula, data, family=binomial())

data$logitPScores <- log(fitted(psModel)/(1-fitted(psModel)))

A preliminary evaluation of common support was performed using histograms and box plots of the distributions of linear propensity scores for the treated and untreated. These graphs are shown in Figures 5.1 and 5.2. They indicate that common support is potentially adequate to estimate the ATT with matching methods, because the distribution of the treated is contained within the distribution of the untreated, and therefore an adequate match could be found for every treated observation. However, the use of a caliper during the matching process allows for a more precise evaluation of the adequacy of common support. The graphs also indicate that estimating the ATE using propensity score matching with these data may be difficult because there are areas of the distribution of the untreated without any treated cases nearby, which could result in poor matching. Therefore, the ATT of a mother working for a company that provides or subsidizes child care will be estimated. In applications of propensity score matching, the ATT is more commonly estimated than the ATE.

---

[1]R code to prepare the data set and to specify the propensity score model in the *psFormula* object is shown on the book's website.

FIGURE 5.1 ● Histograms of Linear Propensity Scores for Treated and Untreated Observations

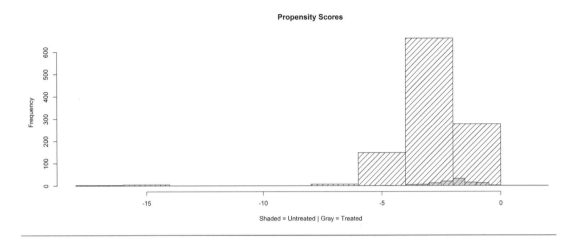

FIGURE 5.2 ● Box Plots of Linear Propensity Scores for Treated and Untreated Observations

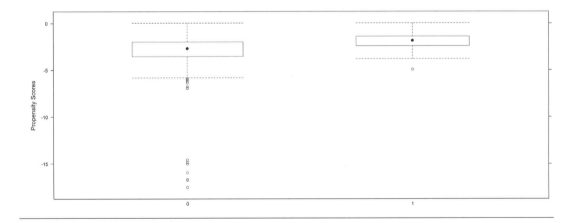

5.4. Propensity Score Matching Algorithms

5.4.1. Greedy Matching

Greedy matching consists of choosing each treated case and searching for the best available match among the untreated cases without accounting for the quality of the match of the entire treated sample. Greedy matching contrasts with genetic matching and optimal matching, discussed later in this chapter, which attempt to optimize global match quality. Greedy matching works well for estimating the ATT when the number of treated cases is substantially smaller than the number of untreated cases available for matching (i.e., the ratio of treated to untreated sample sizes is small) and there is common support for all treated cases. The implementation of greedy matching consists of choosing whether to match with or without replacement, whether to enforce a maximum allowable distance, and whether to allow multiple matching. These options are reviewed below.

Matching with or without replacement. Matching with replacement consists of selecting one or multiple matches for each case (depending on the desired matching ratio) and then returning the matched cases to the pool of observations. In matching without replacement, each case can be used as a match only once. Matching with replacement has the advantage of always matching each treated case to the closest untreated case and therefore produces larger bias reduction than matching without replacement. Also, when performing greedy matching with replacement, the order of matches does not matter, while greedy matching without replacement will produce different results depending on the order in which cases are matched. Matching with replacement performs better when the number of available matches is small (Rosenbaum, 1989), but the difference between these methods tends to disappear as the size of the pool of available matches increases.

One-to-one, fixed ratio, or variable ratio matching. When each treated case has one untreated case matched to it, the procedure is described as one-to-one matching or pair matching. One disadvantage of one-to-one matching is that it discards untreated cases even if they are appropriate matches for the treated cases, reducing the sample size to twice the number of treated cases or fewer if there is lack of common support for some treated cases. However, one-to-one matching does not result in a substantial drop of power, because the power is driven by the size of the smallest group, and the increased homogeneity of the sample increases power (Cohen, 1988).

The use of fixed ratio matching or one-to-k matching, where k specifies a fixed matching ratio larger than 1 (e.g., one-to-two, one-to-three), is not recommended in most situations, because matching to the specified number of untreated cases will occur regardless of whether enough adequate matches are available, leading to an increase in bias. Although the use of a caliper may limit the increase in bias, using a caliper with a fixed ratio larger than one-to-one may result in substantial loss of treated cases, because there may not be enough untreated cases within the caliper to satisfy the specified ratio. If matching with a ratio larger than one-to-one is desired to retain a larger sample size, it is more advantageous to use either variable ratio matching or full matching.

If each single treatment case is matched to one to several untreated cases (i.e., the number of matches varies across treated cases), the method is known as variable ratio matching or one-to-many matching. Research has shown that variable ratio matching removes more bias than one-to-one matching (Cepeda, Boston, Farrar, & Strom, 2003; Gu & Rosenbaum, 1993; Ming & Rosenbaum, 2000). Variable ratio matching is particularly useful if the number of untreated group cases is much larger than the number of treatment cases (Ming & Rosenbaum, 2001). Variable ratio matching is known to outperform one-to-one matching for estimating the treatment effect in general conditions, but the difference in performance between these methods decreases as the number of available matches increases (Cepeda et al., 2003; Gu & Rosenbaum, 1993).

Nearest neighbor or within-caliper matching.   Greedy propensity score matching has been performed using either a nearest neighbor or nearest neighbor within-caliper matching strategy. Matching to the nearest neighbor consists of simply finding the untreated observation with the closest propensity score to the propensity score of each treated observation. The use of a caliper, which is a maximum distance within which matches are allowed, has been shown to improve greedy nearest neighbor matching performance. A caliper for matching is usually defined as a fraction of the standard deviation of the logit of the propensity score. Targeting to remove at least 90% of bias, Rosenbaum and Rubin (1985, p. 37) used a caliper of 0.25 standard deviations. Using a caliper not only improves the quality of matching but also enforces common support, because treated cases without any untreated cases within their caliper are discarded. When nearest neighbor matching within a caliper is used, the closest untreated case to a treated case is only considered an acceptable match if its propensity score lies within the caliper of the treated case.

Implementation of greedy matching.   Two different R packages will be used to demonstrate greedy matching, because their different features may be helpful to researchers. The *MatchIt* package (Ho et al., 2011) is focused on estimating the ATT, and its *matchit* function will be used to demonstrate greedy one-to-one matching with replacement within a 0.25 caliper.

library(MatchIt)

greedyMatching <- matchit(psFormula, distance=data$logitPScores, m.order="largest",

    data = data, method = "nearest", ratio=1,replace=T, caliper=0.25)

In the code above, the argument *distance=data$logitPScores* specifies the variable that contains the logit of the propensity scores. However, providing the logit of the propensity scores is optional, because the *matchit* function is able to fit a variety of models to estimate the propensity score before performing matching. For example, if the argument *distance = "linear.logit"* is provided, the *matchit* function estimates propensity scores using logistic regression and converts the predicted probabilities into logits as shown in Equation (5.1) and then performs matching. However, the advantage of estimating the propensity score in advance of using the *matchit* function as it is done in this example is that better control of the process is obtained, including using approaches to estimate propensity scores that have not been implemented in the *matchit* function.

In the *matchit* function, the argument *method = "nearest"* in combination with *caliper = 0.25* specifies that the greedy method is to be performed by searching for the nearest untreated observation within a caliper of 0.25 standard deviations of each treated observation. The argument *m.order = "largest"* specifies that matching should start from the treated case with the largest propensity score, rather than the smallest or random. This argument reflects the fact that greedy nearest neighbor matching does not optimize global measures of balance, and therefore different results are obtained depending on the order of matching.[2] The *ratio=1* argument specifies one-to-one matching but can be used to specify other fixed matching ratios. The *replace = T* argument specifies matching with replacement, which allows untreated cases to be matched to more than one treated case.

The *Match* function of the *Matching* package of R (Sekhon, 2011) can perform greedy matching with fixed and variable ratio to estimate either the ATT or ATE. For estimating the ATT, matching is used to identify which untreated observations have similar values of propensity scores as treated observations. For estimation of the ATE, matches for treated observations as well as matches for untreated observations are selected. Here it will be used to implement variable ratio greedy matching with replacement to estimate the ATT.

library(Matching)

greedyMatching2 <- with(data, Match(Y=C0338600, Tr=childCare, X=logitPScores,

estimand = "ATT", M = 1, caliper = 0.25, replace=TRUE, ties=TRUE))

In the code above, the arguments *Y, Tr,* and *X* specify the outcome, the treatment, and the propensity scores, respectively. The argument *M = 1* specifies one-to-one matching, but variable ratio matching is performed implicitly by allowing ties with the argument *ties=TRUE,* and therefore if more than one case is an adequate match to another case, all matches are included. The argument *replace=TRUE* specifies that untreated cases can be used for multiple matches, and *caliper = 0.25* sets the maximum allowed distance between a treated and an untreated case to be equal to 0.25 standard deviations.

5.4.2. Genetic Matching

Genetic matching (Diamond & Sekhon, 2013) minimizes a multivariate weighted distance on covariates between treated and untreated cases, where a genetic algorithm is used to choose weights that optimize postmatching covariate balance. Genetic matching can be used without including propensity scores, but propensity scores can be used by themselves or added to the list of covariates. The distance minimized by the genetic matching algorithm is the generalized Mahalanobis distance (GMD) (Diamond & Sekhon, 2013):

$$GMD(X_i, X_j, W) = (X_i - X_j)^T \left(S^{-1/2} \right)^T WS^{-1/2}(X_i - X_j) \qquad (5.2)$$

---

[2]Here the order does not matter because matching with replacement is performed.

In the GMD, X are vectors of covariates for treated case i and untreated case j, and the weight matrix W is included to reflect the relative importance of each covariate to optimize overall covariate balance. W is a diagonal weight matrix with rows and columns equal to the number of covariates. $S^{-1/2}$ is the Cholesky decomposition of S, the variance covariance matrix of the covariates (Sekhon, 2011). T indicates the transpose. The GMD can be understood as a weighted average effect size between treated and untreated groups across all covariates.

The genetic matching algorithm is available in the *Matching* package of R (Sekhon, 2011) with the *GenMatch* function. The *GenMatch* function uses the genetic algorithm to obtain weights that optimize covariate balance. The following code demonstrates genetic matching with replacement to estimate the ATT based on the linear propensity score and 31 covariates, which are stored in the *covariateData* object.

geneticWeights <- GenMatch(Tr=data$childCare, X=covariateData,

  pop.size=1000, fit.func="pvals",

  estimand="ATT", replace=T, ties=T)

For each generation (i.e., iteration), the genetic algorithm sets the weights in W to initial values (the default initial value is 1 in *GenMatch*) and generates as many W matrices as the specified population size in the *pop.size* argument. Because genetic matching optimizes covariate balance asymptotically, it is important to specify a large population size for the genetic optimization. The default of the *GenMatch* function is *pop.size = 100*, which is increased to 1,000 in the following code, but larger values may be necessary. Then, the algorithm matches for each W in a given generation. Next, it computes the loss for each matched sample and selects the W corresponding to the minimum loss. The algorithm requires the specification of a loss function, which is a summary of a measure of covariate balance. The default loss function is specified in *fit.func = "pvals"*, which consists of the maximum of p values from Kolmogorov-Smirnov tests and paired t tests for all covariates. While using p values for covariate balance assessment is problematic because it depends on sample size, it is a good choice for defining the fit function because the sample size is fixed within the optimization (Diamond & Sekhon, 2013). If the convergence criterion is reached, the genetic algorithm returns the matched sample and corresponding W matrix; otherwise, it proceeds to the next generation. Details about the genetic matching algorithm are provided by Sekhon (2011). Once the matrix of weights is obtained with the *GenMatch* function, the actual matching procedure is implemented by the *Match* function using the weight matrix, shown as follows:

geneticMatching <- Match(Y=data$C0338600, Tr=data$childCare, X=covariateData,

  Weight.matrix = geneticWeights, estimand = "ATT",

  M = 1, replace=TRUE, ties=TRUE)

Genetic matching can also be obtained by using the *matchit* function of the *MatchIt* package, which can run *GenMatch* in the background. The following code implements one-to-many genetic matching without replacement based solely on the linear propensity score with the *matchit* function:

geneticMatching2 <- matchit(psFormula, distance=data$logitPScores, data = data,

method = "genetic", pop.size=1000, fit.func="pvals",

estimand="ATT", replace=T, ties=T)

A major strength of genetic matching is that it searchers for matches that optimize covariate balance. Sekhon and Grieve (2009, 2012) found through simulation studies that genetic matching based on covariates without using the propensity score is able to provide adequate covariate balance, and in their studies, it produced better balance than propensity score matching. In another simulation study, Diamond and Sekhon (2013) found that genetic matching on covariates provided greater bias reduction and lower root mean squared error than greedy matching using propensity scores estimated with logistic regression, random forests, and boosted regression trees, in conditions where the treatment assignment model had nonlinear and interaction terms. Therefore, genetic matching without the propensity score could be particularly useful for situations when propensity score matching fails to achieve covariate balance, or propensity score estimation results in complete separation or quasi-complete separation (Allison, 2004) of treated and untreated groups.

5.4.3. Optimal Matching

Optimal matching was proposed by Rosenbaum (1989) as a solution to the problem that greedy matching does not guarantee matches with the minimum total distance between treated and matched groups. Optimal matching produces matches that attain minimal total distances by using network flow optimization methods (Carré, 1979; Ford & Fulkerson, 1962). Hansen (2007) created the *optmatch* package for R, which produces one-to-one, one-to-*k*, and full matching. However, Rosenbaum (1989) cautioned that optimal one-to-one and one-to-*k* matching only guarantees minimum total distance given the constraint of the matching ratio desired. Optimal one-to-one matching is expected to outperform one-to-one greedy matching, but the differences in match quality are small when many matches are available. However, when the treated to untreated ratio is large, one-to-one optimal matching is noticeably better than one-to-one greedy matching (Gu & Rosenbaum, 1993).

The following code uses the *matchit* function of the *MatchIt* package with the argument *method = "optimal"*, which runs the *optmatch* package in the background to perform optimal one-to-one optimal matching without replacement:

optimalMatching <- matchit(psFormula,distance=data$logitPScores, data = data,

method = "optimal", ratio=1)

5.4.4. Full Matching

Full matching (Rosenbaum, 1991) matches each treated case to at least one untreated case and vice versa, without replacement. Therefore, this procedure can be viewed as a propensity score stratification where the number of strata containing at least one treated and one untreated observation is maximized. Differently from one-to-one matching with replacement and variable ratio matching with replacement, the matched sets never overlap and observations are not discarded, which allows the estimation of treatment effects and standard errors with methods appropriate for finely stratified samples (Hansen, 2007). Full matching is particularly helpful when there are large differences in the distributions of propensity scores between treated and untreated (assuming common support is still adequate): In this case, there will be many untreated cases with low propensity scores, so in the lower part of the propensity score distribution, there will be several matches for each treated case. However, in the upper part of the propensity score distribution, there will be few untreated cases to match to each treated case (Hansen, 2007; Stuart & Green, 2008). Full matching has been found to perform better than one-to-many greedy matching in terms of distance within matched sets as well as covariate balance, especially when the number of covariates is large (Gu & Rosenbaum, 1993).

The following code implements optimal full matching using the *matchit* function of the *MatchIt* package with the argument *method = "full"*, running the *optimatch* package in the background:

fullMatching <- matchit(psFormula,distance=data$logitPScores, data = data, method = "full")

Table 5.1 presents a summary of the matching methods implemented in this section, highlighting their unique characteristics. From the methods implemented, genetic, optimal, and full matching optimize distances for the entire sample, while greedy matching does not. From these methods, only genetic matching can optimize covariate balance directly, while optimal and full matching only match based on propensity scores. It is not possible to recommend a single matching algorithm implementation as superior to the others for all situations, because matching algorithm performance depends on the treated and untreated sample sizes, the degree of common support, and the distributions of propensity scores for treated and untreated. Therefore, it is best to implement multiple methods and compare covariate balance between them, as done in the next section.

5.5. Evaluation of Covariate Balance

There are 31 covariates in the propensity score model, but covariance balance is evaluated for the propensity score, continuous covariates, and levels of categorical covariates, so the total number of covariate balance measures obtained is 42. This section

TABLE 5.1 ● List of Matching Methods Used for Example	
Matching Method	**Summary**
One-to-one greedy with replacement and caliper	Match based on closest observation without considering total distance for sample; fast to implement; replacement allows best matches to be used; caliper enforces common support
Variable ratio greedy with replacement and caliper	Match based on closest observation without considering total distance for sample; allows multiple matches per observation
Variable ratio genetic with replacement (propensity score [PS] + covariates)	Match optimizing loss function, which is a summary of a measure of covariate balance
Variable ratio genetic with replacement (PS only)	Match optimizing loss function based on balance of propensity scores, faster than matching on covariates
One-to-one optimal without replacement	Match minimizing global propensity score distance
Full matching	Match entire sample by creating strata with at least one treated and one untreated, minimizing global propensity score distance

provides code to evaluate covariate balance with both the *MatchIt* and *Matching* packages. The following code is for covariate balance evaluation with the *MatchIt* package after one-to-one greedy matching was implemented, but similar code can be used for any matching method implemented with the *MatchIt* package, such as genetic, optimal, and full matching.

balance.greedyMatching <- summary(greedyMatching, standardize=T)

The next piece of code is to evaluate covariate balance with the *MatchBalance* function of the *Matching* package after genetic matching is implemented, but it can be used for greedy matching as well. The argument *match.out = geneticMatching* specifies the object generated by the *Match* function containing the matches, so to use this code to evaluate balance for the greedy matching shown earlier, the only change needed is *match.out = greedyMatching2*.

balance.geneticMatching <- MatchBalance(psFormula, data = data,

match.out = geneticMatching, ks = F, paired=F)

The comparison of covariate balance achieved by different matching methods is shown in Table 5.2. None of the matching methods produced absolute standardized mean differences lower than 0.1 for all covariates, but three produced differences lower than 0.25 standard deviations for all covariates. It is interesting to note that genetic matching with the propensity score performed better than genetic matching with the propensity score plus covariates, but this may not always be the case, so comparing both methods is recommended. At this point, the researcher may proceed with the analysis or go back and try to improve covariate balance. This decision depends on the researcher's chosen target for adequate balance, and different recommendations for what is acceptable covariate balance are presented in Chapter 1. If the target is to obtain standardized mean differences below 0.1 for all covariates, the researcher could attempt to change the propensity score model or change the propensity score estimation method and perform matching again. However, if the target is to obtain standardized mean differences below 0.25, then three of the matching methods shown in Table 5.2 performed adequately. In the next section, the matched data sets from variable ratio genetic with replacement (propensity score + covariates), variable ratio genetic matching with replacement (propensity score only), and full matching will be used to demonstrate a variety of treatment effect estimation methods.

TABLE 5.2 ● Comparison of Covariate Balance Across Matching Methods

Matching Method	Maximum Absolute Standardized Mean Difference	Covariates With Absolute Standardized Mean Difference Above 0.1, n (%)
One-to-one greedy with replacement and caliper	0.21	11 (26.1)
Variable ratio greedy with replacement and caliper	0.30	4 (9.5)
Variable ratio genetic with replacement (PS + covariates)	0.23	12 (28.6)
Variable ratio genetic with replacement (PS only)	0.13	8 (19.0)
One-to-one optimal without replacement	0.28	11 (26.1)
Full matching	0.26	4 (9.5)

Note: PS = propensity score. Results based on 42 standardized mean differences, which include the propensity score, continuous covariates, and values of categorical covariates.

5.6. Estimation of Treatment Effects

Treatment effect estimation methods with propensity score matched samples may differ depending on matching method, nature of the outcome, and whether the researcher decides to use parametric or nonparametric methods. The implementation of propensity score methods separates the design part of the analysis from the analysis of outcome (Rubin, 2005, 2007, 2008). In this chapter, the design part of the analysis consists of propensity score matching. Because of this separation, any parametric or nonparametric method can be used for the analysis of outcomes. In many academic fields, researchers have strong traditions of using specific parametric models for certain outcomes. Ho et al. (2007) recommend using the same parametric models with the propensity score matched samples, because they account for theoretical relationships well known in the field and provide additional bias reduction. An example of a complex parametric model (i.e., structural equation modeling) used with propensity score matching is provided in Chapter 8. In the current chapter, the focus is on simple matching estimators proposed by Abadie and Imbens (2002, 2006), the bias-corrected Abadie and Imbens estimator, and treatment effect estimation based on mean differences and linear regression (Schafer & Kang, 2008).

There is disagreement on whether propensity score matching produces clustering effects that should be accounted for in the outcome analysis. Schafer and Kang (2008) argued that matched samples should be treated as independent data because matching does not produce correlations between outcomes of matched individuals. Stuart (2010) supported Schafer and Kang's argument by adding that propensity score matching does not guarantee that covariate values are the same for matched pairs, only that covariate distributions are similar for treated and matched groups. In contrast, Austin (2011a) argued that because covariates that have similar distributions for matched and treated groups are related to the outcomes, the distributions of outcomes will be more similar for treated and matched samples than for randomly selected samples. With a simulation study of the effect of binary treatments on binary outcomes, Austin found that analyses treating the matched pairs as dependent rather than independent resulted in Type I error rates closer to the .05 alpha level, coverage of 95% confidence intervals closer to 95%, and narrower confidence intervals. Therefore, he recommended that matched samples be analyzed with methods for dependent samples. Although the differences between the results with independent and dependent sample methods in Austin's simulation study were small, they were consistently in favor of treatment matched pairs as dependent samples. Given that additional research is needed on this issue, this chapter includes methods for estimating standard errors for treatment effects that represent both sides of this debate.

The first estimator of the treatment effect appropriate for matching discussed here is the Abadie-Imbens simple matching estimators (Abadie & Imbens, 2002, 2006).

Under Rubin's potential outcomes framework, the treatment effect for a single case i is $\tau_i = Y_i^1 - Y_i^0$, where Y_i^1 is the potential outcome under the treatment condition and Y_i^0 is the potential outcome under the untreated condition (see Chapter 1 for details). Similarly to a missing data problem, propensity score matching can be seen as a method to provide imputations for the potential outcomes:

$$\hat{Y}_i^1 = \begin{cases} Y_i \text{ if } Z_i = 1 \\ \dfrac{1}{M_i} \sum\limits_{j \in J_M(i)} Y_j \text{ if } Z_i = 0 \end{cases} \tag{5.3}$$

$$\hat{Y}_i^0 = \begin{cases} Y_i \text{ if } Z_i = 0 \\ \dfrac{1}{M_i} \sum\limits_{j \in J_M(i)} Y_j \text{ if } Z_i = 1 \end{cases} \tag{5.4}$$

In Equations (5.3) and (5.4), Y_i is the observed outcome of case i, which was either exposed to the treated ($Z_i = 1$) or the untreated ($Z_i = 0$) condition. M_i is the total number of matches for each case; the total set of matches for case i is $J_M(i)$, and the outcome of each matched case j is Y_j. Given the imputed potential outcomes obtained through matching, the ATE can be estimated as the average of the differences between the imputed potential outcomes under the treated and untreated conditions for all n cases, while the ATT can be estimated taking the average difference only for the n_1 treated cases, as shown below (Abadie & Imbens, 2002, 2006):

$$ATE = \frac{1}{n} \sum_1^n \left(\hat{Y}_i^1 - \hat{Y}_i^0 \right) \tag{5.5}$$

$$ATT = \frac{1}{n_1} \sum_{i \in Z_1}^{n_1} \left(\hat{Y}_i^1 - \hat{Y}_i^0 \right) \tag{5.6}$$

Estimates obtained with the matching estimators in Equations (5.5) and (5.6), as well as standard errors estimated with the Abadie and Imbens (2006) method, are provided by the *Matching* package (Sekhon, 2011). The Abadie-Imbens estimators will be demonstrated with the matched sample obtained with genetic matching with the propensity score and 31 covariates. The Abadie-Imbens matching estimators were proposed for general multivariate matching but can be used for propensity score matching. The following code for estimating treatment effects with the Abadie-Imbens estimators using the sample from genetic matching is also applicable to data sets obtained with greedy matching. The *geneticMatching* object was created earlier by sequentially using the functions *GenMatch* and *Match* of the *Matching* package.

summary(geneticMatching)

This code produces the following output:

```
Estimate... 3.7664
AI SE...... 2.6266
T-stat..... 1.4339
p.val...... 0.1516

Original number of observations.............. 1209
Original number of treated obs.............. 107
Matched number of observations.............. 107
Matched number of observations (unweighted). 107
```

The estimate of the ATT is 3.766 (*SE* = 2.626, *p* = .152), indicating that mothers who had a job that provided or subsidized child care did not breastfeed their child longer than if they had a job that did not provide this benefit. The output above indicates that the number of mothers in the treatment condition is 107, and they are matched to 107 untreated mothers. Therefore, for this example, although the algorithm is set to allow multiple matches per treated case, it produced one-to-one matching, because only one untreated observation was identified for each treated observation that optimized balance in the propensity score as well as 31 covariates.

Abadie and Imbens (2002) showed that the matching estimator will be biased if the matching is not exact, but this bias can reduced by regressing the outcomes on covariates only with the matched data. The *Matching* package allows bias adjustment, which is accomplished with the *Match* function by adding the *BiasAdjust=T* argument and *Z=covariateData,* which specifies the data set containing the covariates that will be used for bias adjustment.

geneticMatchingBA <- Match(Y=data$C0338600, Tr=data$childCare, X=covariateData,

BiasAdjust=T, Z=covariateData, Weight.matrix = geneticWeights,

estimand = "ATT", M = 1, replace=TRUE, ties=TRUE)

The code for multivariate genetic matching with bias adjustment for all covariates shown above produces estimates that can be extracted with the *summary* function:

summary(geneticMatchingBA)

```
Estimate... 4.352
AI SE...... 2.7694
T-stat..... 1.5714
p.val...... 0.11608
```

The estimate of the ATT is 4.352 (SE = 2.769, p = .116), showing that bias adjustment did not alter the conclusion obtained without bias adjustment that there is no treatment effect.

The *MatchIt* package (Ho et al., 2011) does not estimate treatment effects directly, but it provides a matched data set with case weights that can be used to estimate the ATT. In one-to-one matching without replacement, all case weights are 1. However, if fixed ratio (greater than one-to-one) or variable ratio matching is done, weights for treated cases are 1 but weights for all untreated cases matched to a treated case are the inverse of the total number of matches the treated case received. Also, if matching is done with replacement, case weights for each untreated case are summed across the multiple matched groups in which it was included. Finally, the weights of the matched cases are multiplied by the ratio of the total number of matched cases and total number of treated cases, which scales the untreated weights to sum to the number of matched cases (Ho, Imai, King, & Stuart, 2014). The following equation implements the calculation of weights described above:

$$w_i = \begin{cases} 1 \text{ if } Z_i = 1 \\ \dfrac{n_0}{n_1} \sum_{m=1}^{n_i} \dfrac{1}{M_m} \text{ if } Z_i = 0 \end{cases} \tag{5.7}$$

where n_i is the number of treated cases that case i was matched to, M_m is the total number of matches including case i that each treated case received, n_0 is the total number of matched cases, and n_1 is the total number of treated cases. If a caliper is used, treated cases without untreated cases within their calipers are dropped before weights are calculated.

Using the matched sample obtained with variable ratio genetic matching with replacement based only on the propensity score, the following code demonstrates the estimation of treatment effects as a difference between weighted means. The function *match.data* of the *MatchIt* package was used to extract the *data.geneticMatching2* matched data set, which is then analyzed with the *survey* (Lumley, 2004) package. First, the *svydesign* function is used to specify the name of the data to be analyzed and the *weights* variable that contains the weights resulting from the variable ratio with replacement matching method.

data.geneticMatching2 <- match.data(geneticMatching2)

library(survey)

design.geneticMatching2 <- svydesign(ids=~1, weights=~weights,

data=data.geneticMatching2)

Then, the *svyglm* function is used with the formula *C0338600~childCare* to fit the simple regression model $Y_i = \beta_0 + \beta_1 Z_i + \varepsilon_i$, where β_1 is the treatment effect.

model.geneticMatching2 <- svyglm(C0338600~childCare, design.geneticMatching2,

family=gaussian())

The code above applies weights as defined in Equation (5.7) to the outcomes but does not implement any method to account for any clustering effects due to matching. The treatment effect is shown with the *summary* function:

summary(model.geneticMatching2)

```
Coefficients:
        Estimate Std. Error t value Pr(>|t|)
(Intercept)      8.916    1.581   5.641  5.5e-08 ***
childCareTRUE    4.607    2.679   1.720   0.087 .
```

With variable ratio genetic matching with replacement, the ATT estimate is 4.607 (*SE* = 2.679, *p* = .087), which is similar to the previous two estimates.

Next, the ATT will be estimated using the data set extracted with the *matched.data* function from the *fullMatching* object, which contains the results of full matching performed earlier with the *matchit* function. Full matching does not drop any observations, so the sample size for the estimation of treatment effects is much larger than with one-to-one matching.

data.fullMatching <- match.data(fullMatching)

After the matched data set is extracted, the *svydesign* function of the *survey* package is used to specify the data and weights to be used to fit the outcome model.

design.fullMatching <- svydesign(ids=~1, weights=~weights,

data=data.fullMatching)

The following code uses a regression model fit with the *svyglm* function of the *survey* package to estimate the ATT as the difference between weighted means, with weights obtained according to Equation (5.7).

model.fullMatching <- svyglm(C0338600~childCare, design.fullMatching, family=gaussian())

summary(model.fullMatching)

```
Coefficients:
        Estimate Std. Error t value Pr(>|t|)
(Intercept)     10.0428   0.8887  11.300   <2e-16 ***
childCareTRUE    3.4806   2.3346   1.491   0.136
```

The analysis results with the data set obtained with full matching show a treatment effect estimate (ATT = 3.481, *SE* = 2.335, *p* = .136) that is lower than those estimated with the methods presented previously, but it agrees with the other results with respect to the estimate not being statistically significant.

The use of a without-replacement matching strategy provides nonoverlapping matched pairs, which allows the use of a design-based method to account for clustering effects. Abadie and Imbens (2008) showed that bootstrapping is not an appropriate estimator for the standard error of treatment effects when matching with replacement is performed. However, Austin and Small (2014) found that bootstrapping matched pairs is an effective method to estimate standard errors when matching without replacement is used. In the following code, standard errors are obtained by bootstrapping the clusters of observations formed by the full matching algorithm. The argument *ids=~subclass* to the *svydesign* function specifies the cluster ids. This strategy is consistent with Austin's recommendation to adjust for pair effects when estimating standard errors from matched data.

design.fullMatching2 <- svydesign(ids=~subclass, weights=~weights,

data=data.fullMatching)

The *as.svrepdesign* function specifies that bootstrapping will be performed with 1,000 replications:

design.fullMatching2 <- as.svrepdesign(design.fullMatching2, type="bootstrap",

replicates=1000)

model.fullMatching2 <- svyglm(C0338600~childCare, design.fullMatching2, family=gaussian())

summary(model.fullMatching2)

```
Coefficients:
        Estimate Std. Error t value Pr(>|t|)
(Intercept)    10.043   0.880 11.413   <2e-16 ***
childCareTRUE   3.481   2.385  1.459   0.148
```

The only difference between the results below and the previous ones is the standard error estimation method, but the difference between the standard errors is very small. The estimate obtained (ATT = 3.481, *SE* = 2.385, *p* = .148) for the effect of the availability of company-provided or subsidized child care on length of breastfeeding is not statistically significant.

5.7. Sensitivity Analysis

Sensitivity analysis consists of examining what magnitude of hidden bias would change inferences about a treatment effect. Rosenbaum (2002) proposed a nonparametric sensitivity analysis method for continuous and ordinal outcomes based on the Wilcoxon signed ranks test. Rosenbaum's sensitivity analysis method is briefly described here and demonstrated with the *rbounds* package in R.

Rosenbaum's sensitivity analysis is based on the principle that if two cases have the same values on observed covariates but different probabilities of treatment assignment, the odds ratio of these cases receiving the treatment is

$$\frac{\pi_j/(1-\pi_j)}{\pi_k/(1-\pi_k)} = \frac{\pi_j(1-\pi_k)}{\pi_k(1-\pi_j)} \tag{5.8}$$

If there is an unobserved confounder, the odds ratio will be larger than 1 and smaller than a constant Γ (gamma) that measures the degree of departure from the absence of hidden bias.

$$\frac{1}{\Gamma} \leq \frac{\pi_j(1-\pi_k)}{\pi_k(1-\pi_j)} \leq \Gamma \tag{5.9}$$

Therefore, the value of Γ can be manipulated to evaluate how large it has to be for inferences about the significance of the treatment effect to change. If Γ has to attain very high values for inferences to change, then it is possible to conclude that the treatment effect is insensitive to hidden bias. Rosenbaum's sensitivity analysis consists of computing p values of the lower and upper bounds of the Wilcoxon signed rank statistic for the outcome difference between treated and untreated groups, under null hypotheses with increasing values of Γ.

The *rbounds* package was designed to work together with the *Matching* package to implement Rosenbaum's sensitivity analysis method. It can handle matched outcomes obtained with packages other than *Matching*, but it can currently handle only one-to-one and fixed ratio matching. Therefore, sensitivity analysis with one-to-one genetic matching will be demonstrated but not with full matching. The following line of code uses the *psens* function of the *rbounds* package to implement the sensitivity analysis with the *geneticMatching* object obtained previously with the *Match* function of the *Matching* package, by varying the sensitivity parameter gamma from 1 to a maximum given by Gamma = 3, in increments of 0.1 specified by the *GammaInc* argument:

psens(geneticMatching, Gamma=3, GammaInc=.1)

```
Rosenbaum Sensitivity Test for Wilcoxon Signed Rank P-Value
 Unconfounded estimate .... 0.1305
Gamma Lower bound Upper bound
  1.0      0.1305      0.1305
  1.1      0.0686      0.2224
  1.2      0.0343      0.3311
  1.3      0.0166      0.4456
  1.4      0.0077      0.5560
  1.5      0.0035      0.6553
  1.6      0.0016      0.7396
  1.7      0.0007      0.8080
  1.8      0.0003      0.8613
  1.9      0.0001      0.9017
  2.0      0.0001      0.9315
  2.1      0.0000      0.9529
  2.2      0.0000      0.9681
  2.3      0.0000      0.9786
  2.4      0.0000      0.9858
  2.5      0.0000      0.9906
  2.6      0.0000      0.9939
  2.7      0.0000      0.9960
  2.8      0.0000      0.9974
  2.9      0.0000      0.9984
           0.0000      0.9990
```

In this particular example, the results show that although the *p* value assuming no hidden bias is not statistically significant, a value equal to 1.2 or larger could lead to a significant *p* value, and therefore the conclusion that there is no effect of availability of company-provided or company-subsidized child care on length of breastfeeding is vulnerable to hidden bias. If the lower bound of the *p* value did not overlap the significance level even with Γ as high as 3, then there would be evidence of the results not being sensitive to hidden bias.

TABLE 5.3 ● Summary of Main Functions Used in This Chapter

Package	Function	Objective
stats	*glm*	Estimate propensity scores with logistic regression
MatchIt	*matchit*	Implement greedy matching and as interface for genetic, optimal, and full matching
MatchIt	*match.data*	Extract the matched data set from the object created with the *matchit* function
Matching	*GenMatch*	Obtain covariate weights for genetic matching

Package	Function	Objective
Matching	*Match*	Implement genetic matching with weights provided by the *GenMatch* function, as well as greedy matching
Matching	*MatchBalance*	Evaluate covariate balance of matching results provided by the *Match* function
survey	*svydesign*	Create an object that specifies the data to be analyzed, strata ids, cluster ids, and weights
survey	*as.svrepdesign*	Add replication weights to an object created with *svydesign* function, to allow bootstrapping
survey	*svyglm*	Estimate treatment effect with a generalized linear model
rbounds	*psens*	Implement Rosenbaum's sensitivity analysis method

5.8. Conclusion

Both multivariate and propensity score matching have been used and studied extensively since seminal work by Rubin in the late 1970s and early 1980s. Therefore, discipline-specific preferences have been developed with respect to how matching is used. For example, in the economics field, matching is performed primarily with replacement (Abadie & Imbens, 2006; Imbens, 2004; Imbens & Wooldridge, 2009), while in medicine, it is performed most commonly without replacement (Austin, 2008; Austin & Small, 2014). Although matching with replacement is able to produce better covariate balance than matching without replacement, it complicates statistical analysis, particularly with respect to estimation of standard errors.

With large samples with many untreated cases available for each treated case, matching with or without replacement makes little difference in covariate balance. This is particularly true when algorithms that optimize covariate balance, such as the genetic and optimal algorithms, are being used. However, as shown in the covariate balance evaluation comparison in Table 5.2, despite the theoretical advantages of optimal, full, and genetic matching over greedy matching, it is not always possible to predict how each matching algorithm will actually perform with respect to covariate balance for a particular sample. Therefore, it is recommended that multiple matching algorithms be implemented and the results are compared. It is common in applications of propensity score matching to report results based on multiple methods, which provides some evidence on how sensitive the conclusions are to matching algorithm choice.

Implementation of a propensity score matching method is more complicated and involves many more choices of algorithms and tuning parameters than implementation of propensity score weighting shown in Chapter 3. This begs the question of whether there are situations when using matching would be preferable over propensity score weighting. First, there are situations when matching is able to produce better covariate balance than weighting, due to a combination of factors, such as differences in sample sizes and the distributions of propensity scores of treated and untreated. Second, when there are difficulties in estimating propensity scores due to nonconvergence or quasi-separation of treated and untreated groups, matching based on covariates without the propensity score with the genetic matching algorithm is possible. Finally, there are situations when a stakeholder of an evaluation project is willing to accept matching as a quasi-experimental design method but not weighting. For example, the current standards of the What Works Clearinghouse (U.S. Department of Education, Institute of Education Sciences, & What Works Clearinghouse, 2013), which is a government organization that reviews educational research, describes matching as a method of quasi-experimental analysis but not weighting. Therefore, if the evaluators of an educational intervention are aiming to obtain a favorable review from the What Works Clearinghouse but cannot perform an experimental design, matching would be an acceptable option.

Study Questions

1. What is the difference between the common support requirements for matching for estimating the ATT and the ATE?

2. Why is it advantageous to match based on the logit of the propensity score rather than the propensity score itself?

3. How is greedy matching performed?

4. How is optimal matching performed?

5. How is genetic matching performed?

6. What is the role of the generalized Mahalanobis distance in genetic matching?

7. In what situation would greedy matching be expected to perform as well as optimal matching?

8. What is the advantage of optimal matching over greedy matching?

9. What is the advantage of genetic matching over optimal and greedy matching?

10. What is the expected difference in performance between one-to-one, one-to-many, and variable ratio matching?

11. How is a caliper used in matching, and what is the advantage of using it?

12. How can common support be strictly enforced in propensity score matching?

13. What is the expected difference in performance between matching with and without replacement?

14. How is full matching performed?

15. Which matching methods require the use of weights and why?

16. Why do some researchers argue that matched samples should be treated as independent samples?

17. Why do some researchers argue that matched samples should be treated as related samples?

18. What is the Abadie-Imbens simple estimator of the ATE for matched samples?

19. How can treatment effects for matched samples be estimated with regression?

20. What is the objective of sensitivity analysis?

21. What is the role of the gamma constant in Rosenbaum's sensitivity analysis?

6

Propensity Score Methods for Multiple Treatments

Learning Objectives

- Describe the generalized propensity score.

- Describe the assumptions of propensity score methods for multiple treatments.

- Compare methods for estimation of generalized propensity scores.

- Describe methods for assessing common support with multiple treatments.

- Describe the calculation of inverse probability of treatment weights.

- Describe the calculation of marginal mean weights through stratification.

- Describe the process of evaluation of covariate balance with multiple treatments.

- Estimate the ATE for pairwise combinations of multiple treatment conditions.

- Estimate the ATE, controlling for covariates in the outcome model.

6.1. Introduction

This chapter addresses research designs where the goal is to compare multiple treatment conditions. For example, a researcher may be interested in the following question: Do employees benefit differently from classroom training, on-the-job training, or online training? In contrast with the previous chapters of this book, where the focus was on whether there was a single treatment effect, this chapter focuses on estimating multiple treatment effects. Under Rubin's causal framework, when there are multiple treatment conditions available, each individual is associated with a vector of potential outcomes with one value for each condition.

Imbens (2000) provided the theoretical foundation for applying propensity score methods to research designs with multiple treatment conditions. He defined weak unconfoundedness as the assumption that the assignment to each treatment condition is independent of the potential outcome of the respective condition. Then, he showed that when weak unconfoundedness is met, estimates of treatment effects are unbiased. The difference between strong ignorability of treatment assignment discussed in Chapter 1 and weak unconfoundedness is that the latter does not require that the assignment to one treatment condition be independent of all potential outcomes. Instead, it requires only pairwise independence of assignment to a specific condition and the potential outcome of that condition.

Imbens (2000) defined the generalized propensity score $P(Z_i = z \mid X)$ as the conditional probability of each individual receiving treatment condition z given observed covariates X. Therefore, there are as many vectors of generalized propensity scores (GPS) as there are treatment conditions. He showed that if the assignment to each treatment condition is weakly unconfounded given observed covariates, it is also weakly unconfounded given the generalized propensity score.

Unbiased estimation of effects for multiple treatment conditions with propensity score methods requires three assumptions: weak unconfoundedness, overlap, and the stable unit treatment value assumption (SUTVA). Weak unconfoundedness is achieved when the generalized propensity score is correctly specified. The overlap assumption requires that the probability of receiving a treatment condition is neither 0 nor 1 for any individual in any treatment condition. This implies that no combination of covariate values should determine exactly which treatment an individual will receive or be excluded from receiving. The SUTVA assumption requires that the potential outcomes of each individual are independent from the treatment assignment of other individuals and that there are no unrepresented treatment conditions (Rubin, 1986). The extent that these assumptions may hold is discussed within the context of the example provided in this chapter.

Multiple propensity score methods have been proposed for removing selection bias in the estimation of the effects of multiple treatment conditions: inverse probability of treatment weighting (IPTW; Imbens, 2000), marginal mean weighting through stratification (MMWTS; Hong, 2012), and matching (Lechner, 2002). The focus of this this chapter is on IPTW and MMWTS for estimating the ATE of discrete treatment conditions. Propensity score methods for continuous treatments are presented in Chapter 7.

6.2. Description of Example

The example for this chapter answers the following research question: Does the assigning of mentors of different areas to new teachers affect the probability that they will continue in the teaching profession in the following year? The treatment has three conditions: (1) No mentor was assigned, (2) a mentor was assigned who was in the same subject area as the teacher, and (3) a mentor was assigned who was in a different subject area from the teacher.

Data on types of mentoring and covariates were obtained from the 1999–2000 School and Staffing Survey (SASS). The sample consists of teachers of public schools with less than 3 years of experience. There are 5,770 teachers in the sample, from which 2,299 (40%) were not assigned a mentor, 2,559 (44%) were assigned a mentor from the same subject area, and 912 (16%) were assigned a mentor from a different subject area. The outcome, which is a binary indicator of whether the teacher left the teaching profession, was obtained from the 2000–2001 Teacher Follow-up Survey (TFS).

The public use SASS data set is provided with missing values already imputed and with missing data indicators available as variables. For the cases with missing data in school or principal variables that had not already been imputed in the SASS data set, single imputation was performed using the *mice* package of the R statistical software (van Buuren & Oudshoorn, 2000).

6.3. Estimation of Generalized Propensity Scores With Multinomial Logistic Regression

To estimate GPS for multiple treatment conditions, multinomial logistic models are used. More specifically, the following baseline-category logit model (Agresti, 2002) is used to estimate the probabilities of teachers having no mentor, mentor from the same subject area, or mentor from a different subject area:

$$\log \frac{P(Z_i = z \mid X)}{P(Z_i = Z \mid X)} = \alpha_z + \beta_z X, \tag{6.1}$$

where $P(Z_i = z \mid X)$ is the probability of condition z, $P(Z_i = Z \mid X)$ is the probability of the reference condition Z, and β_z are the effects of covariates X. The model estimates the effects of covariates on the logit of selecting treatment condition z instead of a reference treatment condition Z. This model, in terms of the probabilities of selecting each treatment condition, is as follows (Agresti, 2002):

$$P(Z_i = z \mid X) = \frac{\exp(\alpha_z + \beta_z X)}{1 + \sum_{z=1}^{C-1} \exp(\alpha_z + \beta_z X)}, \tag{6.2}$$

where C is the total number of conditions, and with $\alpha_z = 0$ and $\beta_z = 0$ for the reference category Z. The probabilities of receiving the treatment conditions sum to 1 for each individual.

The first step in estimating the GPS is to determine which covariates to include in the propensity score model. True confounders of the relationship between type of mentor assignment and the retention of teachers in the profession in the following year may consist of characteristics of the school, the principal, and the teacher.

Strategies for selecting covariates are discussed in detail in Chapter 2. For this example, 76 covariates are included in the propensity score model, from which 15 were measured at the school level, 10 were measured at the principal level, and 51 were measured at the teacher level. Also, five dummy indicators of imputed values were included in the propensity score model (see Chapter 2 for more details on dealing with missing data in propensity score analysis). The following code is used to generate the formula for the generalized propensity score model by using the *paste* function to convert a vector of covariate names into a single character string separated by "+" and then adding the treatment assignment variable as the outcome. The *formula* function converts the character string to a formula object. This strategy for generating the formula is particularly useful when the number of covariates is very large.

psFormula <- paste(covariateNames, collapse="+")

psFormula <- formula(paste("Treat~",psFormula, sep=""))

print(psFormula)

```
Treat ~ TCHEXPER + A0053 + A0054 + A0058 + A0059 + A0060 + A0061 + A0062 +
A0063 + A0065 + TOTTEACH + URBANIC + S0104 + S0105 + S0106 + S0107 +
MINENR + MINTCH + PGMTYPE + REGION + S0284 + STU_TCH + LEP_T + PLAN +
PUPILS + T0059 + T0106 + T0120 + T0124 + T0125 + T0126 + T0127 +
T0150 + T0153 + T0154 + T0156 + T0158 + T0208 + T0293 + T0294 +
T0295 + T0296 + T0297 + T0298 + T0299 + T0300 + T0301 + T0303 +
T0306 + T0307 + T0308 + T0309 + T0310 + T0311 + T0312 + T0315 +
T0320 + T0321 + T0322 + T0324 + T0325 + T0326 + T0327 + T0331 +
T0332 + T0335 + T0336 + T0337 + T0338 + T0339 + T0340 + teachImputed +
principalImputed + schoolImputed + missingPrincipal + missingSchool
```

After covariates are selected and the generalized propensity score model shown above is created, the next step is to fit the multinomial logistic regression model. The model is fit using the *vglm* function of the package *VGAM* (Yee, 2010). The argument *formula = psFormula* indicates the propensity score model. Teacher weights provided by the SASS are used to remove bias due to unequal selection probabilities and response rates. The argument *weights=imputedData$TFNLWGT* specifies the variable containing sampling weights. Also, the argument *family=multinomial* declares that a multinomial logistic regression model should be fit.

require(VGAM)

ps.model <- vglm(formula=psFormula, weights=imputedData$TFNLWGT, family=multinomial,

data=imputedData)

A matrix of GPS can be obtained using the *fitted* function. The fitted values of the multinomial logistic regression model consist of an $n \times 3$ matrix where the probability of treatment assignment for *n* participants is provided for each of the three treatment conditions. Once GPS are estimated, it is important to evaluate the area of common support between different treatments. For each vector of GPS and each pair of treatments being compared, the area of common support is the range of the generalized propensity score distribution of the treatments where there are individuals with similar probabilities of receiving each treatment. Therefore, when there are multiple treatment conditions, common support should hold for all pairs of treatment conditions with respect to each vector of GPS. Poor common support may result in failure to obtain adequate covariate balance but can also limit the generalizability of treatment effects if individuals without common support are removed from the sample. The function *densityplot* of the *lattice* package is used in combination with the *reshape* function to generate the kernel density plot in Figure 6.1.

ps <- data.frame(fitted(ps.model))

library(lattice)

densityplot(~ps|time, groups=Treat, plot.points=F, auto.key=T,

   data = reshape(data.frame(ps,imputedData[,c("CNTLNUM","Treat")]),

   idvar="CNTLNUM",varying=c("noMentor","sameArea","otherArea"), v.names="ps",

   times=c("GPS of No Mentor","GPS of Same Area","GPS of Other Area"),direction="long"),

   ylab = "Generalized Propensity Scores", xlab = "Treatment Conditions")

FIGURE 6.1 ● Kernel Density Plots of the Distribution of GPS Estimated With Multinomial Logistic Regression for Teachers With No Mentor, Mentor in the Same Area, and Mentor in a Different Area

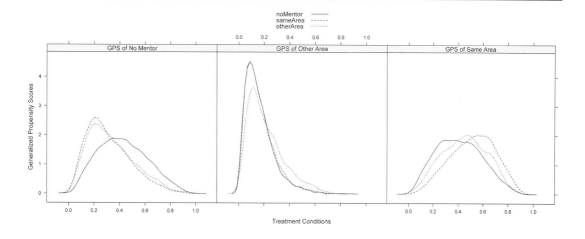

In the kernel density plot in Figure 6.1, the distributions of GPS across the treatment conditions appear to have adequate common support. Evidence of the adequacy of common support is also obtained at a later stage of the analysis, once propensity score methods have been implemented. In propensity score matching, cases without common support are dropped. In propensity score stratification, having a stratum containing few cases receiving one of the treatment conditions indicates poor common support. For inverse probability of treatment weighting, common support problems are harder to diagnose directly, but evidence of common support problems can be obtained by checking whether trimming the distribution of weights at the 99th percentile results in substantial improvement in covariate balance. However, caution is warranted because extreme weights can occur either due to poor common support or because the generalized propensity score model is misspecified. In the latter case, Lee et al. (2011) found that trimming weights can reduce bias of estimates and standard errors, but if there are extreme weights, they recommend that researchers first attempt to improve the model rather than just trimming weights (see Chapter 3 for additional discussion of extreme weights).

6.4. Estimation of Generalized Propensity Scores With Data Mining Methods

Data mining methods can be used to estimate GPS for multiple treatments (see Chapter 2 for a description of these methods). Estimating GPS with data mining methods based on recursive partitioning, such as regression trees, random forests, and generalized boosted modeling (GBM), has the advantage over multinomial logistic regression of automatically identifying interactions and nonlinear effects (Strobl et al., 2009). The use of data mining with multiple treatments can be accomplished by creating a dummy indicator for each treatment condition, where a case receives a value of 1 if exposed to the treatment condition and 0 otherwise. Then, the data mining method is used to predict each dummy indicator, resulting in a vector of predicted probabilities of receiving each treatment condition. Differently from multinomial logistic regression, the sum of the predicted probabilities of all treatments for each individual does not sum to 1. This limitation does not impede the use of data mining methods, because only the predicted probability of the treatment condition that each individual was exposed to is used in the analysis as an estimate of the GPS (McCaffrey et al., 2013). The estimation of GPS for multiple treatments with GBM is demonstrated here with the *twang* package, because it automates the process of creating a dummy indicator for each condition of the treatment, obtaining predicted probabilities, and assessing covariate balance. In the following code, GBM for multiple treatments is implemented by the *mnps* function of the *twang* package.

library(twang)

boost.ps <- mnps(psFormula, data = imputedData, estimand = "ATE", verbose = FALSE,

stop.method = c("es.max"), n.trees = 10000, sampw=imputedData$TFNLWGT)

The *estimand="ATE"* argument specifies that GBM should optimize covariate balance using weights to estimate the ATE (see description of weights in the next section). However, the algorithm also takes into account sampling weights, which are declared with the argument *sampw=imputedData$TFNLWGT*. The convergence criterion is selected with *stop.method=c("es.max")*, which sets the convergence criterion equal to the maximum standardized effect size of the difference between two groups across covariates. The argument *n.trees* sets the GBM algorithm to run for a total of 10,000 trees.

The next step is to diagnose convergence of the GBM algorithm to a minimum value of the convergence criterion. The code *plot(boost.ps, color=F, plots=1,pairwiseMax=F)* produces a plot of the maximum standardized effect size by iteration number, which allows examining whether the convergence criterion reached a minimum value within the requested 10,000 trees. This plot is shown in Figure 6.2 and indicates convergence of the GBM algorithm for all groups. The code *summary(boost.ps)* gives additional

FIGURE 6.2 ● Plot of Convergence of the GBM Algorithm for 10,000 Iterations

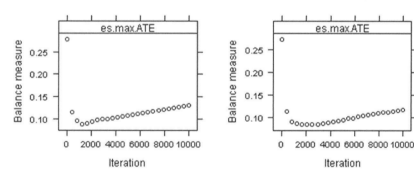

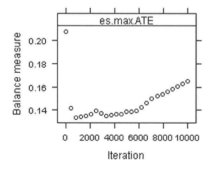

convergence information, showing that the maximum standardized effect size at convergence across all treatment condition comparisons is 0.124.

The next step is to assemble an $n \times 3$ data set of GPS with the *data.frame* function, which then receives variable names with the *names* function. Then, common support is evaluated by examining kernel density plots of GPS by treatment condition. The *twang* package facilitates the generation of plots for evaluating common support. The kernel density plot in Figure 6.3 is obtained with a simple call to the *plot* function, as shown below. Comparing Figure 6.1 and Figure 6.3 indicates that the distributions of propensity scores obtained with multinomial logistic regression and with GBM are very similar.

ps2 <- data.frame(noMentor=boost.ps$psList$noMentor$ps,

sameArea=boost.ps$psList$sameArea$ps,

otherArea=boost.ps$psList$otherArea$ps)

names(ps2) <- c("noMentor","sameArea","otherArea")

plot(boost.ps, color=F, plots = 2, figureRows=1)

FIGURE 6.3 ● Kernel Density Plots of the Distribution of GPS Estimated With GBM for Teachers With No Mentor, Mentor in the Same Area, and Mentor in a Different Area

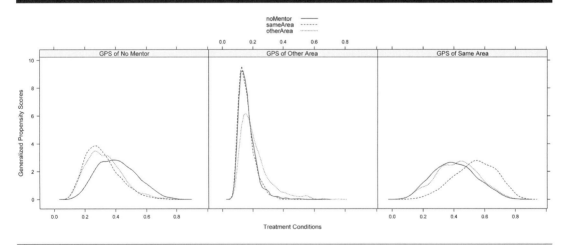

6.5. Propensity Score Weighting for Multiple Treatments

Inverse probability of treatment weights (IPTW) aims to adjust the sample so it is representative of a pseudo-population in which pretreatment variables are balanced (Robins et al., 2000). Imbens (2000) proposed IPTW for estimation of the ATE with multiple treatments where weights are defined as the inverse of the generalized propensity score:

$$w_i = \frac{1}{P(Z_i = z \mid X)},\tag{6.3}$$

where w_i is the weight of participant i. The IPTW can be obtained with a set of calls to the *ifelse* function that assigns the inverse of the probabilities of a treatment condition to the individuals who were exposed to that condition:

imputedData$IPTW <- ifelse(imputedData$Treat=="noMentor", 1/ps$noMentor,

   ifelse(imputedData$Treat=="sameArea", 1/ps$sameArea, 1/ps$otherArea))

To account for the complex sampling design of the SASS, the IPTW should be multiplied by the teacher sampling weights and then divided by the mean of the weights so that the final weights sum to the sample size. This is accomplished with the following code:

imputedData$IPTW.TFNLWGT <- with(imputedData,IPTW*TFNLWGT)

imputedData$finalWeightATE <- with(imputedData,IPTW.TFNLWGT/

   mean(IPTW.TFNLWGT))

The following code prints the summary of final weights:

with(imputedData, by(finalWeightATE,Treat,summary))

```
Treat: noMentor
Min. 1st Qu.  Median   Mean 3rd Qu.   Max.
0.01169 0.17740 0.38590 0.81510 0.89830 18.76000
-----------------------------------------------------------------
Treat: sameArea
Min. 1st Qu. Median  Mean 3rd Qu.  Max.
0.0235 0.2167 0.4473 0.7380 0.8758 8.0130
-----------------------------------------------------------------
Treat: otherArea
Min. 1st Qu.  Median   Mean 3rd Qu.   Max.
0.04265 0.48910 1.12500 2.20100 2.77200 26.25000
```

In the summary shown above, it is important to check if there are no extreme weights, which could dramatically increase the variance of the treatment effect estimates. Although there is no clear guideline of what magnitude of weight is too large, comparing the weights obtained with the total sample size of 5,770 provides some indication that the weights obtained are not extreme. If extreme weights were a concern in this example, they could be stabilized or truncated, as shown in Chapter 3.

6.5.1. Covariate Balance With
Weights From Multinomial Logistic Regression

The evaluation of covariate balance with multiple treatment conditions can be performed between each treatment condition and all the other conditions combined, or between pairs of treatment conditions. The latter strategy is preferable because it allows precise identification of which pair of conditions had covariates with adequate balance. Covariate balance evaluation for multiple treatments can be accomplished using the *bal.stat* function of the *twang* package (Ridgeway et al., 2013). The following code shows the creation of the *pairwise.balance* custom function to implement pairwise covariate balance evaluation with *twang*. The arguments of the function *condition1, condition2, data,* and *iptw* are the name of the first and second treatment conditions to be compared, the data object, and the variable containing the final weights, respectively. The *pairwise.balance* function creates a data set with just two treatment conditions before calling the *bal.stat* function to create a covariate balance table.

```
pairwise.balance <- function(condition1, condition2, data, iptw){

        require(twang)

        data <- subset(data, Treat == condition1 | Treat == condition2)

        data$Treat <- as.numeric(data$Treat==condition1)

        balance.iptw <- bal.stat(data=data, vars=covariateNames, treat.var ="Treat" ,

            w.all = data[,iptw], get.ks=F, sampw = data$TFNLWGT,

            estimand="ATE", multinom=F)

        return(balance.iptw$results) }
```

The following code uses the *pairwise.balance* function with all possible pairs of treatment conditions:

```
balance.iptw <- list(

pair12 <- pairwise.balance("noMentor", "sameArea", imputedData, "finalWeightATE"),

pair13 <- pairwise.balance("noMentor", "otherArea", imputedData, "finalWeightATE"),

pair23 <- pairwise.balance("sameArea", "otherArea", imputedData, "finalWeightATE"))
```

For this example, the covariate balance criterion is that standardized effect sizes should be less than 0.1 standard deviations (Austin, 2011b). The next code takes the absolute values of the standardized effect sizes between pairs of treatment conditions for all covariates and then summarizes covariate balance.

std.eff.iptw <- data.frame(abs(balance.iptw[[1]][5]), abs(balance.iptw[[2]][5]),

abs(balance.iptw[[3]][5]))

summary(std.eff.iptw)

```
   std.eff.sz          std.eff.sz.1         std.eff.sz.2
 Min.   :9.355e-05   Min.   :0.0001057   Min.   :0.0002229
 1st Qu.:4.398e-03   1st Qu.:0.0130202   1st Qu.:0.0142486
 Median :1.166e-02   Median :0.0284777   Median :0.0273534
 Mean   :1.325e-02   Mean   :0.0355310   Mean   :0.0336634
 3rd Qu.:1.935e-02   3rd Qu.:0.0507797   3rd Qu.:0.0478227
 Max.   :4.687e-02   Max.   :0.1870903   Max.   :0.1825487
```

The maximum standardized effect size between the teachers with no mentor and teachers with a mentor in the same area was 0.046, which indicates adequate balance for all covariates. However, between teachers with no mentors and teachers with mentors from other subject areas and mentors from the same area, the maximum was 0.187 with three covariates exceeding 0.1. Between teachers with mentors from the same subject area and teachers with mentors from other subject areas, the maximum was 0.182 with five covariates exceeding 0.1. Across all treatment conditions, the balance criterion of 0.1 was not achieved with six covariates (i.e., T0297, T0300, T0308, T0322, T0325, T0335). This situation can be addressed by respecifying the propensity score model, changing the propensity score estimation method, or including the covariates that did not reach the specified criteria for covariate balance in the outcome model.

6.5.2. Covariate Balance With
Weights From Generalized Boosted Modeling

For the current example, estimation of GPS with GBM was demonstrated in Section 6.4. The *mnps* function of the *twang* package calculates the IPTW and produces plots and tables of covariate balance. Using the *plot* function on the *boost.ps* object created by the *mnps* function, the pairwise plots of covariate balance shown in Figure 6.4 are produced.

plot(boost.ps, plots = 3, color=F, pairwiseMax = F, figureRows = 1)

FIGURE 6.4 ● Covariate Balance Between Treatment Conditions (Columns) by Baseline and Weighted Status (x-axis) and Absolute Standardized Effect Sizes (y-axis)

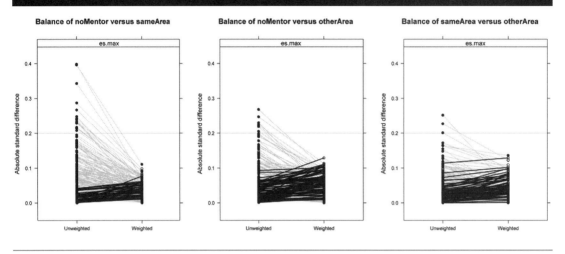

The *bal.table* function creates balance tables containing standardized effect sizes for all covariates and treatment conditions, shown as follows:

balance.boost.ps <- bal.table(boost.ps, digits = 2)

summary.balance.boost <- aggregate(std.eff.sz~tmt1+tmt2+stop.method, data=balance.boost. ps, FUN=max)

balance.above.0.1.gbm <- subset(balance.boost.ps,

   (std.eff.sz > 0.1 & stop.method == "es.max"))

The covariate balance before and after weighting with the IPTW from multinomial logistic regression and GBM is summarized in Table 6.1. It shows that using the IPTW obtained with GBM resulted in better covariate balance than when multinomial logistic regression was used. With GBM, eight covariates had a covariate balance slightly above 0.1: T0154, MINENR, REGION, T0296, T0309, URBANIC, S0284, and T0337. Both multinomial logistic regression and GBM resulted in a covariate balance substantially better than the baseline (i.e., no weighting).

6.5.3. Marginal Mean Weighting
Through Stratification for Multiple Treatment Versions

MMWTS (Hong, 2010, 2012; Hong & Hong, 2008) combines propensity score stratification and weighting. MMWTS applied to the estimation of the ATEs of multiple treatment conditions consists of estimating a vector of propensity scores for each

TABLE 6.1 ● Summary of Covariate Balance		
Pair	**Method**	**Maximum Standardized Effect Size**
Same area–mentor from other area	Baseline	0.240
	MLR	0.182
	GBM	0.120
	MMWTS	0.115
No mentor–mentor from other area	Baseline	0.270
	MLR	0.187
	GBM	0.120
	MMWTS	0.110
No mentor–mentor from same area	Baseline	0.420
	MLR	0.046
	GBM	0.110
	MMWTS	0.092

Note: MLR = multinomial logistic regression; GBM = generalized boosted modeling; MMWTS = marginal mean weighting through stratification.

condition, categorizing each vector into S equal-width strata, and then creating a weight for each observation based on the following equation:

$$w_{zs} = \frac{n_s \Pr(Z = z)}{n_{zs}}, \tag{6.4}$$

where w_{zs} is the marginal mean weight for treatment condition z within stratum s, n_s is the number of units in stratum s, $\Pr(Z = z)$ is the proportion of units in the overall sample that received treatment condition z, and n_{zs} is the number of units in stratum s that actually received the treatment z. The numerator $n_s \Pr(Z = z)$ is an estimate of the number of individuals in stratum s that should have received treatment z if there was no selection bias, while the denominator is the actual number of units within stratum s that received treatment z. Therefore, the weight in Equation (6.4) works like a sampling weight for disproportionate stratified sampling, which adjusts for the fact that some treatment conditions were overrepresented in some strata. The following code creates the custom *mmws.weights* function to calculate the weights for MMWTS, with arguments *id, treat, ps,* and *numb.strata,* which are the vector of case ids, the treatment factor, the vector of generalized propensity scores, and the number of strata desired, respectively. The function works by using a *for* loop to go through the treatment conditions to create strata with the *cut* function and obtain frequency tables of strata and strata by condition to fill in n_s and n_{zs} in Equation (6.4), respectively.

```
mmws.weights <- function(id,treat, ps, numb.strata) {

all.weights <- data.frame(id)

        for (t in levels(treat)) {

                strata = cut(x=ps[,t],breaks=quantile(ps[,t], prob = seq(0, 1, 1/numb.strata)),

                labels=1:numb.strata,include.lowest=T)

                treatment = as.numeric(treat==t)

        treat.by.strata <- data.frame(xtabs(~strata+treatment))

        strata.table <- data.frame(table(strata))

        names(strata.table)[2] <- "Freq.strata"

        treat.by.strata <- merge(treat.by.strata,strata.table)

        print(treat.by.strata)

        treat.by.strata$mm.weight <- ifelse(treat.by.strata$treatment==1,

                mean(treatment)*treat.by.strata$Freq.strata/treat.by.strata$Freq,

                (1-mean(treatment))*treat.by.strata$Freq.strata/treat.by.strata$Freq)

        data.weight <- data.frame(id,treatment,strata)

        data.weight <- merge(treat.by.strata[,c(1,2,5)],data.weight)

        data.weight$mm.weight[data.weight$treatment==0] = 0

        data.weight <- data.weight[,3:4]

        names(data.weight)[1] <- paste("W.",t,sep="")

        all.weights <- merge(all.weights,data.weight) }

        all.weights$mmws <- apply(all.weights[,-1],1,sum)

        return(all.weights[,c("id","mmws")]) }
```

The following code applies the function defined above to the current example to obtain weights for MMWS using the generalized propensity scores with GBM, because they provided better balance than multinomial logistic regression.

mmws <- mmws.weights(imputedData$CNTLNUM, imputedData$Treat, ps2, numb.strata=5)

Then, the data set with weights for MMWS is merged with the SASS data:

names(mmws)[1] <- "CNTLNUM"

imputedData <- merge(imputedData,mmws)

The final weights are the product of the weights from MMWS and the sampling weights, divided by the mean of weights so they sum to the sample size, shown as follows:

*imputedData$mmwsFinal <- with(imputedData,(mmws*TFNLWGT)/mean(mmws*TFNLWGT))*

by(imputedData$mmwsFinal, imputedData$Treat, summary)

```
imputedData$Treat: noMentor
    Min. 1st Qu.  Median   Mean 3rd Qu.     Max.
 0.01848 0.22300 0.47800 0.91700 1.06600 15.17000
------------------------------------------------------------------
imputedData$Treat: sameArea
    Min. 1st Qu.  Median    Mean 3rd Qu.    Max.
0.03433 0.34060 0.69520 1.06900 1.28900 9.26300
------------------------------------------------------------------
imputedData$Treat: otherArea
    Min. 1st Qu.  Median    Mean 3rd Qu.    Max.
0.02992 0.29110 0.60140 1.01500 1.27400 8.28800
```

It can be seen in the summary above that weights are similar across treatment conditions. Table 6.2 shows that no stratum had zero or very few observations, which is evidence of adequate common support for propensity score stratification with five strata. Using five strata is expected to remove at least 90% of bias, but increasing the number of strata will increase bias reduction. However, as the number of strata is increased, the common support may become inadequate because some strata may have zero observations for one of the treatments. Covariate balance was evaluated in the same way as presented earlier for IPTW. Table 6.1 shows that MMWS using the propensity scores estimated with GBM provided the best covariate balance among the methods examined. With MMWS, six covariates had a covariate balance that slightly exceeded 0.1 standard deviations: MINENR, S0284, T0296, T0299, T0324, and T0325.

6.6. Estimation of Treatment Effect of Multiple Treatments

For all the PS methods that result in weights, the ATE of one treatment condition with respect to another condition can be estimated with the following:

TABLE 6.2 ●	Number of Observations per Stratum for Each Treatment Condition		
Stratum	**No Mentor**	**Same Area**	**Other Area**
1	194	190	80
2	331	366	123
3	430	476	148
4	560	665	198
5	784	862	363

$$\Delta_{12} = \frac{\sum_{i=1}^{n1} w_{i1} y_{i21}}{\sum_{i=1}^{n1} w_{i1}} - \frac{\sum_{i=1}^{n2} w_{i2} y_{i2}}{\sum_{i=1}^{n2} w_{i2}}, \tag{6.5}$$

where Δ_{12} is the ATE of Treatment Condition 1 compared with Treatment Condition 2, with 1 and 2 representing any pair of conditions. Also, $n1, n2$ are the number of participants in each treatment condition; w_{i1}, w_{i2} are the weights of the treatments' participants; and y_{i1}, y_{i2} are the outcomes. Because the teachers are nested within schools, clustering effects should be accounted for in the estimation of standard errors (Leite et al., 2015). Using the *survey* package, a cluster-robust estimate of the standard error of Δ_{12} can be obtained with Taylor series linearization (TSL) or replication methods such as jackknife and bootstrapping (Heeringa et al., 2010; Lohr, 1999). Doubly robust versions of the estimator in Equation (6.5), which use covariates to increase robustness to misspecifications of the propensity score model and increase efficiency, are described by Lunceford and Davidian (2004), Kang and Schafer (2007a, 2007b), and Bang and Robins (2005).

The following code is used to estimate the ATE with the estimator in Equation (6.5) for pairwise combinations of teachers having no mentor, a mentor from the same subject area, and a mentor from a different subject area. The weights obtained with MMWTS are used because they provided the best covariate balance. The *svydesign* function of the *survey* package is used to define a design object that contains the data and specifies that the cluster id is the variable *SCHCNTL,* and the final weights are in the variable *mmwsFinal.*

library(survey)

design.IPTW<- svydesign(id = ~SCHCNTL, weights = ~ mmwsFinal, data = imputedData)

Bootstrapping is used to obtain standard errors that account for the clustering of teachers within schools. To allow estimation of standard errors with bootstrapping, the function *as.svrepdesign* adds 1,000 replication weights to the design object:

design.IPTW.boot <- as.svrepdesign(design.IPTW, type=c("bootstrap"),replicates=1000)

The function *svyby* applies the *svymean* function to estimate means or proportions by treatment group. *svymean* detects whether means or proportions should be estimated by checking whether the outcome is numeric or a factor. In this example, the proportions of teachers who left the teaching profession are estimated by combinations of mentoring conditions:

weightedProportions <- svyby(formula=~leftTeaching,by=~Treat,design=design.IPTW.boot,

  FUN=svymean,covmat=TRUE)

print(weightedProportions)

```
              Treat leftTeaching0 leftTeaching1        se1        se2
noMentor   noMentor     0.9701300    0.02986995 0.006570714 0.006570714
sameArea   sameArea     0.9628483    0.03715169 0.005719677 0.005719677
otherArea otherArea     0.9694922    0.03050780 0.007793343 0.007793343
```

The *svycontrast* function is used to obtain pairwise ATE estimates by specifying a weight of 1 for the proportion of one treatment condition and a weight of –1 for the proportion of another treatment condition:

pairwise.ATE <- svycontrast(weightedMeans, contrasts=list(

  sameArea.noMentor= c("sameArea:leftTeaching1"=1,"noMentor:leftTeaching1"=-1),

  sameArea.otherArea=c("sameArea:leftTeaching1"=1,"otherArea:leftTeaching1"=-1),

  otherArea.noMentor=c("otherArea:leftTeaching1"=1,"noMentor:leftTeaching1"=-1)))

```
                      contrast        SE
sameArea.noMentor   0.00728174    0.0082
sameArea.otherArea  0.00664389    0.0096
otherArea.noMentor  0.00063785    0.0101
```

Because the outcome (i.e., teacher left the profession) is a binary variable, the ATEs are differences in proportions of teachers who left the profession between the types of mentor assignment. None of the ATEs obtained by pairwise contrasts between treatment conditions are statistically significant at $\alpha = .05$.

TABLE 6.3 ● Summary of Main Functions Used in This Chapter		
Package	**Function**	**Objective**
VGAM	*vglm*	Fit multinomial logistic regression model to estimate propensity scores for multiple treatment conditions
lattice	*densityplot*	Obtain kernel density plots to evaluate common support
twang	*mnps*	Estimate propensity scores for multiple treatment conditions with generalized boosted modeling
	plot	Obtain plots of convergence, common support, and covariate balance
	bal.stat	Evaluate pairwise covariate balance between treatment conditions
survey	*svydesign*	Declare data, weights, and cluster ids that will be used in the estimation
	as.svrepdesign	Add replication weights to a survey design to enable bootstrapping, jackknife, and balanced repeated replications to estimate standard errors
	svymean	Estimate means and proportions, taking into account a complex survey design
	svycontrast	Estimate treatment effects by taking differences between weighted means or proportions

6.7. Conclusion

This chapter only demonstrated inverse probability of treatment weighting and marginal mean weighting through stratification, but with multiple treatment conditions, pairwise subgroup matching can be performed (Lechner, 2002) by minimizing the difference between GPS. Any matching methods could be used, such as greedy, genetic, optimal matching, and optimal full matching (see Chapter 5). Because optimal full matching can be viewed as an extension of propensity score stratification where the maximum number of strata containing at least two individuals receiving different treatments is defined by the data, it can be used for multiple treatment conditions in the same way that marginal mean weighting through stratification is used in this chapter (e.g., Leite, Aydin, & Gurel, 2013).

The ATE is estimated in this chapter by calculating differences between weighted proportions. Because the outcome of the example shown in this chapter is binary, logistic regression could have been used to estimate odds ratios of treatment conditions. However, logistic regression has a noncollapsibility problem, which means that the coefficients will not be invariant to the removal of a covariate. Therefore, coefficients may change with different logistic models used to estimate the treatment effect not because of omitted confounders but because of noncollapsibility. The issue of noncollapsibility and its distinction from confounding are discussed in detail by Greenland, Robins, and Pearl (1999). An alternative is to use a log binomial model, which is a binomial generalized linear model with the log link that estimates risk differences directly and is collapsible. However, it is numerically unstable because it allows probabilities greater than 1, but solutions to this problem have been proposed (e.g., Marschner, 2012).

Study Questions

1. What is weak unconfoundedness?

2. What is the difference between weak unconfoundedness and strong ignorability of treatment assignment?

3. What are the assumptions necessary for propensity score methods for multiple treatments?

4. What is the generalized propensity score?

5. What are two methods that can be used to estimate generalized propensity scores?

6. How can data mining methods be used to estimate generalized propensity scores?

7. How can common support be assessed with multiple treatments?

8. How can weights based on the generalized propensity score be calculated?

9. How are marginal mean weights through stratification calculated with multiple treatments?

10. How can covariate balance be assessed with multiple treatments?

11. What are two methods to estimate the ATE with multiple treatments?

7

Propensity Score Methods for Continuous Treatment Doses

Learning Objectives

- Describe the weak unconfoundedness assumption in the context of continuous treatments.

- Describe the generalized propensity score.

- Evaluate the effects of continuous treatments with a dose response function.

- Calculate the inverse probability of treatment weight.

- Evaluate covariate balance given the inverse probability of treatment weight.

- Estimate the average treatment effect with inverse probability of treatment weighting.

7.1. Introduction

Three methods have been proposed to estimate the effects of continuous treatments when there is a nonrandom selection mechanism of treatment dosage. Hirano and Imbens (2004) extended previous work by Imbens (2000) to define generalized propensity scores (GPS) for continuous treatments. Robins et al. (2000) proposed inverse probability weighting for removing selection bias in the estimation of the effect of continuous treatments. Although developed independently, these two methods are connected because the formula for inverse probability weights for continuous treatments has the GPS in its denominator. The third approach to estimate the effects of continuous treatments is the propensity function proposed by Imai and Van Dyk (2004). This chapter will focus on inverse probability weighting because it is a very flexible approach that can be used with a variety of models for the outcome and is closely related to the methods demonstrated in Chapters 3, 6, and 9. However, because of the relationship between the GPS and the calculation of the inverse probability weight (IPW), Hirano and Imbens's (2004) proposed definition, estimation, and use of the GPS for continuous treatments are reviewed first. Then, the calculation of inverse probability weights as proposed by Robins et al. (2000) is presented.

7.2. Description of Example

Virtual learning environments such as virtual K–12 schools, e-learning management systems, intelligent tutoring systems, and massive open online courses (MOOCs) provide the opportunity of quick collection of responses to surveys and scales, as well as collection of server logs, click streams, time on task, and discussion posts (U.S. Department of Education, 2012). These data provide opportunities to evaluate whether virtual learning environments lead to improvements in teaching and learning (Institute of Education Sciences, 2014). The objective of this example is to estimate the effect of school participation in the Algebra Nation virtual learning environment on the school-level means of student scores on Florida's Algebra I End-of-Course (EOC) assessment. Algebra Nation is a virtual learning environment that supports students and teachers in meeting mathematics state standards required on the Florida Algebra I EOC assessment. Algebra Nation has video lessons covering algebra concepts, formative assessments, and an interactive student wall. Algebra Nation is a schoolwide program because it is implemented by integrating the school's network system with the Algebra Nation system so that students and teachers can access Algebra Nation from school computers and personal computers, smartphones, and tablets using their school ID and password. Also, Algebra Nation implementation includes offering training to the mathematics teachers in the school about how to use Algebra Nation in their classrooms and sending paper copies of the Algebra Nation workbook to the teachers for distribution and use with their students.[1] The study's population consisted of high schools, middle/high schools, and senior high schools in all school districts in Florida. Data for this example were collected from February to April 2014 and contain observations for 448 schools. The outcome for this example is the school-level means of the student scores on the spring 2014 Algebra I EOC exam.

7.3. Generalized Propensity Scores

Hirano and Imbens (2004) consider a continuous treatment Z where for each individual i receiving treatment dose z, there is a vector of potential outcomes $Y_i(z)$. The individual-level treatment effect is the mean of the vector of potential outcomes

---

[1] See http://www.algebranation.com for more details.

$\mu(z) = E[Y_i(z)]$, which cannot be directly estimated because only one value within the vector of potential outcomes of each individual is observed, and the others are missing.[2] The treatment dose received and the value of the potential outcomes observed for each individual depend on a set of observed confounding variables X, and therefore ignoring these true confounders in the estimation of the average treatment effect at any level of the continuous treatment will result in biased estimates.

Given a set of true confounders X, weak unconfoundedness (Imbens, 2000) is the assumption that the potential outcomes at treatment dose z are independent of the treatment dosage assignment given observed covariates (i.e., $Y_i(z) \perp Z_i(z) | X$), which differs from strong ignorability of treatment assignment because it does not require joint independence for all treatment doses. Extending the work of Imbens (2000), Hirano and Imbens (2004) showed that the GPS can be used to remove the bias due to covariates X if weak unconfoundedness (i.e., weak ignorability of treatment assignment) is achieved. Given a parametric model for the relationship between Z and X, the conditional density of the treatment given covariates is $r(z,x) = f_{Z|X}(z | x)$. The generalized propensity score $r_i(Z,X)$ for each individual i is the conditional density of the treatment evaluated at the individual's specific values of Z and X. For example, if the linear regression model $Z_i = \beta_0 + \beta X_i + \varepsilon_i$ with $e_i \sim N(0, \sigma_i^2)$ is used, then the conditional Gaussian density is

$$r(z,x) = \frac{1}{\sqrt{2\pi\sigma^2}} \exp\left(-\frac{1}{2\sigma^2}(Z_i - \beta_0 - \beta X_i)^2\right). \tag{7.1}$$

A single value $r_i(Z,X)$ of GPS for each treatment value and values of covariates can be estimated using Equation (7.1). Hirano and Imbens (2004) proved that if weak unconfoundedness holds given the covariates X; it also holds given the GPS. More specifically, they proved that if unconfoundedness holds, then for every treatment dose z,

$$f_Z(z | r(Z,X), Y(Z)) = f_Z(z | r(Z,X)), \tag{7.2}$$

where $f_Z(z | .)$ is the conditional density of Z, $r(Z,X)$ is the generalized propensity score, and $Y(Z)$ is the vector of potential outcomes at a dose z.

The method proposed by Hirano and Imbens (2004) to estimate the effects of continuous treatments consists of the following steps: (1) Model the continuous treatment indicator as a function of covariates, (2) obtain the GPS, (3) model the outcomes as a function of treatment and GPS, and (4) estimate the average potential outcome at each treatment dose of interest and plot the dose response function. In this section, these steps are presented and demonstrated for estimating the effect of Algebra Nation participation.

Before proceeding to the first step, it is necessary to define a measure of Algebra Nation participation. For some continuous treatments, such as receiving a dose of a

---

[2] The notation used in this chapter differs from Hirano and Imbens (2004) to keep consistency across the book chapters.

certain medicine, the operational definition of the treatment dose may be straightforward, such as the amount of medicine received per day in milliliters. However, quantifying the use of virtual learning environments such as Algebra Nation at the school level is complex, because Algebra Nation can be used by the teachers with all students in the classroom, by individuals or groups of students in a computer lab, or by students in their home using the school-provided login and password. Furthermore, teachers use Algebra Nation in the schools in a variety of ways such as for a warm-up activity, as review after a lesson, and for remediation. For this example, the ratio of number of logins and number of examinees in each school is used as a continuous measure of the treatment, where number of logins is the sum of teacher and student logins for a school from all sources (classroom, lab, and home computers, smartphones, and tablets), and number of examinees is the number of students in the school who took the Algebra I EOC assessment in the spring of 2014. A ratio is used here to facilitate the interpretation of the treatment dose. This measure of treatment dosage has limitations, such as not distinguishing between teacher logins to show Algebra Nation content to an entire class from individual student logins. The mean number of logins per examinee is 2.50 and the maximum is 25.13 during a time period of 3 months. Because the distribution of logins per examinee is highly skewed, a log transformation is applied to the number of logins per examinee to reduce skewness. Figure 7.1 presents histograms to compare the distributions of the original and log-transformed treatment doses, indicating that the log transformation succeeds in reducing nonnormality.

Once a measurement of the treatment is defined, covariates can be selected that are related to both treatment dosage and the outcome (i.e., true confounders), as well as covariates related just to the outcome to increase efficiency. For this example, 13 covariates are selected, including the school-level means in the Algebra I EOC

FIGURE 7.1 ● Histograms of Total Logins per Examinee in Each School

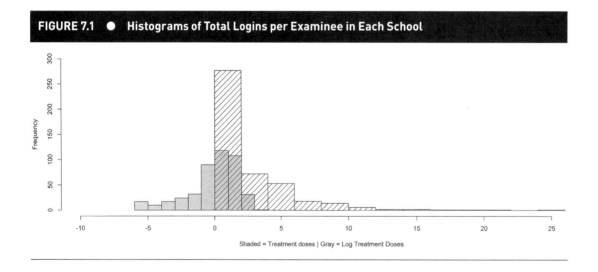

exam in 2012, the number of students, percentage of students eligible for free lunch, percentage of students eligible for reduced-price lunch, and dummy indicators of whether the school was a charter, magnet, or Title I in 2012. The model for doses of treatment is written as a formula and assigned to the *formulaDose* object as follows:

formulaDose <- formula("logLoginsPerExaminee~Charter+Magnet.+

Title.I.School.+locationRural+locationSize+Students.+

SeniorHigh+numOfStud2014+meanScale2012+lev1Perc2012+

lev5Perc2012+perc.free.lunch+perc.reduced.lunch")

To complete the first step of Hirano and Imbens's (2004) method, the linear regression model for the treatment doses as a function of the covariates is fit using the *lm* function:

modelDoses <- lm(formula=formulaDose, data=data)

The second step is to estimate the GPS, which can be obtained using the conditional density shown in Equation (7.1) by evaluating it with specific values of the treatment dose z and the fitted values of the treatment dose (i.e., $\beta_0 - \beta X_i$). The code to calculate the GPS uses the *dnorm* function to obtain the conditional density:

data$GPS <- dnorm(data$logLoginsPerExaminee, mean=modelDoses$fitted,

sd=sd(data$logLoginsPerExaminee))

Hirano and Inbems (2004) evaluated the covariate balance achieved with the GPS by stratifying the sample according to both treatment dose and GPS and performing t tests across the strata. However, this method is cumbersome and relies on significance tests, which are not adequate because covariate balance is a property of the sample, and significance tests refer to the population. One alternative strategy is to stratify based on GPS and fit one regression for each covariate with the treatment dose as the outcome and with GPS strata and the covariate as predictors. Then, standardized regression coefficients can be used as a measure of the effect size of the covariates on treatment dose. Covariate balance is achieved if the effect sizes of the covariates and covariate-by-GPS interactions are small. This strategy is implemented with a *for* loop through all covariates and the *lm* function to fit a regression for each covariate. The *covariateNames* object is a vector of covariate names. The following code creates the *balanceTable* object, which contains the absolute value of standardized coefficients of the regression of treatment doses on the covariates (for dummy-coded categorical covariates, the largest coefficient of the dummy codes is selected).

```
balanceTable <- data.frame()

for (var in 1:length(covariateNames)) {

    balanceFormula <- paste("logLoginsPerExaminee~strataGPS+",covariateNames[var],sep="")

    maxEff <- max(abs(coef(lm(balanceFormula,data))[-(1:5)]))

    balanceTable <- rbind(balanceTable,c(var,maxEff)) }

names(balanceTable) <- c("variable","coef")

balanceTable$variable <- covariateNames

balanceTable$coef <- balanceTable$coef/sd(data$logLoginsPerExaminee)
```

The standardized regression coefficients obtained with the code above are shown in Table 7.1, together with baseline covariate balance and balance with inverse probability of treatment weighting. For this example, covariate balance is considered adequate if the standardized regression coefficient is lower than 0.1, but guidelines for covariate balance evaluation for propensity score analysis with treatment doses are not well established. Although the covariate balance improved substantially compared with the baseline, three covariates (charter school, magnet school, and location size) did not achieve the desired level of balance. These covariate balance results could be improved by changing the GPS model, but for this example analysis, covariate balance will be improved by using inverse probability weighting, shown in Section 7.4.

TABLE 7.1 ● Standardized Coefficients of Regressions of Treatment Dose on Covariates

Variable	Baseline	GPS Strata	IPW
Charter	0.321	0.346	0.200
Magnet	0.459	0.319	0.019
Title I school	0.105	0.024	0.054
Rural school	0.321	0.034	0.007
Location size	0.397	0.215	0.071
Number of students	0.000	0.000	0.000
Senior high	0.064	0.000	0.085
Number of students 2014	0.106	0.038	0.030
Mean scale 2012	0.117	0.077	0.019
Level 1 percent 2012	0.108	0.064	0.027

Variable	Baseline	GPS Strata	IPW
Level 5 percent 2012	0.084	0.093	0.017
Percent free lunch	0.037	0.015	0.068
Percent reduced lunch	0.056	0.067	0.010

The third step in Hirano and Imbens's (2004) method is to model the outcome as a function of the treatment dosage and the GPS. For the current example, the outcome model in Equation 7.3 contains linear and quadratic effects of treatment dose and GPS, as well as the interaction between them. The outcome is the school-level mean Algebra EOC assessment score in 2014.

$$E\left[Y_i \mid Z_i, r_i(Z, X)\right] = \gamma_0 + \gamma_1 Z_i + \gamma_2 Z_i^2 + \gamma_3 r_i(Z, X) + \gamma_4 r_i(Z, X) + \gamma_4 Z_i r_i(Z, X) \tag{7.3}$$

However, the coefficients γ from this outcome model do not have a causal interpretation, and the model is just an intermediate step to obtaining individual treatment effects. The following code estimates the outcome model for the example with the *svyglm* function of the *survey* package (Lumley, 2004). In this particular example, the *lm* or *glm* functions of the *stats* package could have been used instead, because the data do not contain sampling weights.

library(survey)

designAN <- svydesign(id=~1,weights=~1,data =data)

modelOutcome <- svyglm(formula="meanScale2014~logLoginsPerExaminee +

I(logLoginsPerExaminee^2) + GPS + I(GPS^2) +

logLoginsPerExaminee:GPS", design=designAN)

7.3.1. Dose Response Function

The final step of Hirano and Imbens's (2004) method is to obtain individual treatment effects and plot the dose response function. Individual treatment effects are the average potential outcomes at treatment dose z given the coefficients of the outcome model:

$$E\left[Y_i(z)\right] = \frac{1}{N}\sum_{i=1}^{N}\left(\gamma_0 + \gamma_1 z + \gamma_2 z^2 + \gamma_3 r_i(Z, X) + \gamma_4 r_i(Z, X)^2 + \gamma_4 z r_i(Z, X)\right) \tag{7.4}$$

The following code shows a *for* loop to obtain estimates of the average treatment effects at the 1st to 100th percentiles of the treatment dose. The percentiles are obtained with the *quantile* function. The *predict* function is used with *modelOutcome* to obtain the potential outcomes for each percentile of treatment dose with all values of the GPS. The *svyconstrast* function is used to implement the averaging of potential outcomes across all observations for each percentile of treatment dose. The average treatment effects for all percentiles of treatment dosage evaluated are stored in the *all. effects* object. The *svycontrast* function also provides the standard error for each average treatment effect.

all.effects <- data.frame()

for (dose in quantile(data$logLoginsPerExaminee,probs=seq(0.01,1,0.01))) {

effects <- predict(modelOutcome,type="response", vcov=T,

        newdata=data.frame(logLoginsPerExaminee=dose, GPS=data$GPS))

effect <- svycontrast(effects,rep(1/nrow(data),nrow(data)))

all.effects <- rbind(all.effects,effect) }

The following code was used to create Table 7.2. More specifically, it organizes the average treatment effects into a *data.frame,* including also the percentile numbers, the dosage corresponding to each percentile, and confidence intervals.

doseResponses <- data.frame(percentile = seq(1,100,1),

    loginsPerExaminee=quantile(data$loginsPerExaminee,

    probs=seq(0.01,1,0.01)), all.effects)

names(doseResponses)[3] <- "meanAlgebraScore"

doseResponses$lowerCL <- with(doseResponses, meanAlgebraScore – 1.96*SE)

doseResponses$upperCL <- with(doseResponses, meanAlgebraScore + 1.96*SE)

Table 7.2 shows the treatment dose effects corresponding to some percentiles of treatment dosage. The treatment dose effects can be interpreted as the expected values of the outcome if all the participants received each specific dose of treatment. It is possible to verify whether the difference between the treatment effects for two doses is statistically significant by comparing confidence intervals of the effects. For example, Table 7.2 shows that all the confidence intervals overlap, indicating no significant differences between doses. Figure 7.2 is a plot of the dose response function. It shows the treatment dose effects on the mean Algebra EOC scores as a function of log logins per examinee, with confidence intervals indicated by dashed lines. It is noticeable that the confidence intervals are narrower in the middle of the distribution of log logins per examinee, because more schools were available to estimate the treatment dose effects at the middle region of the distribution.

TABLE 7.2 ● Treatment Dose Effects, Standard Errors, and Confidence Intervals for Percentiles of Treatment Doses					
Percentile	Log Logins per Examinee	Mean Algebra EOC Score	Standard Error	Lower Confidence Limit	Upper Confidence Limit
10%	−2.901	395.129	2.698	389.841	400.417
20%	−1.246	397.087	0.985	395.157	399.017
30%	−0.553	397.654	1.049	395.599	399.710
40%	−0.111	397.938	1.078	395.825	400.051
50%	0.297	398.146	1.044	396.100	400.192
60%	0.666	398.291	0.961	396.406	400.175
70%	1.084	398.402	0.846	396.745	400.060
80%	1.458	398.456	0.810	396.868	400.045
90%	1.835	398.467	0.964	396.578	400.356
100%	3.224	398.125	3.132	391.987	404.263

FIGURE 7.2 ● Plot of Treatment Dose Effects on the Mean Algebra EOC Score as a Function of Treatment Dose, With Confidence Intervals

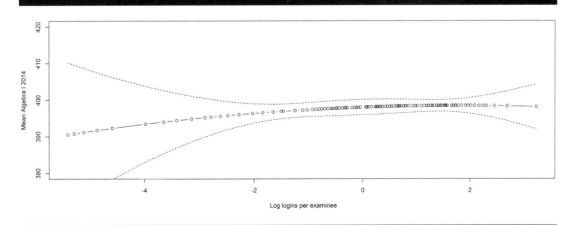

Note. Confidence intervals are indicated by dashed lines.

7.4. Inverse Probability Weighting

Robins et al. (2000) proposed inverse probability weighting to remove selection bias of the estimate of the average treatment effect of a continuous treatment. The bias removal occurs because the IPW of the observations creates a pseudo-population within which a set of individuals receiving dose z of treatment and another set receiving a different dose have similar distributions of covariates. The IPW for continuous treatments is

$$w_i = \frac{f_Z(z)}{f_{Z|X}(z \mid x)},$$
(7.5)

where the denominator $f_{Z|X}(z \mid x)$ is the conditional density of the treatment evaluated at the values of Z and X of individual i. Therefore, the denominator of the weight is the GPS and can be estimated with Equation (7.1). The numerator $f_Z(z)$ is the marginal density of the treatment variable:

$$f_Z(z) = \frac{1}{\sqrt{2\pi\sigma^2}} \exp\left(-\frac{1}{2\sigma^2}\left(Z_i - \mu_i\right)^2\right)$$
(7.6)

The following code calculates the numerator of the IPW of logins per examinee for the current example and then obtains the IPW using the GPS that was previously estimated:

data$numerator <- with(data, dnorm(logLoginsPerExaminee,

mean=mean(logLoginsPerExaminee), sd=sd(logLoginsPerExaminee)))

data$IPW <- with(data, numerator/GPS)

summary(data$IPW)

```
  Min. 1st Qu. Median  Mean 3rd Qu.  Max.
 0.2293 0.8350 0.9960 0.9902 1.1110 7.0680
```

The examination of the weights indicates that extreme weights are not a concern, given that the maximum weight was 7.068. The next step is to evaluate covariate balance. This can be accomplished by running bivariate regressions of the treatment dosage on each covariate and comparing the regression coefficients obtained with and without the use of the IPW. The rationale of this covariate balance evaluation method is that the treatment dose is uncorrelated with the covariates in the pseudo-population generated by weighting observations by the IPW, if the GPS model was correctly specified. Therefore, the standardized coefficients of the regression of the treatment dose on the covariate should be close to zero. The *svyglm* function of the *survey* package is used to fit the regressions with the inverse probability weights. Before these regressions can be fit, the following code is used to create the *designIPW* object, which specifies the data to be analyzed and the variable containing the weights.

designIPW <- svydesign(ids=~1,weights=~IPW,data=data)

The following code obtains the information about covariate balance displayed in Table 7.1. A *for* loop is used to fit one regression with the *svyglm* function for each of the covariates in the example, with the treatment dose as the outcome and the covariate as the predictor.

balanceTableIPW <- data.frame()

for (var in 1:length(covariateNames)) {

    balanceFormula <- paste("logLoginsPerExaminee~",covariateNames[var],sep="")

    maxEffBaseline <- max(abs(coef(svyglm(balanceFormula,designAN))[-1]))

    maxEffIPW <- max(abs(coef(svyglm(balanceFormula,designIPW))[-1]))

    balanceTableIPW <- rbind(balanceTableIPW,c(var,maxEffBaseline,maxEffIPW)) }

names(balanceTableIPW) <- c("variable","coefBaseline","coefIPW")

balanceTableIPW$variable <- covariateNames

balanceTableIPW$coefBaseline <- balanceTableIPW$coefBaseline/

                    sqrt(coef(svyvar(~logLoginsPerExaminee,designAN)))

balanceTableIPW$coefIPW <- balanceTableIPW$coefIPW/

                    sqrt(coef(svyvar(~logLoginsPerExaminee,designIPW)))

The standardized regression coefficients are displayed in Table 7.1, showing that covariate balance improved with the IPW compared with both the baseline and the GPS strata. All covariates have standardized coefficients lower than 0.1, except for the variable indicating that the school was a charter school. This variable is included in the outcome model to provide additional bias reduction.

7.4.1. Estimation of the Average Treatment Effect

The average treatment effect of a continuous treatment can be estimated by weighting observations with the IPW when fitting any parametric model of the outcome as a function of the treatment dose. For example, for a continuous outcome, the following regression model can be used:

$$y_i = \beta_0 + \gamma Z_i + \varepsilon_i , \tag{7.7}$$

where γ is the average treatment effect. For the current example, because the charter school indicator did not meet the target criterion for adequate covariate balance, the outcome model is expanded to include charter school as well as the interaction between charter school and treatment dose:

$$y_i = \beta_{0i} + \gamma Z_i + \beta_1 X + \beta_2 X_i Z_i + \varepsilon_i \tag{7.8}$$

If covariates are included, it is important to center the covariates and add interactions between the covariates and the treatment doses, which will ensure that the coefficient of the treatment dose variable can still be interpreted as the average treatment effect. In the following code, centering of the *Charter* variable is performed with the scale function. Then, the *svydesign* function is used to re-create the *designIPW* object because the *Charter* variable changed. The outcome model is fit with the *svyglm* function, incorporating inverse probability weights and with standard errors obtained with Taylor series linearization (Lumley, 2004, 2010).

data$Charter <- scale(as.numeric(data$Charter=="Yes"),scale=F)

designIPW <- svydesign(ids=~1,weights=~IPW,data=data)

outcomeModelDR <- svyglm(formula= meanScale2014~logLoginsPerExaminee +

Charter + Charter:logLoginsPerExaminee,

design = designIPW, family=gaussian)

summary(outcomeModelDR)

```
Call:
svyglm(formula = meanScale2014 ~ logLoginsPerExaminee + Charter +
  Charter:logLoginsPerExaminee, design = designIPW, family = gaussian)
Survey design:
svydesign(ids = ~1, weights = ~IPW, data = data)
Coefficients:
                          Estimate Std.  Error t   value Pr(>|t|)
(Intercept)                397.42444 0.52839 752.138   <2e-16 ***
logLoginsPerExaminee         0.66387 0.31777   2.089   0.0373 *
Charter                      4.33191 2.25213   1.923   0.0551 .
logLoginsPerExaminee:Charter 0.00714 1.15741   0.006   0.9951
---
Signif. codes: 0 '***' 0.001 '**' 0.01 '*' 0.05 '.' 0.1 ' ' 1
(Dispersion parameter for gaussian family taken to be 115.2521)
Number of Fisher Scoring iterations: 2
```

The estimated coefficient of 0.664 ($SE = 0.318$, $p = .037$) indicates a statistically significant average treatment effect of log logins per examinee on mean Algebra EOC scores. Because of the log scale of the predictor, for an increase in logins per examinee from value x_1 to value x_2, the expected change in mean Algebra EOC scores is $0.664 \log(x_2/x_1)$. For example, an increase of 10% in logins per examinee corresponds to an expected change in mean Algebra EOC scores of $0.664 \log(1.1) = 0.063$. It is also important to keep in mind that this is a school-level effect, so no inference can be made about individual student scores.

TABLE 7.3 ● Summary of Main Functions Used in This Chapter		
Package	**Function**	**Objective**
stats	*lm*	Fit model for the continuous treatment indicator as a function of covariates
stats	*dnorm*	Obtain generalized propensity scores
survey	*svydesign*	Define survey object with data and weights
survey	*svyglm*	Fit model for the outcome
stats	*quantile*	Obtain percentiles of treatment doses
survey	*predict*	Obtain potential outcomes
survey	*svycontrast*	Average potential outcomes for each treatment dose

7.5. Conclusion

The generalized propensity score method proposed by Hirano and Imbens (2004) and the inverse probability weighting method of Robins et al. (2000) were reviewed and demonstrated in this chapter. Both approaches are anchored in Rubin's causal model because they conceptualize the observed outcome of each treatment dose as part of a vector of potential outcomes. However, the generalized propensity score method focuses on estimating treatment effects at many treatment doses to characterize a dose response function, while inverse probability weighting targets estimating the average treatment effect. The inverse probability of treatment weighting method is most flexible because it can be combined with any parametric and nonparametric estimator of the treatment effect that incorporates sampling weights. Furthermore, inverse probability weighting is directly applicable to time-varying treatments, as will be demonstrated in Chapter 9.

Study Questions

1. How does the concept of potential outcomes that is the key part of Rubin's causal model generalize to continuous treatments?

2. What is the assumption of weak unconfoundedness in the context of continuous treatments?

3. What is the generalized propensity score of a treatment dose?

4. What are the steps of Hirano and Imbens's (2000) generalized propensity score method?

5. How are individual treatment responses estimated with the generalized propensity score method?

6. How can the effect of two treatment doses be compared using the generalized propensity score method?

7. How is the dose response function plot constructed?

8. What is the inverse probability weight for continuous treatments?

9. How does the inverse probability weight reduce selection bias?

10. How can covariate balance be evaluated with the inverse probability weight for continuous treatments?

11. How can the average treatment effect be estimated with inverse probability weights for continuous treatments?

12. What are the advantages of including covariates in the model for the outcome with inverse probability weights?

Propensity Score Analysis With Structural Equation Models

Learning Objectives

- Describe the benefits of using structural equation modeling in propensity score analysis.

- Differentiate between a latent confounding variable and an observed confounding variable.

- Describe the importance of measurement invariance of confounders and outcomes across treated and untreated groups.

- Perform measurement invariance testing.

- Perform estimation of propensity scores incorporating factor scores.

- Use structural equation modeling to estimate the treatment effect on a latent outcome.

8.1. Introduction

The use of propensity score methods to estimate treatment effects in observational studies entails a design stage, where propensity scores are estimated and selection bias is removed with a propensity score method (i.e., matching, stratification, weighting), and the analysis stage, where treatment effects are estimated (Rubin, 2005, 2007, 2008). Propensity score analyses may use latent variables rather than observed variables as covariates in the propensity score model in the design stage and/or as the outcome in the analysis stage. These latent variables are usually measured with multiple-item scales, where each item's variance is in part due to the latent variable and in part due to random measurement error. Although it is a common practice to simply sum the scale's items to obtain the outcome for the observational study, such practice not only assumes that the items' measurement error is negligible but also that the items have equal relationships with the latent variable. In other words, using sums of multiple items to measure latent variables in program evaluation assumes that the item scores are highly reliable and none of the items is a better measure of the construct of interest than the others.

There are three contributions that structural equation modeling (SEM) can provide to propensity score analysis when latent variables are confounding variables and/or outcomes: First, in the design stage, the estimation of propensity scores assumes that covariates in the propensity score model are reliably measured (Steiner et al., 2011), and SEM can be used to control for measurement error in latent confounding variables. Second, in the analysis stage, SEM can control for measurement error in latent outcomes. This is important because ignoring the measurement error in latent variables results in biased standard errors (Kaplan, 1999). Third, SEM can provide validity evidence for the measurement of latent confounders and latent outcomes. In particular, SEM can be used to examine whether the measurement of the latent variable of interest is equivalent across treated and untreated groups, which is known in the SEM literature as measurement invariance testing (Meredith, 1993; Raykov, Marcoulides, & Li, 2012), and is similar to the testing of differential item functioning (DIF; Kamata & Vaughn, 2004) in psychometrics research (Kim & Yoon, 2011; Reise, Widaman, & Pugh, 1993; Raju, Laffitte, & Byrne, 2002).

This chapter demonstrates the use of multiple-group SEM to estimate factor scores of latent variables to be included in the propensity score model. It also presents multiple-group SEM combined with propensity score matching to estimate treatment effects with cross-sectional data. Also, multiple-group SEM is used for measurement invariance testing (Meredith, 1993) to determine whether the same latent variable is being measured across treated and untreated groups. This chapter assumes that the reader has some familiarity with structural equation modeling. Short introductions to structural equation modeling can be found in articles by Bollen (2002) and Hox and Bechger (1998). Several books about structural equation modeling are available, such as Bollen (1989), Kaplan (2009), Kline (2011), Raykov and Marcoulides (2006), and Schumacker and Lomax (2010), as well as books on structural equation modeling using R (Beaujean, 2014; Finch & French, 2015).

The design stage of propensity score analysis with latent variables as confounders entails the following steps: (1) Identify observed and latent confounding variables, (2) select indicators for the latent confounding variables, (3) fit the measurement model to indicators of latent confounding variables, (4) assess model fit and respecify model or revise choice of indicators if needed, (5) evaluate whether there is measurement invariance in latent confounding variables, (6) estimate factor scores, (7) use factor scores to estimate propensity scores, (8) implement a propensity score method, and (9) evaluate covariate balance.

The analysis stage of propensity score analysis with a latent outcome consists of these steps: (1) Identify indicators for the latent outcome, (2) fit the measurement model, (3) assess model fit and respecify as needed, (4) evaluate measurement invariance of the latent outcome across treated and control groups, (5) fit the structural equation model for estimation of treatment effects, (6) evaluate fit of the structural equation model, and (7) if the fit is acceptable, interpret the treatment effect estimate.

8.2. Description of Example

In this chapter, the application of structural equation modeling to propensity score analysis is demonstrated with the estimation of the effect of new teacher participation in a network of teachers on their perception of workload manageability, which is a latent variable. Data from the 1999–2000 administration of the School and Staffing Survey (SASS) and the 2000–2001 administration of the Teacher Follow-up Survey (TFS) is analyzed. This is the same data set used for the example in Chapter 6. The SASS implemented a stratified multistage sampling design where a sample of schools was obtained with stratified sampling and teachers were randomly sampled within schools.[1] The example for this chapter uses a subsample of 1,030 new teachers with 0 to 3 years of teaching experience. The treatment indicator is obtained from the following survey question: "In the past 12 months, have you participated in the following activities related to teaching?" where teachers selected the option "Participating in a network of teachers (e.g., one organized by an outside agency or over the Internet)." In the sample of interest, 223 (21.7%) of new teachers reported participating in a teacher network.

8.3. Latent Confounding Variables

For this example, the propensity score analysis removes bias due to 25 covariates. Five of them are latent confounding variables measured at the teacher level: perception of school management, perception of the family background of the students attending the school, perception of student delinquency in the school, perception of student participation, and perception of teacher support. The indicators measuring each latent covariate are shown in Table 8.1. These indicators have a 4-point Likert response scale from *strongly agree* to *strongly disagree*. Cronbach's alpha estimates, which are estimates of the reliability of measurement for the latent variables, are shown in Table 8.1. They range from 0.87 to 0.6.

---

[1] For this example, the sampling weights will not be used, because the *MatchIt* package used for optimal matching does not accept sampling weights.

TABLE 8.1 ● Latent Variables and Indicators		
SASS Variable Number	**Indicator Description**	**Factor Loading**
Perception of school management: $\alpha = 0.87$		
T0299	The principal lets staff members know what is expected of them.	0.805
T0300	The school administration's behavior toward the staff is supportive and encouraging.	0.801
T0306	My principal enforces school rules for student conduct and backs me up when I need it.	0.784
T0307	The principal talks with me frequently about my instructional practices.	0.693
T0310	The principal knows what kind of school he/she wants and has communicated it to the staff.	0.863
T0312	In this school staff members are recognized for a job well done.	0.768
Perception of family background: $\alpha = 0.84$		
T0335	Problem—parental involvement	0.821
T0336	Problem—poverty	0.743
T0337	Problem—unprepared students	0.938
T0338	Problem—student health	0.760
Perception of student delinquency: $\alpha = 0.81$		
T0325	Problem—physical conflicts	0.713
T0326	Problem—theft	0.723
T0327	Problem—vandalism	0.785
T0331	Problem—weapons	0.758
T0332	Problem—disrespect for teachers	0.838
Perception of student participation: $\alpha = 0.8$		
T0321	Problem—student tardiness	0.791
T0322	Problem—student absenteeism	0.877
T0324	Problem—class cutting	0.825

SASS Variable Number	Indicator Description	Factor Loading
Perception of teacher support: $\alpha = 0.72$		
T0308	Rules for student behavior are consistently enforced by teachers in this school even for students who are not in their classes.	0.820
T0309	Most of my colleagues share my beliefs and values about what the central mission of the school should be.	0.671
T0311	There is a great deal of cooperative effort among the staff members.	0.736
Workload manageability: $\alpha = 0.60$		
F0105	Some of the classes or sections I taught were too large.	0.796
F0108	I often felt that my teaching workload was too heavy.	0.353
F0113	There was not enough time available for planning and preparation during a typical week at the school.	0.606
F0116	There was not enough uninterrupted class time available for instruction.	0.486

Note: α = Cronbach's alpha.

Raykov (2012) showed that if latent confounding variables included in the propensity score model are unreliably measured, the estimated propensity scores will not balance the latent confounding variables across treated and control groups. To address this problem, multiple-group SEM (Green & Thompson, 2012) is used to obtain factor scores that are more reliable measures of the latent confounding variables than simple summations of indicators. Multiple-group SEM consists of simultaneously fitting separate SEM models to treated and untreated groups, allowing means, variances, and covariances of latent variables to differ across treatment groups. Then, the factor scores are included in the propensity score model as covariates. The multiple-group SEM for a latent confounding variable, which is a multiple-group confirmatory factor analysis (CFA) model, in this example is as follows (Bovaird & Koziol, 2012):

$$
\begin{aligned}
X_{ikg} &= c, \text{if } \tau_c < X_{ikg}^\star < \tau_{c+1} \\
X_{ikg}^\star &= \lambda_k \xi_{ig} + \delta_{ik} \\
E(X_{kg}) &= \lambda_k \mu_g
\end{aligned}
\tag{8.1}
$$

where X_{ikg} is the observed ordinal response of participant i in group g (i.e., $g = 0$ for the untreated group and $g = 1$ for the treated group) on indicator k for the latent confounding variable,[2] X_{ikg}^* is the score on a continuous latent response variable under-lying X_{ikg}, and τ_c is a threshold that categorizes X_{ikg}^* into X_{ikg}. ξ_i is the factor score of participant i on the latent confounding variable. $E(X_{kg})$ is the mean of the indicator k and μ_g is the mean of the latent confounding factor for group g. In this model, each indictor measures a single latent confounding variable. The factor loading is λ_k, which quantifies the strength of the relationship between the observed scores of the indicator and the latent confounding variable. The measurement error is δ_{ik}.

With this multiple-group CFA model, the thresholds τ_c and factor loadings λ_k are estimated, as well as the means of ξ_g, covariance matrices of ξ_g, and δ_{ik}, which are both random factors assumed to be normally distributed. For this example, the covari-ance matrix of measurement errors δ_{ki} is diagonal, establishing the assumption that the measurement error of each indicator is uncorrelated to the measurement error of other indicators. Violation of this assumption would result in a decrease of model fit, but it is possible to allow correlated residuals to account for systematic effects on the indicators not accounted for by the latent variables in the model, such as method effects (see Leite, Svinicki, & Shi, 2010, for an example). The multiple-group CFA model for the five latent confounding variables in this example is shown in Figure 8.1. This model is estimated using the *lavaan* package in R. The model specification is shown as follows. It consists of a single character string, but with one line per equation. The latent variable names are presented to the right of the =~ sign, and the indicators are presented to the left, separated by a + sign.

library(lavaan)

model <- 'PSCHMAN =~ T0299 + T0300 + T0306 + T0307 + T0310 + T0312

      PFAMBACK =~ T0335 + T0336 + T0337 + T0338

      PSTUDEL =~ T0325 + T0326 + T0327 + T0331 + T0332

      PSTUPAR =~ T0321 + T0322 + T0324

      PTEACSUP =~ T0308 + T0309 + T0311'

Estimation of SEM models with ordinal indicators is commonly performed with the mean and variance-adjusted weighted least squares (WLSMV) estimator or robust maximum-likelihood estimator, but other estimators are also available (Beauducel & Herzberg, 2006; Olsson, Foss, Troye, & Howell, 2000). In the following code, the *cfa* function of the *lavaan* package is used to estimate the multiple-group CFA model in Figure 8.1 using the WLSMV estimator. First, a vector of indicator names is created, which is then used with the *ordered* argument of the *cfa* function to declare which indicators have an ordinal scale. The *group* argument is used to specify the treatment indicator, and the *group.equal* argument is used to indicate that factor loadings and thresholds should be equal across groups, enforcing the strong factorial invariance assumption (see discussion of this assumption later in this chapter).

---

[2] The subscript to indicate multiple latent confounding variables is omitted to simplify notation.

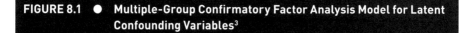

FIGURE 8.1 ● Multiple-Group Confirmatory Factor Analysis Model for Latent Confounding Variables[3]

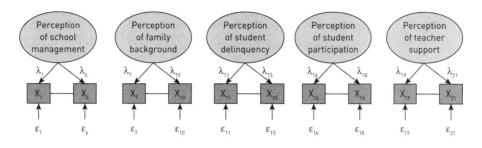

indicator.names <- c("T0299", "T0300", "T0306", "T0307", "T0310", "T0312",

"T0335", "T0336", "T0337", "T0338",

"T0325", "T0326", "T0327", "T0331", "T0332",

"T0321", "T0322", "T0324",

"T0308", "T0309", "T0311")

mgCFA <- cfa(model, ordered=indicator.names, group="treat", data=data, estimator="WLSMV", group.equal=c("loadings", "thresholds"))

mgCFA.fit <- fitMeasures(mgCFA)

mgCFA.estimates <- parameterEstimates(mgCFA, standardized=T)

In the code above, a large number of model fit measures are obtained with the *fitMeasures* function. Here the focus will be on the most commonly used fit measures. The non-significant chi-square statistic indicates exact fit of the model to the data, while fit indices indicate close fit. For this example, the decision about whether there is close fit is based on whether the comparative fit index (CFI) and Tucker-Lewis Index (TLI) are equal to or greater than 0.95 and the root mean square error of approximation (RMSEA) is equal to or smaller than 0.05. In addition, a nonsignificant *p* value for the test of RMSEA < .05 is considered evidence of close fit. These criteria, based on the work of Hu and Bentler (1999), are widely used to evaluate model fit of SEM, although research has shown that they are too conservative (Marsh, Hau, & Wen, 2004; Marsh, Hau, & Grayson, 2005) and not sensitive to certain types of model misspecification (Fan & Sivo, 2005, 2007; Heene, Hilbert, Freudenthaler, & Bühner, 2012; Leite & Stapleton, 2011). For the multiple-group CFA of the latent confounding variables, the fit information is $\chi^2 = 900.614$ ($df = 411$, $p < .05$),

---

[3] Figures 8.1, 8.3, and 8.4 were created using Microsoft PowerPoint. In R, the diagram and DiagrammeR packages are capable of creating these figures.

CFI = 0.99, TLI = 0.99, and RMSEA = 0.048 (p = .759). Therefore, it is possible to conclude that the CFA for the five latent confounding variables does not have exact fit but has close fit based on the values of CFI, TLI, and RMSEA. Because model fit is acceptable, factor scores based on this multiple-group CFA can be obtained for the propensity score model.

Besides adequate model fit, it is also necessary to evaluate the assumption that the indicators of the latent confounding variables measure the constructs equally well across treated and untreated groups. More specifically, it is necessary to evaluate whether strong factorial invariance (Meredith, 1993; Millsap & Meredith, 2007), also known as scalar invariance, holds across treated and untreated groups. For constructs with categorical indicators, strong factorial invariance is a level of measurement invariance that requires that factor loadings and thresholds be the same across groups. To test that this requirement holds, an adjusted likelihood ratio test is used to compare a multiple-group CFA constraining factor loadings and thresholds to equality across groups and an identical model without these constraints. For the current example, the nonsignificant likelihood ratio test (χ^2 = 54.03, df = 53, p = .435) indicates that the requirement of strong factorial invariance holds.[4]

8.4. Estimation of Propensity Scores

Once the multiple-group CFA model for the latent confounding variable is estimated and its adequacy of model fit and measurement invariance requirements are verified, factor scores can be obtained for inclusion in the propensity score model. The following code shows the use of the *predict* function to obtain factor scores for the five latent confounding variables, which are then used in the propensity score model. The *predict* function returns a list containing separate sets of propensity scores for untreated and treated groups, which are then combined into a single set with the *rbind* function[5] and combined with the data using the *cbind* function.

factor.scores <- predict(mgCFA)

data <- cbind(data, rbind(factor.scores[[1]],factor.scores[[2]]))

covariateNames = c("LEP_T", "PLAN", "T0059", "T0106", "T0120", "T0122", "T0124",

"T0125", "T0126", "T0127", "T0147", "T0150", "T0153", "T0154", "T0158", "T0248",

"T0250", "T0208", "PSCHMAN", "PFAMBACK", "PSTUDEL" , "PSTUPAR",

"PTEACSUP", "PUPILS", "teachImputed")

psFormula <- paste(covariateNames, collapse="+")

psFormula <- formula(paste("treat~",psFormula, sep=""))

---

[4] Example code to test for measurement invariance is shown on the book's website.
[5] The data had been sorted by the treated group indicator prior to the analysis, which allows stacking of propensity scores for the two groups.

In the propensity score model shown below, the factor scores of latent confounding variables are *PSCHMAN, PFAMBACK, PSTUDEL, PSTUPAR,* and *PTEACSUP*. It is also important to note that the variable *teachImpute*d is a dummy indicator of whether the teacher had some missing responses that were imputed.

print(psFormula)

```
treat ~ LEP_T + PLAN + T0059 + T0106 + T0120 + T0122 + T0124 +
   T0125 + T0126 + T0127 + T0147 + T0150 + T0153 + T0154 + T0158 +
   T0248 + T0250 + T0208 + PSCHMAN + PFAMBACK + PSTUDEL + PSTUPAR +
   PTEACSUP + PUPILS + teachImputed
```

The following code estimates propensity scores with logistic regression implemented with the *glm* function. Other propensity score estimation methods also could have been used, such as random forests and generalized boosted modeling. After the propensity score model is fit, propensity scores are saved into the *pScores* variable using the *fitted* function, and a summary of the propensity scores is printed.

psModel <- glm(psFormula, data=data, family=binomial)

data$pScores <- fitted(psModel)

with(data,by(pScores,treat,summary))

```
treat: 0
    Min.    1st Qu.    Median      Mean    3rd Qu.      Max.
0.0000001 0.1114000 0.1735000 0.1968000 0.2596000 0.6484000
-----------------------------------------------------------------
treat: 1
   Min. 1st Qu.  Median    Mean 3rd Qu.    Max.
0.05012 0.19770 0.26450 0.28760 0.35420 0.71220
```

Once propensity scores are estimated, common support can be examined by comparing the propensity score distributions of teachers in networks and teachers not in networks. The minimum propensity score for teachers not in networks is very close to zero. However, the maximum propensity scores of the two groups are similar. The kernel density plot in Figure 8.2 shows that the distributions are similar, providing preliminary evidence that common support is adequate.

8.5. Propensity Score Methods

This section shows the implementation and evaluation of covariate balance for propensity score matching and propensity score weighting, which are used in later sections with structural equation models. Propensity score matching to estimate the ATT of participation in a network of teachers is first implemented with the *matchit* function

FIGURE 8.2 ● **Kernel Density Plot of the Distributions of Propensity Scores for New Teachers in a Network and Not in a Network**

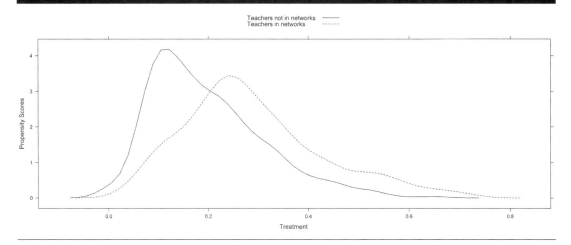

of the *MatchIt* package (Ho et al., 2011) using one-to-one genetic matching[6] without replacement, which is discussed in Chapter 2. The code for this matching strategy is below. Matching is performed based on the logit of the propensity score, declared in the *distance=data$logitPScores* argument, to avoid poor matching due to compression of the scale of the propensity score around 0 and 1. The arguments *method = "genetic", ratio=1, replace=F,* and *ties=F* specify that one-to-one genetic matching without replacement is to be performed. In this sample, the treated group has 223 teachers, and the untreated group has 807 teachers. Therefore, there are 3.62 untreated teachers for each treated teacher, and this large ratio of untreated to treated observations is favorable for matching without replacement (see Chapter 5 for a discussion of the merits of different matching algorithms).

library(MatchIt, Matching)

geneticMatching <- matchit(psFormula,distance=data$logitPScores,

   data = data, method = "genetic", pop.size=1000,

   replace=F, ties=F, ratio=1)

For this example, covariate balance is considered acceptable if the standardized mean differences between treated and untreated are less than 0.1 standard deviations. In the next code, the *summary* function with the *standardize = T* argument produces a covariate balance table containing standardized differences between teachers in a

---

[6] The *MatchIt* package uses the *Matching* package to implement genetic matching. The *Matching* package requires that the treatment indicator be in true/false format.

network and not in a network for all covariates. The *match.data* function extracts the matched data set. The *quantile* and *abs* functions are used to print quintiles of the distribution of absolute values of the standardized mean difference across treated and matched groups, to allow examination of balance across all covariates.

balance.optimalMatching <- summary(optimalMatching, standardize=T)

matchedData <- match.data(optimalMatching)

quantile(abs(balance.geneticMatching$sum.matched$"Std. Mean Diff."),na.rm=T)

```
        0%         25%         50%         75%        100%
0.00000000  0.02396904  0.03229208  0.05103580  0.10943550
```

With one-to-one genetic matching, only one covariate had a standardized mean difference exceeding 0.10, which was 0.109 for the covariate *LEP_T* (i.e., percentage of students with limited English proficiency taught in most recent full week), so the covariate balance was considered adequate. The original sample size is 1,030, but the matched data set has only 446 cases with 223 in each treatment group.

Propensity weights for estimating the ATT are also calculated. These weights are 1 for teachers who participated in a network and the odds of participation (i.e., the propensity score divided by 1 minus the propensity score) for teachers who were not in a network. Chapter 3 provides details of propensity score weighting. Covariate balance evaluation is performed with the *bal.stat* function of the *twang* package (Ridgeway et al., 2013). The code to obtain weights and evaluate covariate balance is the following:

data$psWeight <- with(data,ifelse(treat==1,1,pScores/(1-pScores)))

library(twang)

balance.psWeight <- bal.stat(data=data, vars=covariateNames, treat.var ="treat" ,

                w.all = data$psWeight, get.ks=F, sampw =1,

                estimand="ATT", multinom=F)

balance.psWeight <- balance.psWeight$results

quantile(abs(balance.psWeight$std.eff.sz),na.rm=T)

```
         0%          25%          50%          75%          100%
0.0009732788  0.0069210080  0.0150721909  0.0235585797  0.0392812790
```

With propensity score weights, the maximum standardized mean difference in a covariate between groups is 0.04. Therefore, for this example, propensity score weighting provided better covariate balance than propensity score matching.

8.6. Treatment Effect Estimation With Multiple-Group Structural Equation Models

Multiple-group SEM is helpful in the analysis stage of propensity score analysis with latent outcomes because it allows estimating the treatment effect as the difference between latent variable means. It also allows flexibility with respect to whether the groups have equal or different variances of the latent outcomes. The latent outcome for the example analysis is workload manageability, which is measured by four indicators shown in Table 8.1. The multiple-group SEM model to estimate the treatment effect on a single latent outcome is shown in Equation (8.2).

$$
\begin{aligned}
Y_{ikg} &= c, \text{ if } \tau_c < Y_{ikg}^* < \tau_{c+1} \\
Y_{ikg}^* &= \lambda_k \eta_{ig} + \delta_{ikg} \\
E(Y_{kg}) &= \lambda_k \kappa_g
\end{aligned}
\tag{8.2}
$$

where Y_{ikg} is the observed ordinal response of participant i of group g on indicator k for the latent outcome η_i (i.e., workload manageability), Y_{ikg}^* is the continuous underlying response variable, and τ_c is a threshold. $E(Y_{kg})$ is the mean of the indicator k of the latent outcome of group g, and κ_g is the mean of the latent outcome variable for group g. There is no group subscript in the factor loading λ_k and the threshold τ_c because the strong factorial invariance assumption implies that they are the same across groups. Identification of latent means is obtained by setting the latent mean for one group to zero (i.e., $\kappa_0 = 0$), and the freely estimated latent mean of the other group (i.e., κ_1) is interpreted as the difference between means. Therefore, κ_1 is the treatment effect, which for the current example is the ATT.

The multiple-group SEM in Equation (8.2) will be expanded to include two predictors of workload manageability, which are the LEP_T variable that did not reach a balance of 0.1 after matching, and the logit of the propensity score. Therefore, an additional equation is added to specify the relationship between the latent outcome variable and the covariates, as shown in Equation (8.3). The model is also presented in Figure 8.3.

$$
\eta_i = v_g + \beta_{1g} X_1 + \beta_{2g} X_2 + \zeta_i
\tag{8.3}
$$

In this model, X_1 is LEP_T and X_2 is the logit of the propensity score. In general, including covariates in the outcome model is helpful because the doubly robust property may be achieved, where the treatment effect is unbiased if either the propensity score model or the outcome model is correctly specified. In Equation (8.3), the intercept of one group (i.e., v_0) is set to zero and the intercept of the other group (i.e., v_1) is the ATT. For the intercept of the treated group to be interpretable as the ATT (Schafer & Kang, 2008), the covariates are centered on the mean of the treated group, and the

FIGURE 8.3 ● Multiple-Group Structural Equation Model to Estimate the Effect of Participation in Teacher Networks on Workload Manageability

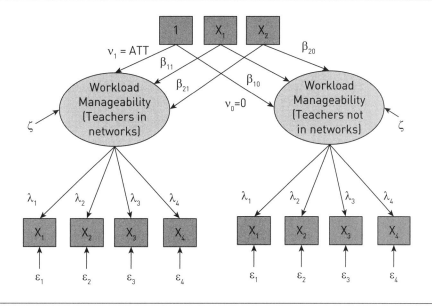

regression coefficients of the covariates are allowed to vary between groups, which is equivalent to adding treatment-by-covariate interactions in the model. The following code centers the two continuous covariates on the mean of the treated group:

matchedData$LEP_T = with(matchedData, LEP_T - mean(LEP_T[treat==1]))

matchedData$logitPScores = with(matchedData, logitPScores - mean(logitPScores[treat==1]))

Before the treatment effect is estimated, it is important to examine whether there is strong factorial invariance across treated and untreated groups for the measurement of workload manageability. If there is strong factorial invariance, then the differences in means of the indicators correspond to the differences in means in the latent variable (Millsap & Olivera-Aguillar, 2012). Without this level of measurement invariance, the ATT is not interpretable. A likelihood ratio test can be used to compare two versions of the multiple-group SEM shown in Equation (8.2), one enforcing strong factorial invariance and another allowing thresholds and loadings to vary across groups. This test is not statistically significant ($\chi^2 = 13.93$, $df = 14$, $p = .45$), indicating that the required level of invariance holds across groups.[7]

---

[7] The code for invariance testing is shown in the book's website.

Using the data obtained with genetic matching ($n = 446$), the following code fits the multiple-group SEM for the estimation of the ATT, controlling for two covariates and enforcing strong factorial invariance:

mgSEMmodel <- 'WORKMAN =~ F0108 + F0105' + F0113 + F0116

    WORKMAN ~ LEP_T + logitPScores'

mgSEMoutcome <- sem(mgSEMmodel, ordered=c("F0108", "F0105", "F0113", "F0116"),

     data=matchedData, group="treat", estimator="WLSMV",
     group.equal=c("loadings","thresholds"))

summary(mgSEMoutcome, fit.measures=TRUE, standardized=TRUE)

The chi-square statistic for this model ($\chi^2 = 42.928$, $df = 30$, $p = .059$) is not statistically significant, indicating exact fit to the data. The fit indices (CFI = 0.971, TLI = 0.973, RMSEA = 0.044 [$p = .997$]) also indicate excellent model fit. The estimate of the ATT is 0.123 ($SE = 0.097$, $p = .604$). Therefore, the effect of new teachers participating in a network of teachers is not statistically significant at $\alpha = .05$. The standardized coefficient is 0.143 and, if significant, could be interpreted as the effect size of participation in a network of teachers on workload manageability in standard deviation units.[8]

8.7. Treatment Effect Estimation With Multiple-Indicator and Multiple-Causes Models

The multiple-indicator and multiple-causes model (MIMIC) can be used to estimate treatment effects on latent variables instead of the multiple-group SEM. The MIMIC model consists of including a dummy indicator of the treatment effect on a single-group structural equation model. The MIMIC model has the limitations compared with the multiple-group SEM of assuming that the treatment has an effect on means but not on variances (i.e., that the variances of the latent outcome are identical across groups) and not allowing explicit testing of measurement invariance. The MIMIC model is

$$
\begin{aligned}
Y_{ik} &= c, \text{ if } \tau_c < Y_{ik}^* < \tau_{c+1} \\
Y_{ik}^* &= \lambda_k \eta_i + \delta_{ik} \\
\eta_i &= \delta Z_i + \zeta_i
\end{aligned}
\tag{8.4}
$$

where indicators of the latent outcome are Y_{ik}, the treatment effect is δ, the residual of the latent variable is ζ_i, and the other terms are as defined previously.

For this example, the MIMIC model is demonstrated with propensity score weighting to estimate the ATT using the entire sample ($n = 1,030$). The MIMIC model is

---

[8] All parameter estimates are available in the book's website.

shown in Figure 8.4. The *lavaan.survey* package (Oberski, 2014) allows using weights for refitting a model originally fit with the *lavaan* package. The *lavaan.survey* package can implement pseudo-maximum likelihood, weighted least squares, and diagonally weighted least squares estimation. Differently from the multiple-group SEM model demonstrated previously, the MIMIC model implemented here does not contain any covariates in addition to the treatment indicator. Including covariates is not needed in this analysis because propensity score weighting succeeds in achieving acceptable covariate balance in all covariates. Covariates could be included in the MIMIC model both to increase power and to achieve a doubly robust property. However, it would also be necessary to include treatment-by-covariate interactions and center continuous covariates on the mean of the treatment group to ensure the interpretation of the treatment effect as the ATT is maintained (Schafer & Kang, 2008). The code to fit the MIMIC model with the *lavaan* package and then refit it including propensity score weights with the *lavaan.survey* package[9] is shown as follows:

MIMICmodel <- 'WORKMAN =~ F0108 + F0105 + F0113 + F0116

> *WORKMAN ~ treat'*

MIMIC <- sem(MIMICmodel, data=data2, estimator="MLR")

library(survey)

surveyDesign <- svydesign(ids=~1, weights=~psWeight, data = data2)

library(lavaan.survey)

weighted.MIMIC <- lavaan.survey(MIMIC, surveyDesign, estimator="MLMV")

summary(weighted.MIMIC, fit.measures=TRUE, standardized=TRUE)

For the MIMIC model estimated with the *lavaan.survey* package, pseudo-maximum-likelihood estimation is used with robust standard errors and chi-square statistics. The fit information obtained with the robust chi-square statistic indicates no exact fit (χ^2 = 15.257, *df* = 5, *p* = .01) but supports close fit (CFI = 0.951, TLI = 0.902, RMSEA = 0.045 [*p* = .60]) of the model to the data, so this model is retained. The standardized estimated ATT is 0.165 (*SE* = 0.103, *p* = .086), which is not statistically significant at α = .05. It is interesting to note that, for this example, the ATT estimate obtained with the multiple-group SEM is similar to the one obtained with the MIMIC model. This similarity is desirable, because it shows that the estimate was not sensitive to different model specifications.

---

[9] The current version of the *laavan.survey* package does not accept categorical indicators, so the indicators of workload manageability were treated as continuous. The object *data2* contains the data in numeric format.

FIGURE 8.4 ● Multiple-Indicators and Multiple-Causes Model to Estimate the ATT of Participation in Teacher Networks on Workload Manageability

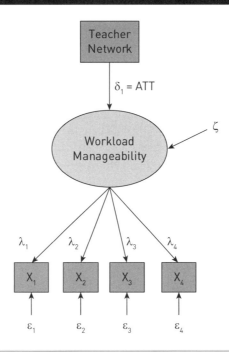

TABLE 8.2 ● Summary of Main Functions Used in This Chapter

Package	Function	Objective
lavaan	*cfa*	Fit confirmatory factor analysis models for latent covariates and latent outcome
lavaan	*sem*	Fit structural equation models to estimate the ATT
MatchIt	*matchit*	Perform one-to-one optimal matching without replacement
twang	*bal.stat*	Evaluate covariate balance with ATT weights
survey	*svydesign*	Define an object containing the data and ATT weights
lavaan.survey	*lavaan.survey*	Refit the structural equation modeling including ATT weights in the estimation

8.8. Conclusion

This chapter demonstrates the use of structural equation modeling in propensity score analysis to handle latent confounding variables and latent outcome variables measured with error. It is desirable to have latent variables that are measured by multiple indicators and with individual scores for these indicators available for the analysis. However, if only a single indicator or composite (i.e., mean, sum) of multiple indicators is available, it is still possible to adjust the latent variable for measurement error. This is done in SEM by fixing the factor loading of the single indicator of the latent variable to 1 and its error variance to $\mathrm{var}(\varepsilon_k) = (1 - \rho_{xx})\mathrm{var}(X_k)$ (Bollen, 1989), where ρ_{xx} is a reliability estimate, such as Cronbach's alpha.

One shortcoming of the analyses shown in this chapter is that factor scores had to be estimated and then used in a logistic regression model to estimate propensity scores. The estimation of factor scores introduces error, and it would be preferable if the propensity score model was a SEM that had the treatment indicator as an endogenous variable.[10] Jakubowski (2014) found through a Monte Carlo simulation study that using true factor scores in propensity score estimation followed by matching removes all bias due to latent confounders, but using estimated factor scores performs only slightly better than including the indicators of the latent variables directly into the propensity score model. However, they used CFA to estimate factor scores, which assumes strict factorial invariance as well as equality of means, variances, and covariances of the latent variables across treatment groups. In this chapter, multiple-group CFA was used instead, assuming strong factorial invariance and allowing means, variances, and covariances of latent variables as well as residual variances to differ between groups. It is not known to what extent the poor performance of estimated factor scores observed by Jakubowski (2014) generalizes to factor scores from multiple-group CFA. Therefore, more research is needed about how to include latent variables in propensity score analysis.

In addition to CFA and multiple-group CFA, scores on latent variables for inclusion in the propensity score model or in the outcome model can be obtained using item response theory (IRT) models (Lord & Novick, 1968). Many IRT models, such as the two-parameter logistic model, the graded response model, the generalized partial-credit model, and the nominal response model, have been shown to be equivalent to CFA models (Huggins-Manley & Algina, 2015; Kamata & Bauer, 2008; Takane & De Leeuw, 1987). Although this chapter focuses on continuous latent variables, categorical latent variables (i.e., latent classes) can be used in propensity score analyses in a variety of ways, such as to reduce selection bias by identifying clusters of similar individuals (Haviland & Nagin, 2005; Haviland, Nagin, & Rosenbaum, 2007; Haviland, Nagin, Rosenbaum, & Tremblay, 2008), or membership in latent classes can be either the treatment or outcome of interest (Butera, Lanza, & Coffman, 2014; Lanza, Coffman, & Xu, 2013).

---

[10] This is not currently implemented in the *lavaan* package, but it is available in the *Mplus* software.

Although not addressed in this chapter, SEM has many capabilities with respect to estimating mediation (Muthén & Asparouhov, 2015) and moderation (Marsh, Wen, Hau, & Nagengast, 2013) involving latent variables, in both single-level (Little, Card, Bovaird, Preacher, & Crandall, 2007) and multilevel models (Preacher, Zyphur, & Zhang, 2010). These capabilities can be combined with propensity score analysis (Coffman, 2011; Jo, Stuart, MacKinnon, & Vinokur, 2011) to evaluate nuances of the effect of treatments, while controlling for selection bias.

Study Questions

1. Why is it important to consider latent covariates in propensity score analysis?

2. How can confirmatory factor analysis be used in the design stage of propensity score analysis?

3. What is the consequence of ignoring measurement error of latent covariates?

4. What is the role of structural equation modeling in the analysis stage of a propensity score analysis?

5. Why is measurement invariance important in propensity score analysis with latent covariates and latent outcomes?

6. What level of measurement invariance is required for the use of latent covariates and latent outcomes in propensity score analysis?

7. What is the consequence of measurement error in the estimate of a treatment effect on a latent outcome?

8. What is the consequence of lack of measurement invariance in the estimate of a treatment effect on a latent outcome?

9. How can multiple-group structural equation models be used to estimate treatment effects with propensity score matching?

10. How can the multiple-indicators and multiple-causes model be used to estimate treatment effects with propensity score methods?

9

Weighting Methods for Time-Varying Treatments

Learning Objectives

- Describe the weighting strategies for time-varying treatments.

- Calculate inverse probability weights and stabilized inverse probability weights.

- Describe the importance of weight stabilization.

- Describe the role of treatment history in the calculation of weights.

- Estimate the average treatment effect with regression with cluster-robust standard errors.

- Estimate the average treatment effect with generalized estimating equations.

9.1. Introduction

The previous chapters addressed estimation of effects of time-invariant treatments, which are nonrandomly assigned to participants only once. For time-invariant treatments, removing selection bias with propensity score methods requires a single measurement of confounding variables. Although the focus of these chapters was the estimation of the treatment effect on an outcome measured at a single time after assignment, the propensity score methods discussed can be used for estimation of treatment effects on multiple measurements across time. This is the case because after selection bias is removed in the design stage of propensity score analysis, treatment effects can be estimated with any number of future outcomes in the analysis stage.

With time-varying treatments, which are treatments that can be repeated at multiple occasions, each individual's probability of receiving the treatment at a certain time depends on the treatment history, previous outcomes, time-invariant covariates, and time-varying covariates. By the end of the study, each individual has a treatment sequence. For example, a study with two treatment opportunities may have individuals with treatment sequences equal to [0,0], [1,1], [0,1], and [1,0]. A researcher may be interested in estimating treatment effects that contrast different pairs or combinations of the possible sequences.

In this chapter, inverse probability of treatment weighting (IPTW; Robins et al., 2000) is demonstrated to remove selection bias in the estimation of effects of time-varying treatments. This method was developed separately from the literature on propensity score analysis, but there are many similarities between propensity score weighting in cross-sectional studies described in Chapter 3 and the IPTW method for longitudinal studies described here. In longitudinal studies, it is also necessary to account for clustering effects by individual. These clustering effects occur because there are many measurements for each individual, and consequently there is a within-individual correlation structure. The combination of IPTW to remove selection bias and generalized estimating equations (GEEs; Liang & Zeger, 1986) to estimate treatment effects accounting for clustering effects is known as marginal structural models (Hernán et al., 2000; Robins et al., 2000) and has been extensively used in epidemiology. Besides GEEs, there are other methods to estimate treatment effects accounting for within-individual correlations in longitudinal data in combination with IPTW, such as regression estimation with cluster-robust standard errors (Heeringa et al., 2010; Wolter, 2007), fixed-effects models (Allison, 2009), and mixed-effects (i.e., multilevel, hierarchical linear) models (Goldstein, 2003; Raudenbush & Bryk, 2002; Snijders & Bosker, 2012). In this chapter, the calculation of weights to remove selection bias in longitudinal studies with time-varying treatments will be demonstrated, as well as the estimation of treatment effects with weighted regression with cluster-robust standard errors and GEEs.

9.2. Description of Example

The objective of this example is to estimate the effect of self-employment on job satisfaction using data from the National Longitudinal Survey of Youth 1979 (NLSY79). Global job satisfaction is measured in the NLSY79 by a single question about one to five jobs per year, from 1994 to 2012, with each survey wave occurring every 2 years. The measures of global job satisfaction in the NLSY79 have been used in a variety of studies, such as Judge and Hurst's (2008) study of the effect of core self-evaluations on job satisfaction. Self-employment is a self-selected time-varying condition measured in each survey wave. The sample contains 9,150 individuals measured at 10 waves from 1994 to 2012. Custom sampling weights for analyses over these 10 years, including individuals who participated in all or any of these waves, were obtained from the NLS Investigator website (U.S. Bureau of Labor Statistics, 2016).

9.3. Inverse Probability of Treatment Weights

In studies of time-varying treatments, time-varying confounders influence selection into treatment and the outcome. Also, the effect of these confounders may change with each treatment opportunity. The probability of treatment assignment may also depend on the outcome measured prior to each treatment opportunity and the treatment history of participants. IPTW allows removal of bias due to time-varying and time-invariant covariates, as well as history of treatment. The effect of weighting is to create a pseudo-population, where each person is duplicated according to his or her weight. Observations associated with the largest weights would be from individuals exposed to the condition despite low probability of exposure or individuals not exposed to the condition despite high probability of exposure. The inverse probability of treatment weight w_{ti} of individual i exposed to treatment condition z at time t is

$$w_{ti} = \frac{1}{\prod_{t=0}^{T} P(Z_{ti} = z \mid Z, W, X)}, \tag{9.1}$$

where $Z_{ti} = z$ indicates treatment status at time t, with $z = 1$ if treated and $z = 0$ if untreated; Z is a vector of previous treatment indicators; W are time-varying covariates (including the previous outcomes); and X are time-invariant covariates. Therefore, $P(Z_{ti} = z \mid Z, W, X)$ is the conditional probability of receiving treatment z at time t, and $\prod_{t=0}^{T} P(Z_{ti} = z \mid Z, W, X)$ is the probability of the treatment sequence received by person i.

The process of implementing IPTW begins with the identification of covariates related to both treatment assignment and the outcome (i.e., true confounders) for inclusion as predictors of the probability of treatment assignment. For the current example, the specification of the model for the probability of self-employment was informed by Schiller and Crewson's (1997) research on the origins of entrepreneurship. Using data from the NLSY79, they examined variables that predict the probability of self-employment as well as whether the effect of these variables varied across males and females. They found that gender, age, ethnicity, locus of control, urbanicity, having a mother with a managerial job, and years employed, unemployed, and self-employed had either a main effect or an interaction with gender on the probability of self-employment. Therefore, Schiller and Crewson's results are used in this example to select variables that had significant main effects and/or interactions and specify a model for the probability of self-employment at each measurement time. The selected variables included both time-invariant covariates (e.g., gender, age at the start of the study, locus of control) and time-varying covariates (e.g., urbanicity, marriage status, and divorce). These variables are expected to also affect global satisfaction. In addition, the model includes the total number of measurement occasions prior to the current year that the participant was self-employed, as a measure of treatment history. The probability of treatment at time t is estimated with the following logistic regression model for each treatment opportunity:

$$\text{logit}(Z_{ti} = 1 \mid Z, W, X) = \upsilon + \sum_{j=1}^{t-1} \beta_j Z_{ji} + \sum_{k=1}^{K} \gamma_k W_{ki} + \sum_{l=1}^{L} \pi_l X_{li}, \qquad (9.2)$$

where β_j are coefficients of dummy indicators Z_{ji} of prior treatment opportunities, γ_k are the coefficients of time-varying covariates W_{ki}, and π_l are the coefficients of time-invariant covariates X_{li}. Although dummy indicators of all previous treatments could potentially be included in the model, multicollinearity and quasi-separation problems may occur because of strong correlations between adjacent treatments or outcomes. One alternative to avoid these problems, which is implemented for this example, is to replace the dummy indicators Z_{ji} of prior treatment opportunities by the total number of treatments received by the individual up to time t and the most recent outcome. Another alternative is to include a single dummy indicator Z_{t-1i} of whether the individual received treatment on the previous measurement.

It is also possible to estimate the propensity scores for all treatment occasions simultaneously by organizing the data in a long format with treatment exposure indicators for all times stacked as a single vector. For the current example, the data are in long format, but the logistic regression model for the predicted probability of treatment assignment is fit separately to the data for each year. The data set contains 10 years of data collection between 1994 and 2012. The *ipwtm* function of the *ipw* package (Van der Wal & Geskus, 2011) is used to estimate the probability of treatment assignment at each year according to Equation (9.2) and then calculate the inverse probability of treatment weight, as shown in Equation (9.2). The logistic regression model was specified based on the results of Schiller and Crewson's (1997) study. In the following code, the argument *exposure = selfEmploy* indicates which variable is the time-varying treatment indicator. The indicator of measurement wave is declared in the *timevar=timeRecoded* argument, and time is coded from 0 to 9. Sampling weights are specified with the *weights=data.long$normWeight* argument. The *denominator* argument specifies the denominator of Equation (9.1), and the numerator is 1.

require(ipw)

iptw <- ipwtm(exposure = selfEmploy,timevar=timeRecoded,

  family = "binomial", link="logit", weights=data.long$normWeight,

  denominator = ~ cumSE+age + female + mngr.m + rotter.index + white + degree +

    divorce + experience + married + urban +

    age:female + mngr.m:female + rotter.index:female +

    white:female + degree:female + divorce:female +

experience:female + married:female + urban:female,

    id = id, type = "all", data = data.long)

quantile(iptw$ipw.weights)

0%	25%	50%	75%	100%
1.02e+00	1.13e+00	1.25e+00	1.53e+00	9.47e+08

The quintiles of the weights shown above indicate that the maximum weight is 9.47e+08. The occurrence of extreme weights like this one is common in IPTW. Extreme weights result in biased estimates and large standard errors of the treatment effect. This problem can sometimes be solved by using stabilized weights (Hernán et al., 2000), which are shown in the next section.

9.4. Stabilized Inverse Probability of Treatment Weights

In this section, stabilized inverse probability of treatment weights (SIPTW) are calculated. They have the advantage over IPTW of reducing extreme values. The SIPTW are defined as follows:

$$sw_{ti} = \prod_{t=1}^{T} \frac{P(Z_{ti} = z \mid Z)}{P(Z_{ti} = z \mid Z, W, X)} \tag{9.3}$$

The numerator of SIPTW is the probability that the individual was exposed to condition z at a time t given indicators of previous exposure. The denominator is the probability that the individual was exposed to condition z at time t given indicators of previous exposure and time-invariant and time-varying covariates. SIPTW are obtained with the *ipwtm* function. The only difference from the code used for IPTW is the addition of the *numerator= ~1 + cumSE* argument, which defines a logistic regression model for estimating $P(Z_{ti} = z \mid Z)$ in the numerator of Equation (9.3). In this model, the predictor *cumSE* is the total number of previous measurement waves in which the respondent was self-employed.

siptw <- ipwtm(exposure = selfEmploy, timevar=timeRecoded, weights=data.long$normWeight,

    family = "binomial", link="logit", numerator= ~1 + cumSE,

    denominator = ~ cumSE+ age + female + mngr.m + rotter.index + white + degree +

        divorce + experience + married + urban +

        age:female + mngr.m:female + rotter.index:female +

white:female + degree:female + divorce:female +

experience:female + married:female + urban:female,

id = id, type = "all", data = data.long)

quantile(siptw$ipw.weights)

```
0%      25%    50%    75%    100%
0.0101 0.9599 1.0020 1.0342 22.4729
```

The quintiles above show that the maximum stabilized weight is 22.47, which is a dramatic reduction of extreme weights compared with IPTW. However, Talbot, Atherton, Rossi, Bacon, and Lefebvre (2015) caution that using SIPTW according to Equation (9.3), which has the probability of treatment conditional on treatment history as the numerator, may result in biased treatment effect estimates. This may occur because the equation for SIPTW includes treatment history in both the numerator and denominator, and therefore SIPTW does not control for confounding due to treatment history. To obtain unbiased treatment effects using SIPTW, the treatment history must be part of the outcome model. For situations where the treatment history is not included in the outcome model, Talbot et al. (2015) demonstrated that using a basic stabilization where the numerator is the proportion treated at time t results in unbiased treatment effect estimates. The formula for the basic stabilized inverse probability of treatment weights (BSIPTW) is

$$bsw_{ti} = \prod_{t=1}^{T} \frac{P(Z_{ti} = z)}{P(Z_{ti} = z \mid Z, W, X)} \tag{9.4}$$

The calculation of BSIPTW is obtained with the *ipwtm* function, using the same code as provided earlier for the IPTW, but with the inclusion of the *numerator= ~1* argument. This argument specifies that $P(Z_{ti} = z)$ is estimated with a logistic regression model containing only an intercept.

bsiptw <- ipwtm(exposure = selfEmploy,timevar=timeRecoded, weights=data.long$normWeight,

family = "binomial", link="logit", numerator= ~1,

denominator = ~ cumSE+age + female + mngr.m + rotter.index + white + degree +

divorce + experience + married + urban +

age:female + mngr.m:female + rotter.index:female +

white:female + degree:female + divorce:female +

experience:female + married:female + urban:female,

id = id, type = "all", data = data.long)

quantile(bsiptw$ipw.weights)

```
    0%      25%      50%      75%      100%
8.55e-08  4.61e-01 6.18e-01 7.85e-01  1.99e+03
```

The quintiles above show that the maximum basic stabilized weight is 1,990, which demonstrates that the BSIPTW does not provide as much reduction of extreme weights as the SIPTW.

9.5. Evaluation of Covariate Balance

The next step is to evaluate covariate balance, which for the current example will only be performed with the SIPTW, but the same R code can also be used for IPTW and BSIPTW. Before covariate balance is evaluated, the SIPTW are multiplied by the sampling weights, producing final weights that remove both selection bias and sampling bias:

data.long$finalWeight <- with(data.long, siptw*normWeight)

The covariate balance evaluation can be accomplished by calculating standardized mean differences for each of the covariates included in the model across all measurement waves. Covariate balance is checked with the *bal.stat* function of the *twang* package (Ridgeway et al., 2013).

require(twang)

balance <- bal.stat(data=data.long, var=colnames(data.long)[c(3:5,11:13,15:16,19)],

treat.var="selfEmploy", w.all=data.long$finalWeight,

sampw=data.long$normWeight, get.means=T,

get.ks=F, estimand="ATE", multinom=F)

summary(balance$results$std.eff.sz)

```
Min.    1st Qu. Median  Mean 3rd Qu. Max.
-0.0659 -0.0104 0.0068 0.0101 0.0341 0.1250
```

The summary of the covariate balance evaluation with SIPTW shown above indicates that the maximum standardized mean difference is 0.125. For this example, the criterion for covariate balance is that the standardized mean difference between treated and control groups should be less than 0.1 (Austin, 2011b). Only one covariate, the number of weeks that the respondent was tenured in the longest lasting job in that year, does not have a covariate balance below 0.1. Although it may be possible to modify the model for the probability of treatment assignment so that the covariate balance is further improved, the inclusion of the number of weeks of tenure in the outcome model is used in this example to provide additional bias removal.

9.6. Estimation of Treatment Effects

The estimation of the effects of self-employment on general satisfaction is demonstrated below using weighted regression with adjustment for clustering effects and GEEs. These methods are marginal models in the sense that they are models for the mean μ_i of all individuals with the same values of the covariates, and the correlations between observations obtained from the same individual are considered nuisance parameters. Fixed-effects and mixed-effects[1] models can also be used to estimate time-varying treatment effects accounting for the correlations between multiple observations of the same participant, but they require more assumptions. A detailed discussion of the differences between these models is provided by Gardiner, Luo, and Roman (2009).

The estimation of treatment effects is demonstrated in this section using SIPTW, because they provided smaller weights compared with IPTW and BSIPTW. To address the potential for bias pointed out by Talbot et al. (2015) with respect to using SIPTW without including treatment history in the outcome model, the number of treated waves up to the current wave will be included in the outcome model. In addition, because the covariate balance for the experience variable is not below the target difference of 0.1 standard deviations, the experience variable will be included as a covariate in the outcome models.

9.6.1. Weighted Regression With Cluster-Robust Standard Errors

To estimate the effect of self-employment on general satisfaction, the following regression model is used:

$$y_{ti} = \beta_0 + \beta_1 Z_{ti} + \beta_2 Z_{t-1i} + \beta_3 W_{ti} + \beta_4 T_{ti} + \beta_4 Z_{ti} Z_{t-1i} + \beta_5 Z_{ti} W_{ti} + \beta_4 Z_{ti} T_{ti} + \varepsilon_i, \qquad (9.5)$$

where y_{ti} is a measurement of general satisfaction, Z_{ti} is a dummy indicator of self-employment at time t, Z_{t-1i} is the grand-mean centered number of waves prior to the current one with reported self-employment, W_{ti} is the grand-mean centered number of weeks that the respondent is tenured in the longest lasting job in that year, and T_{ti} is an indicator of time coded from zero to indicate 1994 to nine to indicate 2012. The covariates are grand-mean centered, and interactions with the treatment are included to ensure that the coefficient β_1 is the ATE of self-employment on general satisfaction (Schafer & Kang, 2008). Grand-mean centering is implemented with this code:

data.long$cumSE <- with(data.long, cumSE - mean(cumSE))

data.long$experience <- with(data.long, experience - mean(experience))

---

[1] Currently, the R packages *plm* for fixed-effects models and *lme4* for mixed-effects models do not include sampling weights in the estimation, which prevented demonstrating the use of IPTW with these models in R.

Before estimating the model in Equation (9.5), a design object is created with the *svydesign* function, specifying that the *id* variable contains the individual identification numbers, *finalWeight* contains the weights, and the data set is *data.long*. Model estimation is performed with the *svyglm* function of the *survey* package using iteratively reweighted least squares estimation. Standard errors are estimated with Taylor series linearization, taking into account the clustering of measurements, which is similar to using sandwich estimators (Lumley, 2004). This correction for clustering only affects the standard errors, so the regression coefficients are identical to those that would be obtained if clustering was ignored (McNeish, Stapleton, & Silverman, in press). Details on Taylor series linearization for estimation of standard errors with data containing weights and clusters are provided in the book by Wolter (2007).

require(survey)

design.iptw <- svydesign(ids=~id, nest=F, weights =~finalWeight, data=data.long)

glm.iptw <- svyglm(genSatis~selfEmploy+cumSE+experience+timeRecoded+

        selfEmploy:cumSE + selfEmploy:experience+selfEmploy:timeRecoded,

        design.iptw)

summary(glm.iptw)

```
Call:
svyglm(formula = genSatis ~ selfEmploy + cumSE + experience +
  timeRecoded + selfEmploy:cumSE + selfEmploy:experience +
  selfEmploy:timeRecoded, design.iptw)
Survey design:
svydesign(ids = ~id, nest = F, weights = ~finalWeight, data = data.long)
Coefficients:
                       Estimate Std. Error   t value  Pr(>|t|)
(Intercept)             3.28311    0.00725    453.14   < 2e-16 ***
selfEmploy              0.19372    0.01879     10.31   < 2e-16 ***
cumSE                   0.02181    0.00553      3.94   8.1e-05 ***
experience              0.04518    0.00403     11.22   < 2e-16 ***
timeRecoded             0.00616    0.00111      5.53   3.3e-08 ***
selfEmploy:cumSE        0.00618    0.00817      0.76   0.449
selfEmploy:experience  -0.02596    0.01151     -2.26   0.024      *
selfEmploy:timeRecoded -0.02490    0.00438     -5.68   1.4e-08 ***
---
Signif. codes: 0 '***' 0.001 '**' 0.01 '*' 0.05 '.' 0.1 ' ' 1
(Dispersion parameter for gaussian family taken to be 0.427)
Number of Fisher Scoring iterations: 2
```

In the results shown above, self-employment (*selfEmploy*), the number of measurement waves self-employed (*cumSE*), the number of weeks that the respondent was tenured in the longest lasting job in that year (*experience*), and the passing of time (*timeRecoded*) all had significant positive main effects on global satisfaction. However, self-employment also had negative interactions with the *experience* and *timeRecoded* variables. Therefore, these results indicate that although self-employed individuals have higher global satisfaction than individuals not self-employed, they have a slower rate of increase in satisfaction over time and over their tenure in their position than individuals not self-employed.

9.6.2. Generalized Estimating Equations

In this section, the model specification and estimation with GEEs for the example are presented. A friendly description of GEEs and demonstration with R are presented in Chapter 12 of the book by Zuur, Ieno, Walker, Saveliev, and Smith (2009). A complete description of GEEs can be obtained in the book on GEEs by Hardin and Hilbe (2013). GEEs require the specification of a function for the means, conditional on covariates. For this example, the means of general satisfaction are a function of self-employment, history of self-employment, and experience, as shown in the following model:

$$\mu_{ti} = E(Y_{it} \mid Z_{ti}, Z_{t-1i}, W_{ti})$$
$$g(\mu_{ti}) = \beta_0 + \beta_1 Z_{ti} + \beta_2 Z_{t-1i} + \beta_3 W_{ti} + \beta_4 T_{ti} + \beta_4 Z_{ti} Z_{t-1i} + \beta_5 Z_{ti} W_{ti} + \beta_4 Z_{ti} T_{ti} + \varepsilon_i \tag{9.6}$$

where μ_{it} is the marginal expectation of the outcome (Hardin & Hilbe, 2013). In addition, GEEs require a variance function and a correlation structure between two observations of the same individual. For this example, the variance function and correlation structure are

$$V(Y_{ti}) = \mathrm{var}(Y_{ti} \mid Z_{ti}, Z_{t-1i}, W_{ti})$$
$$cor(Y_{it2}, Y_{it1}) = \alpha^{t2-t1} \tag{9.7}$$

where $t2$ and $t1$ are the indexes of two measurement waves. For this example, the correlation structure used is first-order autoregressive (AR1). Other correlation structures, such as exchangeable, stationary, and unstructured (see Hardin & Hilbe, 2013, for details), could be used. However, GEEs are robust to misspecification of the correlation structure (Zeger, Liang, & Albert, 1988), so identifying the correct one is not critical, and the estimates are expected to be unbiased with the AR1 structure chosen. Once the model for the conditional means shown in Equation (9.6) and the variance and correlation components specified in Equation (9.7) are defined, parameter estimates are obtained with GEEs by solving

$$\sum_{i=1}^{N} D_i V_i^{-1}(Y_i - \mu_i) = 0, \tag{9.8}$$

where D_i is a matrix of first derivatives of μ_i with respect to regression coefficients, and V_i is an estimate of the covariance matrix obtained with the AR1 correlation structure specified in Equation (9.7). V_i is estimated through an iterative procedure, and once it converges, regression coefficients are obtained that are consistent and asymptotically normally distributed. It should be noted that GEEs do not produce the same coefficients as the weighted regression model shown in the previous section. The following code implements generalized estimating equations using the *geeglm* function of the *geepack* package (Halekoh, Hojsgaard, & Yan, 2006). The AR1 correlation structure is specified by the *corstr = "ar1"* argument.

library(geepack)

gee.iptw <- geeglm(genSatis~selfEmploy+cumSE+experience+timeRecoded+

  selfEmploy:cumSE + selfEmploy:experience+selfEmploy:timeRecoded,

  data = data.long, weights = data.long$finalWeight, family = gaussian,

  id = data.long$id, waves=data.long$time, corstr = "ar1")

summary(gee.iptw)

```
Call:
geeglm(formula = genSatis ~ selfEmploy + cumSE + experience +
  timeRecoded + selfEmploy:cumSE + selfEmploy:experience +
  selfEmploy:timeRecoded, family = gaussian, data = data.long,
  weights = data.long$finalWeight, id = data.long$id, waves = data.
long$time,
  corstr = "ar1")
 Coefficients:
                       Estimate Std.err  Wald Pr  (>|W|)
(Intercept)             3.28057  0.00739 1.97e+05 < 2e-16 ***
selfEmploy              0.12342  0.02044 3.65e+01 1.6e-09 ***
cumSE                   0.01767  0.00533 1.10e+01 0.00092 ***
experience              0.01179  0.00369 1.02e+01 0.00140 **
timeRecoded             0.00685  0.00116 3.50e+01 3.4e-09 ***
selfEmploy:cumSE        0.01383  0.00782 3.13e+00 0.07696 .
selfEmploy:experience  -0.02720  0.01435 3.59e+00 0.05800 .
selfEmploy:timeRecoded -0.01799  0.00457 1.55e+01 8.3e-05 ***
---
Signif. codes: 0 '***' 0.001 '**' 0.01 '*' 0.05 '.' 0.1 ' ' 1
Estimated Scale Parameters:
        Estimate Std.err
(Intercept) 0.429 0.00414
Correlation: Structure = ar1 Link = identity
Estimated Correlation Parameters:
        Estimate Std.err
alpha        0.53 0.00965
Number of clusters: 9150 Maximum cluster size: 10
```

In the results shown above, the main effects are all positive and statistically significant but smaller in magnitude than those estimated with weighted regression. The interactions between self-employment and experience, as well as self-employment and tenure, are not statistically significant. The interaction between self-employment and time is negative and significant. Therefore, the results of GEEs allow the conclusion that global satisfaction increases with time and length of tenure, and self-employed individuals have higher global satisfaction than individuals not self-employed, but the increase in satisfaction with time occurs at a slower rate for self-employed individuals.

9.7. Conclusion

Like the methods discussed in this book for time-invariant treatments, the main challenge in the application of weighting methods for time-varying treatments is the identification of the key confounders for the propensity score model. Another key issue is that the measurement of the outcome should be equivalent across measurement waves. Therefore, the issue of measurement invariance discussed in Chapter 8 is also relevant to this chapter.

This chapter demonstrated IPTW and shows the problem of extreme weights, which occurs frequently in designs with many treatment waves. To address extreme weights, SIPTW and BSIPTW were presented. SIPTW provides the largest reduction of extreme weights and is recommended for most situations. In addition to these strategies, marginal mean weighting through stratification (MMWTS; Hong, 2010, 2012; Hong & Hong, 2008) can also be used with time-varying treatments to remove selection bias without having extreme weights. MMWTS is demonstrated in Chapter 4 with a time-invariant treatment, and its extension for time-varying treatments is presented by Hong (2012).

This chapter presented and demonstrated estimation of the average treatment effect of time-varying treatments with weighted regression and GEE. Readers interested in comparisons between these methods, as well as other alternatives to analyze clustered data, should consult Gardiner et al. (2009), Huang (2016), and McNeish at al. (in press). These methods generalize to multiple treatments and continuous treatments,

TABLE 9.1 ● Summary of Main Functions Used in This Chapter		
Package	**Function**	**Objective**
ipw	*ipwtm*	Estimate IPTW, SIPTW, and BSIPTW
twang	*bal.stat*	Evaluate covariate balance
survey	*svydesign*	Define object with data set, cluster ids, and weights
	svyglm	Treatment effect estimation with regression with cluster-robust standard errors
geepack	*geeglm*	Treatment effect estimation with generalized estimating equations

and therefore the implementation of methods in Chapters 6 and 7 can be integrated with the current chapter. Finally, it is recommended that key covariates are always included in the outcome model, not only because they can increase power to detect the treatment effect but also because including covariates in the outcome model allows double robustness of treatment effect estimates (see Chapter 3).

Study Questions

1. What is the difference between modeling the probability of treatment assignment of time-varying treatments compared with time-invariant treatments?

2. How does the inverse probability of treatment weight accomplish reduction of selection bias in the estimation of the treatment effect of time-varying treatments?

3. What is the difference between inverse probability of treatment weights and stabilized inverse probability of treatment weights?

4. Why is it advantageous to use stabilized inverse probability of treatment weights instead of inverse probability of treatment weights?

5. What is the difference between stabilized inverse probability of treatment weights and basic stabilized inverse probability of treatment weights?

6. What issue with stabilized inverse probability of treatment weights does the basic stabilized inverse probability of treatment weights address?

7. What are two possible outcome models for estimating the effects of time-varying treatments?

8. What is the role of the choice of correlation structure in generalized estimating equations?

10

Propensity Score Methods With Multilevel Data

Learning Objectives

- Describe the differences between pooling estimated treatment effects across clusters and marginal estimation of treatment effects across clusters.

- Describe the assumptions of propensity score analysis with multilevel data.

- Estimate propensity score data using a multilevel logistic regression model.

- Estimate propensity scores using a logistic regression model with fixed cluster effects.

- Implement propensity score weighting for estimation of treatment effects with multilevel data.

10.1. Introduction

It is quite common in the social sciences that data have a multilevel structure. For example, data on student achievement usually are obtained from a sample of students clustered within classrooms, which in turn are clustered within schools, school districts, and states. Similarly, data on employee performance can be obtained from workers clustered within departments, branches, stores, factories, and organizations. Some clustered data sets are obtained by sampling methods that specifically use the multilevel structure of the observations, such as cluster and multistage sampling (Kish, 1965; Lohr, 1999), while others are generated by simple random sampling or non-probabilistic methods but maintain a clustered structure. For a researcher interested in using multilevel data to estimate a treatment effect with propensity score methods, it is critical to understand whether the nonrandom treatment assignment occurred at the individual or cluster level and which individual- and/or cluster-level covariates may be related to treatment assignment.

In research designs where the treatment assignment is at the cluster level, only confounders at the cluster or higher level are of concern. For example, if a school is selected to participate in a schoolwide program, then selection may be due to school, neighborhood, and district confounders. These confounders could include individual-level covariates aggregated to the cluster level. However, in research designs where the treatment assignment is at the individual level, the propensity score model should account for both individual- and cluster-level confounders (Arpino & Mealli, 2011; Kelcey, 2011b; Leite et al., 2015; Li, Zaslavsky, & Landrum, 2013; Thoemmes & West, 2011).

Two general strategies can be used for propensity score analysis of individual-level treatment effects with multilevel data: (1) Estimate propensity scores within clusters, estimate a treatment effect for each cluster, and pool the treatment effect estimates, and (2) estimate propensity scores and treatment effect marginally across clusters. Estimating within-cluster effects is advantageous when cluster sizes are large (Kim & Seltzer, 2007) because it removes the confounding effects of both observed and unobserved cluster-level confounders. The cluster sizes should be large enough to allow adequate common support of propensity score distributions within clusters. However, if cluster sizes are not large, marginal estimation of the treatment effect across clusters should be used. This strategy can be implemented accounting for cluster effects in the propensity score model, in the outcome model, or both. In survey data obtained with multistage sampling, cluster sizes are typically small and therefore marginal estimation of the treatment effect is usually more feasible. In this chapter, the focus is on marginal estimation of the effect of an individual-level treatment with multilevel data. An example of the estimation of treatment effect for a cluster-level treatment (i.e., school) is provided in Chapter 7.

For propensity score analysis of binary treatments with multilevel data, the strong ignorability of treatment assignment assumption is needed, which states that the potential outcome distributions are independent of treatment assignment given covariates. For analysis of treatment assignment of individuals within clusters, the treatment assignment should also be independent of cluster membership, and no participant should have a probability of treatment assignment of 0 or 1. In addition, the stable unit treatment value assumption (SUTVA; Rubin, 1986) is required, which states that the potential outcomes of each individual are independent of both the assignment mechanism and the treatment status of others, and there are no unrepresented versions of the treatment. Propensity score analysis for research designs where individuals within clusters are assigned to a treatment are particularly vulnerable to SUTVA violations because of close proximity, regular communication, and shared resources.

This chapter demonstrates different models and estimation methods for propensity score analysis with multilevel data. In particular, the analyses in this chapter include fitting multilevel models, fixed-effects models, and regression models with cluster-robust standard errors. Short comparisons of these methods are provided in articles by Gardiner et al. (2009), Huang (2016), and McNeish et al. (in press).

10.2. Description of Example

The example for this chapter is inspired by the study by Claessens (2012) of the effect of center-based care in kindergarten on child academic and social outcomes, using data from the 1996 Early Childhood Longitudinal Study (ECLS-K). She found that students who attended a child care center either before or after school during the kindergarten year had higher mathematics achievement scores. Claessens's estimates were obtained with a regression model conditioning on a large number of covariates, and standard errors were obtained with cluster-robust methods.

In the current example, the objective is to use propensity score methods to estimate the effect of attending a child care center during the kindergarten year on mathematics scores in the spring of kindergarten. The example's data are from the 2011 ECLS-K, which followed a cohort of students in the kindergarten class of 2010–2011. The sample for the 2011 ECLS-K was obtained with three-stage stratified sampling: In the first stage, 90 geographic areas that are counties or groups of contiguous counties were selected using stratified sampling with strata based on geographic and demographic characteristics. In the second stage, public and private schools were sampled. In the third stage, within each school, a sample of students was obtained. Therefore, the kindergarten data have a three-level structure with students nested within schools, which in turn are nested within counties. The sample for this study includes 12,684 students from 848 schools.

The sample excluded students who changed schools between the first and second waves of the 2011 ECLS-K, had missing data on the treatment indicator, or were the only participant in the school. Missing data on covariates and the outcome were imputed separately for treated and untreated groups using the *mice* package (van Buuren & Oudshoorn, 2000) with predictive mean matching (White et al., 2011) as the univariate method. The individual proportion of missing values was included as a variable in the data set prior to imputation (see Chapter 2 for more details on dealing with missing data).

10.3. Estimation of Propensity Scores With Multilevel Data

Arpino and Mealli (2011), Thoemmes and West (2011), and Leite et al. (2015) performed simulation studies to compare models for estimation of propensity scores with multilevel data. They all reached the conclusion that both the multilevel logistic regression model and the logistic regression model with fixed cluster effects can be used to estimate propensity scores that result in unbiased estimates of treatment effects.

In addition, both Leite et al. (2015) and Li et al. (2013) found that logistic regression ignoring clustering to estimate propensity scores performs satisfactorily if the clustered structure of the data is accounted for in the outcome model.

In research situations with individual treatment assignment within clusters, the effects of individual-level covariates on the probability of treatment assignment may vary across clusters. In the estimation of propensity scores, the following options can be used to deal with this variation: (1) If multilevel logistic regression models are used to estimate propensity scores, include random slopes of covariates in the model; (2) if logistic regression with fixed cluster effects is used, include covariate-by-cluster interactions in the model; and (3) ignore the variation of covariate effects across clusters. Although research on these three approaches is not extensive, some studies have found that ignoring variation of covariate effects across clusters when estimating marginal treatment effects does not result in a substantial increase of bias (Gurel & Leite, 2014; Kelcey, 2011b; Leite et al., 2015).

10.3.1. Multilevel Logistic Regression

With multilevel data, propensity scores can be estimated with a multilevel logistic model that includes individual-level and cluster-level covariates (Kim & Seltzer, 2007). This is an example of a two-level logistic model:

$$\text{logit}\,(Z_{ij} = 1 \mid X, W) = \beta_0 + \sum_{m=1}^{M} \beta_m X_{mij} + \sum_{n=1}^{N} \pi_n W_{nj} + s_{0j} + \sum_{m=1}^{M} s_{mj} X_{mij}, \tag{10.1}$$

where Z_{ij} is the treatment indicator, β_0 is the intercept, β_m are the effects of the individual-level covariates X_m, π_n are the fixed effects of cluster-level covariates W_n, s_{0j} is a normally distributed random intercept, and s_{mj} are normally distributed random slopes of the individual-level covariates with a mean of zero and covariance matrix Σ. This multilevel model assumes that all individual-level and cluster-level true confounders of the treatment effects are included, with appropriate specifications of the functional form of the relationship between covariates and the logit of treatment assignment. In addition, it assumes that the random intercepts and random slopes are uncorrelated with cluster-level predictors. For the current example, a three-level logistic model is used where students are at Level 1, schools at Level 2, and counties at Level 3:

$$\text{logit}\,(Z_{ijk} = 1 \mid X, W) = \beta_0 + \sum_{m=1}^{M} \beta_m X_{mij} + \sum_{n=1}^{N} \pi_n W_{nj} + s_{0j} + s_{0k}, \tag{10.2}$$

where s_{0k} is the random intercept of counties, and the other terms are as defined previously. This propensity score model has 26 individual-level covariates, including student achievement and behavioral assessments in the fall of kindergarten, child demographics, parent demographics, enrichment opportunities at home, family size, distance from school, and the proportion of missing values in the case. It also includes 7 school-level covariates: percentage eligible for free and reduced-price lunch, percentage of minority students in school, percentage of students from the school's neighborhood, percentage with special needs, whether the school participates in the USDA's breakfast program, percentage attending under public school choice, and location type (i.e., city, suburb, town, rural). There are no county-level covariates available in the public data, and aggregating school-level covariates to the county level would not provide representative means because only a small sample of schools was selected per county.

The multilevel model in Equation (10.2) is estimated using the *glmer* function[1] of the *lme4* package (Bates, Maechler, & Bolker, 2011). The treatment indicator is the *treated* variable, with values of 1 indicating students attending a child care center and 0 otherwise. In the *formula* argument, random intercepts of schools are specified with *(1 | S1_ID)*, and the random intercepts of counties are specified with *(1 | W1_2P0PSU)*, where *S1_ID* and *W1_2P0PSU* are school and county id variables, respectively. The *family = binomial* argument defines that the model is logistic. The *control* argument is used in this code to change the optimizer, which may assist in achieving convergence, but the default optimizer is usually adequate. The *fitted* function is then used to obtain the propensity scores.

require(lme4)

ps.model <- glmer(formula = treated ~ X1RTHETK1 + X1MTHETK1 + X1TCHAPP +

X1TCHCON + X1TCHPER + X1TCHEXT + X1TCHINT + X1ATTNFS + X1INBCNT +

X_CHSEX_R + X_RACETH_R + X2DISABL2 + P1HSCALE + C1ENGHM + X12MOMAR +
X1NUMSIB + P1OLDMOM + P1CHLDBK + P2DISTHM + P1NUMPLA + T2PARIN +
X12PAR1ED_I + X12PAR2ED_I + X2INCCAT_I + X1PAR1EMP + S2LUNCH +
X2KRCETH + S2NGHBOR + S2OUTSID + S2USDABR + S2PUBSOC + X1LOCALE +
prop.missing +

   (1 | S1_ID) + (1 | W1_2P0PSU),

   family = binomial, data = data,

   control=glmerControl(optimizer="bobyqa",optCtrl=list(maxfun=2e5)))

data$ps <- fitted(ps.model)

with(data, by(ps, treated, summary))

```
treated: 0
    Min.   1st Qu.    Median      Mean   3rd Qu.      Max.
0.001775  0.036340  0.089160  0.141500  0.201600  0.923700
-------------------------------------------------------------------------
treated: 1
    Min.   1st Qu.    Median      Mean   3rd Qu.      Max.
0.006985  0.248900  0.420300  0.435000  0.616200  0.970400
```

[1] Sampling weights were not used in model fitting because *lmer4* does not accept sampling weights. To account for oversampling of Asians, the variable *race* was included in the propensity score model.

The summary information shown above as well as in Figure 10.1 provides evidence that common support is adequate, because most of the distribution of the treated group is contained within the distribution of the untreated group.

The multilevel model in Equation (10.2) fit to the data for the example contains two random intercepts and no random slopes. Therefore, it assumes that the effects of individual-level covariates on treatment assignment do not vary between clusters (i.e., there is no covariate-by-cluster interaction). It is difficult to include random slopes in the propensity score model because the number of covariates is typically large and a multilevel model with several random slopes would be unlikely to converge. However, Kelcey (2009, 2011b), Leite et al. (2015), and Gurel and Leite (2014) found that using a multilevel logistic regression model without random slopes to estimate propensity scores resulted in adequate bias removal even when there was substantial variation of the effects of covariates on treatment assignment across clusters.

FIGURE 10.1 ● Kernel Density Plot of Propensity Scores Obtained With Multilevel Logistic Regression for Children in Center-Based Child Care and Children in Other Child Care Arrangements

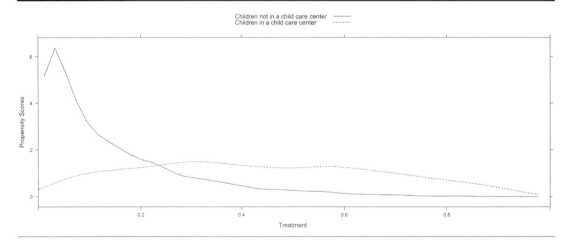

10.3.2. Logistic Regression With Fixed Cluster Effects

A logistic regression model with fixed cluster effects can also be used to estimate propensity scores with multilevel data (Arpino & Mealli, 2011). The fixed-effects model cannot include cluster-level covariates because their effects are captured by the dummy-coded cluster indicators. In the following model, there are $J - 1$ dummy-coded cluster indicators g_j, each with a fixed effect δ_j.

$$\text{logit}\,(Z_{ij} = 1 \mid X, g) = \beta_0 + \sum_{m=1}^{M} \beta_m X_{mij} + \sum_{j=1}^{J-1} \delta_j g_j. \tag{10.3}$$

The logistic regression with fixed cluster effects has two main advantages over the multilevel logistic regression model to estimate propensity scores: (1) It removes all confounding due to cluster-level covariates without requiring including any cluster-level covariates in the model (Arpino & Mealli, 2011), while the multilevel logistic regression model requires that the research identify and measure the true confounders at the cluster level. (2) It allows any correlations between individual-level predictors and the fixed cluster effects, while the multilevel logistic regression model assumes that X_{mij} and s_{0j} are uncorrelated. Disadvantages of logistic regression with fixed cluster effects include the following: (1) convergence difficulty if the number of clusters is large; (2) if the data set has many small clusters, propensity score estimates that are unstable and/or predicted probabilities equal to 0 or 1 (Li et al., 2013); and (3) the requirement that there be at least two observations per cluster. For the current example, the *glm* function is used to fit a logistic regression model with fixed effects of schools and counties:

ps.model2 <- glm(treated ~ X1RTHETK1 + X1MTHETK1 + X1TCHAPP + X1TCHCON +

>*X1TCHPER + X1TCHEXT + X1TCHINT + X1ATTNFS + X1INBCNT + X_CHSEX_R +*
>*X_RACETH_R + X2DISABL2 + P1HSCALE + C1ENGHM + X12MOMAR +*
>*X1NUMSIB + P1OLDMOM + P1CHLDBK + P2DISTHM + P1NUMPLA + T2PARIN +*
>*X12PAR1ED_I + X12PAR2ED_I + X2INCCAT_I + X1PAR1EMP + prop.missing +*
>*S1_ID + W1_2P0PSU, data=data, family=binomial)*

data$ps2 <- fitted(ps.model2)

with(data, by(ps2, treated, summary))

```
treated: 0
  Min.  1st Qu. Median    Mean   3rd Qu.   Max.
0.00000  0.01442 0.07209 0.13830   0.20560 0.97610
-------------------------------------------------------------------
treated: 1
   Min.   1st Qu.  Median    Mean   3rd Qu.    Max.
0.005595  0.258000 0.441900 0.458900  0.643300 1.000000
```

The summary above and in Figure 10.2 shows that the propensity scores estimated with logistic regression with fixed cluster effects had several values very close to 0 and 1 (the values above are rounded to six decimal places), indicating overlap problems. Therefore, for the remainder of this chapter, analyses are conducted using the propensity scores estimated with multilevel logistic regression. It is interesting to note that despite the overlap problems of the propensity scores estimated with logistic regression with fixed cluster effects, their correlation with the propensity scores estimated with multilevel logistic regression was 0.93, indicating that the choice between these two sets of propensity scores may not matter much in this example.

Data mining methods such as random forests (Breiman, 2001), generalized boosted modeling (McCaffrey et al., 2004), and neural networks (Setoguchi et al., 2008) could be used for propensity score estimation with multilevel data. Because these methods automatically detect interactions, adding the cluster indicator as a covariate would allow examination of covariate-by-cluster interactions that improve prediction of treatment assignment. Research on data mining methods for propensity score estimation with multilevel data is still incipient.

FIGURE 10.2 ● Kernel Density Plot of the Distribution of Propensity Scores Obtained With Logistic Regression With Fixed Cluster Effects for Children in Center-Based Child Care and Children in Other Child Care Arrangements

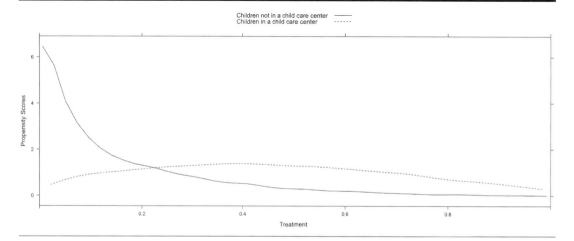

10.4. Propensity Score Weighting

For this example, the propensity score weight to estimate the ATE discussed in Chapter 3 is implemented. This inverse probability of treatment weight is calculated with

$$w_{ij} = \frac{Z_{ij}}{\hat{e}_{ij}(X,W)} + \frac{1-Z_{ij}}{1-\hat{e}_{ij}(X,W)}, \tag{10.4}$$

where w_{ij} is the weight for individual i in cluster j, and the estimated propensity score $\hat{e}_{ij}(X,W)$ is

$$\hat{e}_i(X,W) = \frac{\exp(\text{logit}(Z_{ij} = 1 \mid X,W))}{1+\exp(\text{logit}(Z_{ij} = 1 \mid X,W))}. \tag{10.5}$$

In this chapter, the example focuses on the estimation of the ATE, but the weight to estimate the ATT as defined in Chapter 3 could also be used. The following code obtains the ATE weight by using the *ifelse* function to assign the inverse of the propensity score to the treated or the inverse of 1 minus the propensity score to the untreated:

data$psw <- with(data, ifelse(treated==1, 1/ps, 1/(1-ps)))

This code normalizes the propensity score weights by dividing them by the mean of the weights, which results in weights with a mean of 1 and that sum to the sample size.

data$psw <- data$psw/mean(data$psw)

with(data, by(psw, treated, summary))

```
treated: 0
  Min. 1st Qu. Median  Mean 3rd Qu.   Max.
 0.5431 0.5626 0.5952 0.6623 0.6790 7.1050
----------------------------------------------------------------------
treated: 1
  Min. 1st Qu. Median  Mean 3rd Qu.   Max.
 0.5586 0.8798 1.2900 2.3210 2.1780 77.6100
```

The summary above shows that the largest weight for children not in a child care center is 7.1, and for children in a child care center, it is 77.61. One common problem with inverse probability of treatment weights is the occurrence of extreme weights. Considering that the sample size is 12,684, and a person with a weight of 77.61 is representing only 0.6% of the sample, extreme weights are not a problem for this example analysis. If extreme weights were likely to be a problem, truncating or stabilizing weights would be possible solutions, as discussed in Chapter 3. The next step is evaluation of covariate balance, which is implemented with the *bal.stat* function of the *twang* package:

require(twang)

psw.balance <- bal.stat(data=data, var=list.predictors, treat.var="treated", w.all=data$psw,

    sampw=1, get.means=T, get.ks=F, estimand="ATE", multinom=F)

psw.balance.table <- psw.balance$results

summary(abs(psw.balance.table$std.eff.sz))

```
    Min.   1st Qu.    Median     Mean   3rd Qu.      Max.
 0.0003039 0.0168700 0.0386400 0.0468600 0.0763700 0.1469000
```

The code above obtains a summary of covariate balance, which indicates that the maximum standardized effect size was 0.146. For this example, the criterion for considering covariate balance adequate is 0.1 standard deviations. Given the indication that this criterion was not met for all 33 covariates in the propensity score model, the following code is used to identify which covariates did not meet the criterion:

psw.balance.table[abs(psw.balance.table$std.eff.sz)>0.1,1:5]

	tx.mn	tx.sd	ct.mn	ct.sd	std.eff.sz
X_RACETH_R:1	0.4600186	0.4983989	0.51556796	0.4997576	-0.1114557
X12MOMAR:1	0.5965733	0.4905849	0.65930498	0.4739430	-0.1278711
X12MOMAR:2	0.4034267	0.4905849	0.34069502	0.4739430	0.1278711
X2INCCAT_I	-0.1254207	1.0580547	-0.02047026	0.9892312	-0.1025320
S2LUNCH	0.1835800	1.0139658	0.03578982	0.9937127	0.1469140
prop.missing	0.1205476	0.8823170	0.01025371	1.0673762	0.1118881

The covariates that did not achieve a covariate balance of 0.1 were the white category of race (variable *X_RACETH_R*), whether the parents are married (variable *X12MOMAR*), parental income (variable *X2INCCAT_I*), proportion of missing data (variable *prop.missing*), and percentage of students in the school with free or reduced-price lunch (*S2LUNCH*). The researcher has three options at this point: (1) modify the propensity score model, (2) change the propensity score estimation method, or (3) proceed with the analysis but include the covariates that did not meet the criterion for covariate balance in the outcome model to remove bias by conditioning. Options 1 and 2 are usually preferable because they allow the use of a simpler outcome model and take better advantage of the propensity score method to remove bias. In this example, the third option is used to demonstrate the process of outcome model specification with covariates.

10.5. Treatment Effect Estimation

The estimation of the treatment effects with multilevel data depends on whether the chosen strategy is to pool cluster-specific treatment effects or estimate a marginal treatment effect. For pooling treatment effects across clusters, Li et al. (2013) presented a nonparametric clustered estimator that is based on weighting the mean of the within-cluster treatment effects. For estimating marginal treatment effects, a multilevel model can be used, such as the multilevel model with random intercept and random slope of treatment presented in Leite et al. (2015):

$$y_{ij} = \gamma_0 + \gamma_1 Z_{ij} + u_{0j} + u_{1j}Z_{ij} + \varepsilon_{ij}$$
$$\varepsilon_{ij} \sim N(0,\sigma^2), u_{0j}, u_{1j} \sim N(0,\Phi)$$

(10.6)

where y_{ij} is the outcome of participant i in cluster j, γ_0 is the intercept, γ_1 is the treatment effect, Z_{ij} is the treatment indicator, u_{0j} is the random intercept of cluster j with variance τ, and ε_{ij} is an individual-level residual with variance σ^2. This model includes a random intercept u_{0j} and a random slope u_{1j} of the treatment effect, which have a covariance matrix Φ. This model assumes that the individual-level residuals ε_{ij} are uncorrelated with the random intercepts, random slopes, and the treatment effect indicator. Leite et al. (2015) demonstrated estimation of treatment effects with multilevel models and propensity score weights using the Mplus statistical software (Muthén & Muthén, 2013). However, the estimation of a multilevel model with sampling weights and propensity score weights has not been implemented in the two major packages for multilevel modeling in R, which are *lme4* (Bates et al., 2011) and *nlme* (Pinheiro & Bates, 2000). These packages incorporate variance weights but not sampling weights, and even though the fixed-effect estimates are the same with either type of weight, standard error estimates are different (Snijders & Bosker, 2012). Therefore, the alternative is to estimate treatment effects using weighted regression with cluster-adjusted standard errors. For the current example, the outcome is mathematics achievement at the spring of kindergarten. The following linear regression model will be used to estimate the treatment effect:

$$Y_{ij} = \beta_0 + \beta_1 X_{1ij} + \beta_2 X_{2ij} + \beta_3 X_{i3j} + \beta_4 X_{4ij} + \pi_1 W_{1j} + \gamma Z_{ij} + \varepsilon_{ij}, \quad (10.7)$$

where β_0 is the intercept; β_1, β_2, β_3, and β_4 are the coefficients of individual-level covariates X_{1ij} (white race), X_{2ij} (married parents), X_{3ij} (income), and X_{4ij} (proportion missing) respectively; $\neq_1$ is the coefficient of the school-level covariate W_{1j} (percent free lunch); Z_{ij} is indicator of center-based child care; and γ is the treatment effect. Before fitting the model, indicators of white race and married status are mean-centered, so that the estimate of γ can be interpreted as the ATE. Continuous covariates are in standardized scale, so they did not need to be mean-centered. Also, the outcome variable *X2MTHETK1* (mathematics achievement in spring of kindergarten) was standardized and the treatment indicator *treated* was converted to a 0/1 numeric scale to facilitate adding interaction terms in the model.

data$white <- scale(as.numeric(data$X_RACETH_R==1),scale=F)

data$married <- scale(as.numeric(data$X12MOMAR==1),scale=F)

data$X2MTHETK1 <- scale(data$X2MTHETK1)

data$treated <- as.numeric(data$treated==1)

The following code sets up the survey design with the *svydesign* function, which consists of declaring the two cluster id variables with the *ids* argument, the propensity score weights with the *weights* argument, and the data. Then, estimates of the ATE with the model in Equation (10.7) are obtained using the *svyglm* function of the *survey* package. Cluster-robust standard errors are estimated with Taylor series linearization. In the *formula* argument, the variable *treated* is connected to the other variables with *, which produces all main effects and all two-way interactions with *treated*.

library(survey)

psw.design <- svydesign(ids=~W1_2P0PSU+S1_ID,

    nest=T,

    weights =~psw,

    data=data)

psw.outcome.model <- svyglm(formula = X2MTHETK1~(white+married+X2INCCAT_I+

    prop.missing+S2LUNCH)*treated,

    family=gaussian(), design=psw.design)

summary(psw.outcome.model)

```
Call:
svyglm(formula = X2MTHETK1 ~ (white + married + X2INCCAT_I +
  prop.missing + S2LUNCH) * treated, family = gaussian(), design = psw.
design)
Survey design:
svydesign(ids = ~W1_2P0PSU + S1_ID, nest = T, weights = ~psw,
  data = data)
Coefficients:
                      Estimate  Std. Error  t value   Pr(>|t|)
(Intercept)          -0.007521   0.005056    -1.488   0.167717
white                 0.131165   0.019821     6.617   5.95e-05 ***
married               0.223423   0.024309     9.191   3.42e-06 ***
X2INCCAT_I            0.229207   0.005320    43.085   1.09e-12 ***
prop.missing         -0.061578   0.010196    -6.040   0.000125 ***
S2LUNCH              -0.085236   0.020863    -4.086   0.002195 **
treated               0.038181   0.027815     1.373   0.199856
white:treated         0.151637   0.019998     7.583   1.88e-05 ***
married:treated      -0.205682   0.029744    -6.915   4.12e-05 ***
X2INCCAT_I:treated   -0.078169   0.048921    -1.598   0.141156
prop.missing:treated -0.036421   0.018483    -1.970   0.077088 .
S2LUNCH:treated      -0.038878   0.025079    -1.550   0.152121
---
Signif. codes: 0 '***' 0.001 '**' 0.01 '*' 0.05 '.' 0.1 ' ' 1
(Dispersion parameter for gaussian family taken to be 0.8266558)
Number of Fisher Scoring iterations: 2
```

In the results shown above, the ATE of attending a child care center during kindergarten on mathematics achievement is not statistically significant ($\gamma = 0.038$, $SE = 0.028$, $p = .200$). There are significant positive main effects of white race, married parents, and income. These indicate that white children and those with married parents perform better in the mathematics assessment and that achievement is expected to increase as the income of parents increases. However, there is a significant interaction between white race and attending a child care center, indicating that white children who attend a child care center are expected to have higher mathematics achievement than white children who do not. There is a negative interaction between having married parents and attending a child care center. This effect shows that children of married parents attending a child care center perform worse in mathematics than those not attending. The coefficients in the results shown above are all standardized, indicating that the significant main and interaction effects are all of moderate to large size.

There is a negative main effect of proportion missing and school percentage of children with free or reduced-price lunch. The effect of proportion of missing data indicates that children who had more missing data in the covariates had lower mathematics achievement. This finding deserves further investigation,[2] because it may indicate dependence between the children's mathematics growth trajectory and the nonresponse patterns, which is a type of missing not at random (MNAR) mechanism (Enders, 2010). The negative effect of percentage of children with free or reduced-price lunch indicates that children in schools with low-income child populations have lower mathematics scores.

TABLE 10.1 ● Summary of Main Functions Used in This Chapter		
Package	**Function**	**Objective**
lme4	*glmer*	Fit a multilevel logistic regression model to estimate propensity scores
stats	*glm*	Fit a logistic regression model with fixed cluster effects
twang	*bal.stat*	Evaluate covariate balance with propensity score weighting
survey	*svydesign*	Set up a survey design object that incorporates the data, two clustering variables, and the propensity score weight
survey	*svyglm*	Fit a regression model with cluster-robust standard errors obtained with Taylor series linearization

10.6. Conclusion

In this chapter, the application of propensity score weighting with multilevel data to estimate the ATE of center-based child care during kindergarten on mathematics achievement was presented. Two models to estimate propensity scores with multilevel data were reviewed: the multilevel logistic regression model and the logistic regression

---

[2] Mixture models for MNAR data, such as the pattern mixture model (Little, 1995) and shared parameter mixture model (Gottfredson, Bauer, & Baldwin, 2014), could be useful for growth modeling of 2011 ECLS-K data.

model with fixed cluster effects. Although this chapter focuses on weighting, other propensity score methods such as stratification and a variety of matching methods could be used. Matching can be done either only allowing matches within clusters or allowing matches across clusters. Matching within clusters has the advantage of keeping cluster-level confounders constant for each cluster, and therefore the propensity score model needs to include only individual-level covariates. However, with within-cluster matching, common support and adequate covariate balance may be difficult to achieve if cluster sizes are small. Matching across clusters increases the number of possible matches, potentially improving common support and covariate balance, but the propensity score model for matching across clusters should include both individual-level and cluster-level confounders. Therefore, with all propensity score methods with multilevel data, cluster sizes are important in determining if pooling of effects estimated within clusters or marginal estimation of treatment effects across clusters is the most feasible option.

Study Questions

1. What is the main advantage of pooling estimated treatment effects across clusters over marginal estimation of treatment effects across clusters?

2. What is the main limitation of pooling estimated treatment effects across clusters?

3. When is marginal estimation of treatment effects across clusters recommended instead of pooling estimated treatment effects across clusters?

4. What is the difference between the propensity score model specification for an individual-level treatment and the propensity score model specification for a cluster-level treatment?

5. Why is the stable unit treatment value assumption particularly vulnerable to violation when individuals are nested within clusters?

6. What are two types of models that can be used for propensity score estimation with multilevel data?

7. How can variation in individual-level covariate effects on treatment assignment across clusters be accounted for in propensity score models?

8. What is one advantage of a logistic regression model with fixed cluster effects over a multilevel logistic regression model for propensity score estimation?

9. What is one advantage of a multilevel logistic regression model over a logistic regression model with fixed cluster effects for propensity score estimation?

10. What approaches can be used for marginal estimation of treatment effects across clusters that account for cluster effects on the outcome?

• References •

Abadie, A., & Imbens, G. W. (2002). *Simple and bias-corrected matching estimators for average treatment effects* (Technical Working Paper T0283). Cambridge, MA: NBER.

Abadie, A., & Imbens, G. W. (2006). Large sample properties of matching estimators for average treatment effects. *Econometrica, 74*(1), 235–267.

Abadie, A., & Imbens, G. W. (2008). On the failure of the bootstrap for matching estimators. *Econometrica, 76*(6), 1537–1557.

Agresti, A. (1996). *An introduction to categorical data analysis*. New York, NY: John Wiley.

Agresti, A. (2002). *Categorical data analysis* (2nd ed.). Hoboken, NJ: John Wiley.

Allison, P. D. (2004). Convergence problems in logistic regression. In M. Altman, J. Gill, & M. McDonald (Eds.), *Numerical issues in statistical computing for the social scientist* (pp. 238–252). New York, NY: John Wiley.

Allison, P. D. (2009). *Fixed effects regression models*. Los Angeles, CA: Sage.

An, W. (2010). Bayesian propensity score estimators: Incorporating uncertainties in propensity scores into causal inference. *Sociological Methodology, 40*(1), 151–189.

Arpino, B., & Mealli, F. (2011). The specification of the propensity score in multilevel observational studies. *Computational Statistics & Data Analysis, 55*(4), 1770–1780.

Asparouhov, T. (2006). General multi-level modeling with sampling weights. *Communications in Statistics: Theory and Methods, 35*(3), 439–460.

Austin, P. C. (2008). A critical appraisal of propensity-score matching in the medical literature between 1996 and 2003. *Statistics in Medicine, 27*(12), 2037–2049.

Austin, P. C. (2011a). Comparing paired vs non-paired statistical methods of analyses when making inferences about absolute risk reductions in propensity-score matched samples. *Statistics in Medicine, 30*(11), 1292–1301.

Austin, P. C. (2011b). An introduction to propensity score methods for reducing the effects of confounding in observational studies. *Multivariate Behavioral Research, 46*(3), 399–424.

Austin, P. C., & Small, D. S. (2014). The use of bootstrapping when using propensity-score matching without replacement: A simulation study. *Statistics in Medicine, 33*, 4306–4319.

Bai, H. (2013). A bootstrap procedure of propensity score estimation. *The Journal of Experimental Education, 81*(2), 157–177.

Bang, H., & Robins, J. M. (2005). Doubly robust estimation in missing data and causal inference models. *Biometrics, 61*(4), 962–973.

Barnard, J., Frangakis, C. E., Hill, J. L., & Rubin, D. B. (2003). Principal stratification approach to broken randomized experiments. *Journal of the American Statistical Association, 98*(462), 299–323.

Bates, D., Maechler, M., & Bolker, B. (2011). lme4: Linear mixed-effects models using S4 classes. Retrieved from http://cran.cnr.berkeley.edu/web/packages/lme4/index.html

Beauducel, A., & Herzberg, P. Y. (2006). On the performance of maximum likelihood versus means and variance adjusted weighted least squares estimation in CFA. *Structural Equation Modeling: A Multidisciplinary Journal, 13*(2), 186–203.

Beaujean, A. A. (2014). *Latent variable modeling using R: A step-by-step guide*. New York, NY: Routledge.

Berk, R. (2006). An introduction to ensemble methods for data analysis. *Sociological Methods & Research, 34*, 263–295.

Bodnar, L. M. (2004). Marginal structural models for analyzing causal effects of time-dependent treatments: An application in perinatal epidemiology. *American Journal of Epidemiology, 159*(10), 926–934.

Bollen, K. A. (1989). *Structural equations with latent variables*. New York, NY: John Wiley.

Bollen, K. A. (2002). Latent variables in psychology and the social sciences. *Annual Review of Psychology, 53*(1), 605.

Borra, C., Iacovou, M., & Sevilla, A. (2012). The effect of breastfeeding on children's cognitive and noncognitive development. *Labour Economics, 19*(4), 496–515.

Bovaird, J. A., & Koziol, N. A. (2012). Measurement models for ordered-categorical indicators. In R. H. Hoyle (Ed.), *Handbook of structural equation modeling* (pp. 495–531). New York, NY: Guilford.

Breiman, L. (2001). Random forests. *Machine Learning, 45*, 5–32.

Brookhart, M. A., Schneeweiss, S., Rothman, K. J., Glynn, R. J., Avorn, J., & Sturmer, T. (2006). Variable selection for propensity score models. *American Journal of Epidemiology, 163*(12), 1149–1156.

Brumback, B. A., Hernán, M. A., Haneuse, S. J., & Robins, J. M. (2004). Sensitivity analyses for unmeasured confounding assuming a marginal structural model for repeated measures. *Statistics in Medicine, 23*(5), 749–767.

Butera, N. M., Lanza, S. T., & Coffman, D. L. (2014). A framework for estimating causal effects in latent class analysis: Is there a causal link between early sex and subsequent profiles of delinquency? *Prevention Science: The Official Journal of the Society for Prevention Research, 15*(3), 397–407.

Campbell, D. T., & Stanley, J. C. (1966). *Experimental and quasi-experimental designs for research.* Chicago, IL: Rand McNally.

Carnegie, N. B., Harada, M., Dorie, V., & Hill, J. (2016). treatSens: Sensitivity analysis for causal inference. Retrieved from https://cran.r-project.org/web/packages/treatSens/index.html

Carnegie, N. B., Harada, M., & Hill, J. L. (2016). Assessing sensitivity to unmeasured confounding using a simulated potential confounder. *Journal of Research on Educational Effectiveness, 9*(3), 395–420.

Carré, B. (1979). *Graphs and networks.* New York, NY: Oxford University Press.

Cepeda, M. S., Boston, R., Farrar, J. T., & Strom, B. L. (2003). Optimal matching with a variable number of controls vs. a fixed number of controls for a cohort study:

Trade-offs. *Journal of Clinical Epidemiology, 56*, 230–237.

Claessens, A. (2012). Kindergarten child care experiences and child achievement and socioemotional skills. *Early Childhood Research Quarterly, 27*(3), 365–375.

Cochran, W. (1968). The effectiveness of adjustment by subclassification in removing bias in observational studies. *Biometrics, 24*, 295–313.

Coffman, D. L. (2011). Estimating causal effects in mediation analysis using propensity scores. *Structural Equation Modeling: A Multidisciplinary Journal, 18*(3), 357–369.

Cohen, J. (1988). *Statistical power analysis for the behavioral sciences.* Hillsdale, NJ: Lawrence Erlbaum.

Cole, S. R. (2005). Marginal structural models for estimating the effect of highly active antiretroviral therapy initiation on CD4 cell count. *American Journal of Epidemiology, 162*(5), 471–478.

Cook, T. D., & Campbell, D. T. (1979). *Quasi-experimentation: Design and analysis issues for field settings.* Chicago, IL: Rand-McNally.

Cornfield, J., Haenszel, W., Hammond, E., Lilienfeld, A., Shimkin, M., & Wynder, E. (1959). Smoking and lung cancer: Recent evidence and a discussion of some questions. *Journal of the National Cancer Institute, 22*, 173–203.

Cuong, N. V. (2013). Which covariates should be controlled in propensity score matching? Evidence from a simulation study. *Statistica Neerlandica, 67*(2), 169–180.

Dehejia, R. H., & Wahba, S. (1999). Causal effects in nonexperimental studies: Reevaluating the evaluation of training programs. *Journal of the American Statistical Association, 94*, 1053–1062.

Diamond, A., & Sekhon, J. S. (2013). Genetic matching for estimating causal effects: A general multivariate matching method for achieving balance in observational studies. *The Review of Economics and Statistics, 95*, 932–945.

Dugoff, E. H., Schuler, M., & Stuart, E. A. (2014). Generalizing observational study results: Applying propensity score methods to complex surveys. *Health Services Research, 49*, 284–303.

Enders, C. K. (2010). *Applied missing data analysis.* New York, NY: Guilford.

Fan, X., & Sivo, S. A. (2005). Sensitivity of fit indexes to misspecified structural or measurement model components: Rationale of two-index strategy revisited. *Structural Equation Modeling, 12*(3), 343–367.

Fan, X., & Sivo, S. A. (2007). Sensitivity of fit indices to model misspecification and model types. *Multivariate Behavioral Research, 42*(3), 509–529.

Faraway, J. J. (2006). *Extending the linear model with R: Generalized linear, mixed effects and nonparametric regression models.* Boca Raton, FL: Chapman Hall/CRC.

Finch, W. H., & French, B. F. (2015). *Latent variable modeling with R.* New York, NY: Routledge.

Ford, L., & Fulkerson, D. (1962). *Flows in networks.* Princeton, NJ: Princeton University Press.

Fox, J. (2002). *An R and S-Plus companion to applied regression.* Thousand Oaks, CA: Sage.

Fox, J. (2008). *Applied regression analysis and generalized linear models* (2nd ed.). Los Angeles, CA: Sage.

Gardiner, J. C., Luo, Z., & Roman, L. A. (2009). Fixed effects, random effects and GEE: What are the differences? *Statistics in Medicine, 28*(2), 221–239.

Gelman, A., Jakulin, A., Pittau, M. G., & Su, Y.-S. (2008). A weakly informative default prior distribution for logistic and other regression models. *Annals of Applied Statistics, 2,* 1360–1383.

Goldstein, H. (2003). *Multilevel statistical models.* New York, NY: Halsted.

Gottfredson, N. C., Bauer, D. J., & Baldwin, S. A. (2014). Modeling change in the presence of nonrandomly missing data: Evaluating a shared parameter mixture model. *Structural Equation Modeling: A Multidisciplinary Journal, 21*(2), 196–209.

Graham, J. W. (2009). Missing data analysis: Making it work in the real world. *Annual Review of Psychology, 60,* 549–576.

Green, S. B., & Thompson, M. S. (2012). A flexible structural equation modeling approach for analyzing means. In R. H. Hoyle (Ed.), *Handbook of structural equation modeling* (pp. 393–416). New York, NY: Guilford.

Greenland, S., Robins, J. M., & Pearl, J. (1999). Confounding and collapsibility in causal inference. *Statistical Science, 14*(1), 29–46.

Gu, X. S., & Rosenbaum, P. R. (1993). Comparison of multivariate matching methods: Structures, distances, and algorithms. *Journal of Computational and Graphical Statistics, 2,* 405–420.

Guo, S., & Fraser, M. W. (2015). *Propensity score analysis: Statistical methods and applications* (2nd ed.). Thousand Oaks, CA: Sage.

Gurel, S., & Leite, W. L. (2012, April). *The performance of propensity score methods to estimate the average treatment effect in observational studies with selection bias: A Monte Carlo simulation study.* Paper presented at the annual meeting of

the American Educational Research Association, Vancouver, BC.

Gurel, S., & Leite, W. L. (2014, April). *Evaluation of propensity score strategies with multilevel data when treatment assignment mechanism varies between clusters.* Paper presented at the annual meeting of the American Educational Research Association, Philadelphia, PA.

Hahs-Vaughn, D. L., & Onwuegbuzie, A. J. (2006). Estimating and using propensity score analysis with complex samples. *The Journal of Experimental Education, 75,* 31–65.

Halekoh, U., Hojsgaard, S., & Yan, J. (2006). The R Package geepack for generalized estimating equations. *Journal of Statistical Software, 15*(2), 1–11.

Hansen, B. B. (2007). Optmatch: Flexible, optimal matching for observational studies. *R News, 7*(2), 18–24.

Harder, V. S., Stuart, E. A., & Anthony, J. C. (2010). Propensity score techniques and the assessment of measured covariate balance to test causal associations in psychological research. *Psychological Methods, 15*(3), 234–249.

Hardin, J. W., & Hilbe, J. M. (2013). *Generalized estimating equations* (2nd ed.). Boca Raton, FL: CRC Press.

Haviland, A. M., & Nagin, D. S. (2005). Causal inferences with group based trajectory models. *Psychometrika, 70*(3), 557–578.

Haviland, A. M., Nagin, D. S., & Rosenbaum, P. R. (2007). Combining propensity score matching and group-based trajectory analysis in an observational study. *Psychological Methods, 12*(3), 247–267.

Haviland, A. M., Nagin, D. S., Rosenbaum, P. R., & Tremblay, R. E.

(2008). Combining group-based trajectory modeling and propensity score matching for causal inferences in nonexperimental longitudinal data. *Developmental Psychology, 44*(2), 422–436.

Heene, M., Hilbert, S., Freudenthaler, H. H., & Bühner, M. (2012). Sensitivity of SEM fit indexes with respect to violations of uncorrelated errors. *Structural Equation Modeling: A Multidisciplinary Journal, 19*(1), 36–50.

Heeringa, S. G., West, B. T., & Berglund, P. A. (2010). *Applied survey data analysis.* Boca Raton, FL: CRC Press.

Hernán, M. A., Brumback, B., & Robins, J. M. (2000). Marginal structural models to estimate the causal effect of zidovudine on the survival of HIV-positive men. *Epidemiology, 11,* 561–570.

Hill, J. (2004). *Reducing bias in treatment effect estimation in observational studies suffering from missing data* (ISERP Working Papers). New York, NY: Institute for Social and Economic Research and Policy, Columbia University.

Hill, J., Weiss, C., & Zhai, F. (2011). Challenges with propensity score strategies in a high-dimensional setting and a potential alternative. *Multivariate Behavioral Research, 46*(3), 477–513.

Hirano, K., & Imbens, G. W. (2004). The propensity score with continuous treatments. In D. B. Rubin, A. Gelman, & X.-L. Meng (Eds.), *Applied Bayesian modeling and causal inference from incomplete-data perspectives: An essential journey with Donald Rubin's statistical family* (pp. 73–84). New York, NY: John Wiley.

Ho, D. E., Imai, K., King, G., & Stuart, E. A. (2007). Matching as nonparametric preprocessing for reducing model dependence in parametric causal inference. *Political Analysis, 15*(3), 199–236.

Ho, D. E., Imai, K., King, G., & Stuart, E. A. (2011). MatchIt: Nonparametric preprocessing for parametric causal inference. *Journal of Statistical Software, 42*(8), 1–28.

Ho, D. E., Imai, K., King, G., & Stuart, E. A. (2014). How exactly are the weights created? Retrieved October 22, 2014, from http://r.iq.harvard.edu/docs/matchit/2.4-20/How_Exactly_are.html

Holland, P. W. (1986). Statistics and causal inference. *Journal of the American Statistical Association, 81*(396), 945–960.

Honaker, J., King, G., & Blackwell, M. (2011). Amelia II: A program for missing data. *Journal of Statistical Software, 45*(7), 1–47.

Hong, G. (2010). Marginal mean weighting through stratification: Adjustment for selection bias in multilevel data. *Journal of Educational and Behavioral Statistics, 35*(5), 499–531.

Hong, G. (2012). Marginal mean weighting through stratification: A generalized method for evaluating multivalued and multiple treatments with nonexperimental data. *Psychological Methods, 17*(1), 44–60.

Hong, G., & Hong, Y. (2008). Reading instruction time and homogeneous grouping in kindergarten: An application of marginal mean weighting through stratification. *Educational Evaluation and Policy Analysis, 31*(1), 54–81.

Hox, J. J., & Bechger, T. A. (1998). An introduction to structural equation modeling. *Family Science Review, 11*, 354–373.

Hu, L., & Bentler, P. M. (1999). Cutoff criteria for fit indexes in covariance structure analysis: Conventional criteria versus new alternatives. *Structural Equation Modeling, 6*, 1–55.

Huang, F. L. (2016). Alternatives to multilevel modeling for the analysis of clustered data. *The Journal of Experimental Education, 84*(1), 175–196.

Huber, M. (2011). Identification of average treatment effects in social experiments under alternative forms of attrition. *Journal of Educational and Behavioral Statistics, 37*(3), 443–474.

Huggins-Manley, A. C., & Algina, J. (2015). The partial credit model and generalized partial credit model as constrained nominal response models, with applications in Mplus. *Structural Equation Modeling: A Multidisciplinary Journal, 22*, 308–318.

Imai, K., & Ratkovic, M. (2014). Covariate balancing propensity score. *Journal of the Royal Statistical Society, Series B, 76*, 243–263.

Imai, K., & Van Dyk, D. A. (2004). Causal inference with general treatment regimes: Generalizing the propensity score. *Journal of the American Statistical Association, 99*(467), 854–866.

Imbens, G. W. (2000). The role of the propensity score in estimating dose-response functions. *Biometrika, 87*(3), 706–710.

Imbens, G. W. (2004). Nonparametric estimation of average treatment effects under exogeneity: A review. *Review of Economics & Statistics, 86*(1), 4–29.

Imbens, G. W. (2010). An economist's perspective on Shadish (2010) and West and Thoemmes (2010). *Psychological Methods, 15*(1), 47–55.

Imbens, G. W., & Wooldridge, J. M. (2009). Recent developments in the econometrics of program evaluation. *Journal of Economic Literature, 47*(1), 5–86.

Ingels, S. J., Pratt, D. J., Rogers, J. E., Siegel, P. H., Stutts, E. S., & Owings, J. A. (2004). *Education Longitudinal Study of 2002: Base year data file user's manual* (NCES2004-405). Washington, DC: National Center for Education Statistics, U.S. Department of Education.

Institute of Education Sciences. (2014). *Request for applications: Education research and development center program*. Washington, DC: U.S. Department of Education. Retrieved from http://ies.ed.gov/funding/pdf/2015_84305C.pdf

Jacknowitz, A. (2008). The role of workplace characteristics in breastfeeding practices. *Women & Health, 47*(2), 87–111.

Jakubowski, M. (2014). Latent variables and propensity score matching: A simulation study with application to data from the Programme for International Student Assessment in Poland. *Empirical Economics, 48*, 1287–1325.

Jin, H., Barnard, J., & Rubin, D. B. (2010). A modified general location model for noncompliance with missing data: Revisiting the New York City School Choice Scholarship Program using principal stratification. *Journal of Educational and Behavioral Statistics, 35*(2), 154–173.

Jin, H., & Rubin, D. B. (2009). Public schools versus private schools: Causal inference with partial compliance. *Journal of Educational and Behavioral Statistics, 34*(1), 24–45.

Jo, B., Stuart, E. A., MacKinnon, D. P., & Vinokur, A. D. (2011). The use of propensity scores in mediation analysis. *Multivariate Behavioral Research, 46*(3), 425–452.

Joffe, M. M., Ten Have, T. R., Feldman, H. I., & Kimmel, S. E. (2004). Model selection, confounder control, and marginal structural models: Review and new applications. *American Statistician, 58*(4), 272–279.

Judge, T. M., & Hurst, C. (2008). How the rich (and happy) get richer (and happier): Relationship of core self-evaluations to trajectories in attaining work success. *Journal of Applied Psychology, 93*, 849–863.

Kamata, A., & Bauer, D. J. (2008). A note on the relation between factor analytic and item response theory models. *Structural Equation Modeling, 15*, 136–153.

Kamata, A., & Vaughn, B. K. (2004). An introduction to differential item functioning analysis. *Learning Disabilities: A Contemporary Journal, 2*(2), 49–69.

Kang, J. D. Y., & Schafer, J. L. (2007a). Demystifying double robustness: A comparison of alternative strategies for estimating a population mean from incomplete data. *Statistical Science, 22*(4), 523–539.

Kang, J. D. Y., & Schafer, J. L. (2007b). Rejoinder: Demystifying double robustness: A comparison of alternative strategies for estimating a population mean from incomplete data. *Statistical Science, 22*(4), 574–580.

Kaplan, D. (1999). An extension of the propensity score adjustment method for the analysis of group differences in MIMIC models. *Multivariate Behavioral Research, 34*(4), 467–492.

Kaplan, D. (2009). *Structural equation modeling: Foundations and extensions* (2nd ed.). Newbury Park, CA: Sage.

Kaplan, D., & Chen, J. (2012). A two-step Bayesian approach for propensity score analysis: Simulations and case study. *Psychometrika, 77*(3), 581–609.

Kaplan, D., & Chen, J. (2014). Bayesian model averaging for

propensity score analysis. *Multivariate Behavioral Research, 49*(6), 505–517.

Kelcey, B. M. (2009). *Improving and assessing propensity score based causal inferences in multilevel and nonlinear settings* (Doctoral dissertation). Ann Arbor: University of Michigan. ProQuest Dissertations and Theses database. (304929925)

Kelcey, B. M. (2011a). Covariate selection in propensity scores using outcome proxies. *Multivariate Behavioral Research, 46*(3), 453–476.

Kelcey, B. M. (2011b, April). *Propensity score matching within versus across schools.* Paper presented at the annual meeting of the American Educational Research Association, New Orleans, LA.

Kemple, J. J., & Willner, C. J. (2008). *Career academies long-term impacts on labor market outcomes, educational attainment, and transitions to adulthood.* New York, NY: MDRC.

Kim, E. S., & Yoon, M. (2011). Testing measurement invariance: A comparison of multiple-group categorical CFA and IRT. *Structural Equation Modeling: A Multidisciplinary Journal, 18*(2), 212–228.

Kim, J., & Seltzer, M. (2007). *Causal inference in multilevel settings in which selection processes vary across schools.* Los Angeles, CA: Center for Study of Evaluation (CSE).

Kish, L. (1965). *Survey sampling.* New York, NY: John Wiley.

Kline, R. B. (2011). *Principles and practice of structural equation modeling* (3rd ed.). New York, NY: Guilford.

Krueger, R. A., & Casey, M. A. (2008). *Focus groups: A practical guide for applied research* (4th ed.). Thousand Oaks, CA: Sage.

Lanza, S. T., Coffman, D. L., & Xu, S. (2013). Causal inference in latent class analysis. *Structural Equation Modeling: A Multidisciplinary Journal, 20*(3), 361–383.

Lechner, M. (2002). Program heterogeneity and propensity score matching: An application to the evaluation of active labor market policies. *Review of Economics & Statistics, 84*(2), 205–220.

Lee, B. K., Lessler, J., & Stuart, E. A. (2011). Weight trimming and propensity score weighting. *PLoS ONE, 6*(3), 1–6.

Leite, W. L., & Aydin, B., (2016, April). *A comparison of methods for imputation of missing covariate data prior to propensity score analysis.* Paper presented at the American Education Research Association Conference, Washington, DC.

Leite, W. L., Aydin, B., & Gurel, S. (2013, April). *A comparison of propensity score methods for evaluating the effects of programs with multiple versions.* Paper presented at the annual meeting of the American Educational Research Association, San Francisco, CA.

Leite, W. L., Jimenez, F., Kaya, Y., Stapleton, L. M., MacInnes, J. W., & Sandbach, R. (2015). An evaluation of weighting methods based on propensity scores to reduce selection bias in multilevel observational studies. *Multivariate Behavioral Research, 50*(3), 265–284.

Leite, W. L., Sandbach, R., Jin, R., MacInnes, J. W., & Jackman, M. G. (2012). An evaluation of latent growth models for propensity score matched groups. *Structural Equation Modeling: A Multidisciplinary Journal, 19*(3), 437–456.

Leite, W. L., & Stapleton, L. M. (2011). Detecting growth shape misspecifications in latent growth models: An evaluation of fit indexes. *The Journal of Experimental Education, 79*(4), 361–381.

Leite, W. L., Svinicki, M., & Shi, Y. (2010). Attempted validation of the scores of the VARK: Learning styles inventory with multitrait-multimethod confirmatory factor analysis models. *Educational and Psychological Measurement, 70*(2), 323–339.

Li, F., Zaslavsky, A. M., & Landrum, M. B. (2013). Propensity score weighting with multilevel data. *Statistics in Medicine, 32*, 3373–3387.

Li, L., Shen, C., Wu, A. C., & Li, X. (2011). Propensity score-based sensitivity analysis method for uncontrolled confounding. *American Journal of Epidemiology, 174*(3), 345–353.

Liang, K. Y., & Zeger, S. L. (1986). Longitudinal data analysis using generalized linear models. *Biometrika, 73*, 13–22.

Lingle, J. A. (2011). *Evaluating the performance of propensity scores to address selection bias in a multilevel context: A Monte Carlo simulation study and application using a national dataset.* ProQuest Information & Learning. Retrieved from http://search.ebscohost.com/login .aspx?direct=true&db=psyh& AN=2011-99011-030&site=ehost-live Available from EBSCOhost psyh database

Little, R. J. A. (1995). Modeling the drop-out mechanism in repeated-measures studies. *Journal of the American Statistical Association, 90*(431), 1112–1121.

Little, T. D., Card, N. A., Bovaird, J. A., Preacher, K. J., & Crandall, C. S. (2007). Structural equation modeling of mediation and moderation with contextual factors. In T. D. Little, J. A. Bovaird, & N. A. Card (Eds.), *Modeling*

contextual effects in longitudinal studies (pp. 207–230). Mahwah, NJ: Lawrence Erlbaum.

Loh, W. (2011). Classification and regression trees. *WIREs Data Mining and Knowledge Discovery, 1*, 14–23.

Lohr, S. (1999). *Sampling: Design and analysis*. Pacific Grove, CA: Duxbury Press.

Lord, F., & Novick, M. (1968). *Statistical theories of mental test scores*. Reading, MA: Addison-Wesley.

Lumley, T. (2004). Analysis of complex survey samples. *Journal of Statistical Software, 9*(8), 1–19.

Lumley, T. (2010). *Complex surveys: A guide to analysis using R*. New York, NY: John Wiley.

Lumley, T. (2014). Combining multiple imputations. Retrieved December 23, 2014, from http://watson.nci.nih.gov/ cran_mirror/web/packages/mitools/ vignettes/smi.pdf

Lunceford, J. K., & Davidian, M. (2004). Stratification and weighting via the propensity score in estimation of causal treatment effects: A comparative study. *Statistics in Medicine, 23*, 2937–2960.

Marschner, I. C. (2012). Relative risk regression: Reliable and flexible methods for log-binomial models. *Biostatistics, 13*(1), 179–192.

Marsh, H. W., Hau, K., & Grayson, D. (2005). Goodness of fit in structural equation models. In A. Maydeu-Olivares & J. J. McArdle (Eds.), *Contemporary psychometrics: A festschrift for Roderick P. McDonald* (pp. 275–340). Mahwah, NJ: Lawrence Erlbaum.

Marsh, H. W., Hau, K.-T., & Wen, Z. (2004). In search of golden rules: Comment on hypothesis-testing approaches to setting cutoff values

for fit indexes and dangers in overgeneralizing Hu and Bentler's (1999) findings. *Structural Equation Modeling, 11*(3), 320–341.

Marsh, H. W., Wen, Z., Hau, K., & Nagengast, B. (2013). Structural equation models of latent interaction and quadratic effects. In G. R. Hancock & R. O. Mueller (Eds.), *Structural equation modeling: A second course* (2nd ed., pp. 267–308). Greenwich, CT: Information Age Publishing.

Maxwell, S. E. (2010). Introduction to the special section on Campbell's and Rubin's conceptualizations of causality. *Psychological Methods, 15*(1), 1–2.

McCaffrey, D. F., Griffin, B. A., Almirall, D., Slaughter, M. E., Ramchand, R., & Burgette, L. F. (2013). A tutorial on propensity score estimation for multiple treatments using generalized boosted models. *Statistics in Medicine, 19*, 3388–3414.

McCaffrey, D. F., Ridgeway, G., & Morral, A. R. (2004). Propensity score estimation with boosted regression for evaluating causal effects in observational studies. *Psychological Methods, 9*, 403–425.

McCandless, L. C., Gustafson, P., Austin, P. C., & Levy, A. R. (2009). Covariate balance in a Bayesian propensity score analysis of beta blocker therapy in heart failure patients. *Epidemiologic Perspectives & Innovations, 6*, 5.

McNeish, D., Stapleton, L. M., & Silverman, R. D. (in press). On the unnecessary ubiquity of hierarchical linear modeling. *Psychological Methods*.

Meredith, W. (1993). Measurement invariance, factor analysis and factorial invariance. *Psychometrika, 58*(4), 525–543.

Millsap, R. E., & Meredith, W. (2007). Factorial invariance: Historical perspectives and new problems. In R. Cudeck & R. C. MacCallum (Eds.), *Factor analysis at 100: Historical developments and future directions* (pp. 131–152). Mahwah, NJ: Lawrence Erlbaum.

Millsap, R. E., & Olivera-Aguillar, M. (2012). Investigating measurement invariance using confirmatory factor analysis. In R. H. Hoyle (Ed.), *Handbook of structural equation modeling* (pp. 380–392). New York, NY: Guilford.

Ming, K., & Rosenbaum, P. R. (2000). Substantial gains in bias reduction from matching with a variable number of controls. *Biometrics, 56*(1), 118–124.

Ming, K., & Rosenbaum, P. R. (2001). A note on optimal matching with variable controls using the assignment algorithm. *Journal of Computational and Graphical Statistics, 10*(3), 455–463.

Mitra, R., & Reiter, J. P. (2016). A comparison of two methods of estimating propensity scores after multiple imputation. *Statistical Methods in Medical Research, 25*(1), 188–204.

Muthén & Muthén. (2013). Mplus (Version 7.0). Los Angeles, CA: Author.

Muthén, B. O., & Asparouhov, T. (2015). Causal effects in mediation modeling: An introduction with applications to latent variables. *Structural Equation Modeling: A Multidisciplinary Journal, 22*(1), 12–23.

Na, C., & Gottfredson, D. C. (2013). Police officers in schools: Effects on school crime and the processing of offending behaviors. *Justice Quarterly, 30*(4), 619–650.

National Center for Education Statistics. (2014). Education

Longitudinal Study of 2002 (ELS: 2002). Retrieved from http://nces .ed.gov/surveys/els2002/

Oberski, D. L. (2014). lavaan.survey: An R package for complex survey analysis of structural equation models. *Journal of Statistical Software, 57*, 1–27.

Olsson, U. H., Foss, T., Troye, S. V., & Howell, R. D. (2000). The performance of ML, GLS, and WLS estimation in structural equation modeling under conditions of misspecification and nonnormality. *Structural Equation Modeling, 7*(4), 557–595.

Orr, M. T. (2005). Career academies as a professionally engaging and supportive teaching experience. *Education and Urban Society, 37*, 453–489.

Petersen, M. L., Deeks, S. G., Martin, J. N., & van der Laan, M. J. (2007). History-adjusted marginal structural models for estimating time-varying effect modification. *American Journal of Epidemiology, 166*(9), 985–993.

Pfeffermann, D. (1993). The role of sampling weights when modeling survey data. *International Statistical Review, 61*, 317–337.

Pinheiro, J. C., & Bates, D. M. (2000). *Mixed-effects models in S and S-Plus*. New York, NY: Springer-Verlag.

Preacher, K. J., Zyphur, M. J., & Zhang, Z. (2010). A general multilevel SEM framework for assessing multilevel mediation. *Psychological Methods, 15*, 209–233.

Puma, M. J., Olsen, R. B., Bell, S. H., & Price, C. (2009). *What to do when data are missing in group randomized controlled trials*. Washington, DC: National Center for Education Evaluation and Regional Assistance, Institute of Education Sciences, U.S. Department of Education.

Quigley, M. A., Hockley, C., Carson, C., Kelly, Y., Renfrew, M. J., & Sacker, A. (2012). Breastfeeding is associated with improved child cognitive development: A population-based cohort study. *The Journal of Pediatrics, 160*(1), 25–32.

Rabe-Hesketh, S., & Skrondal, A. (2006). Multilevel modelling of complex survey data. *Journal of the Royal Statistical Society: Series A (Statistics in Society), 169*(4), 805–827.

Raju, N. S., Laffitte, L. J., & Byrne, B. M. (2002). Measurement equivalence: A comparison of methods based on confirmatory factor analysis and item response theory. *Journal of Applied Psychology, 87*(3), 517–529.

Raudenbush, S. W., & Bryk, A. S. (2002). *Hierarchical linear models: Applications and data analysis methods* (2nd ed.). Thousand Oaks, CA: Sage.

Raykov, T. (2012). Propensity score analysis with fallible covariates: A note on a latent variable modeling approach. *Educational and Psychological Measurement, 72*, 715–733.

Raykov, T., & Marcoulides, G. A. (2006). *A first course in structural equation modeling* (2nd ed.). Mahwah, NJ: Lawrence Erlbaum.

Raykov, T., Marcoulides, G. A., & Li, C. H. (2012). Measurement invariance for latent constructs in multiple populations: A critical view and refocus. *Educational and Psychological Measurement, 72*(6), 954–974.

Reise, S. P., Widaman, K. F., & Pugh, R. H. (1993). Confirmatory factor analysis and item response theory: Two approaches for exploring measurement invariance. *Psychological Bulletin, 114*(3), 552–566.

Rickles, J. H. (2011). Using interviews to understand the assignment mechanism in a nonexperimental study: The case of eighth grade algebra. *Evaluation Review, 35*(5), 490–522.

Ridgeway, G., McCaffrey, D., Morral, A., Burgette, L., & Griffin, B. A. (2013). Toolkit for weighting and analysis of nonequivalent groups: A tutorial for the twang package. Retrieved from http://cran.r-project.org/web/packages/twang/vignettes/twang.pdf

Robins, J. M., Hernán, M. A., & Brumback, B. (2000). Marginal structural models and causal inference in epidemiology. *Epidemiology, 11,* 550–560.

Rodgers, J. L. (1999). The bootstrap, the jackknife, and the randomization test: A sampling taxonomy. *Multivariate Behavioral Research, 34*(4), 441–456.

Rojewski, J. W., Lee, I. H., & Gemici, S. (2010). Using propensity score matching to determine the efficacy of secondary career academies in raising educational aspirations. *Career and Technical Education Research, 35*(1), 3–27.

Rosenbaum, P. R. (1989). Optimal matching for observational studies. *Journal of the American Statistical Association, 84*(408), 1024.

Rosenbaum, P. R. (1991). A characterization of optimal designs for observational studies. *Journal of the Royal Statistical Society, Series B, 53,* 597–610.

Rosenbaum, P. R. (2002). *Observational studies.* New York, NY: Springer.

Rosenbaum, P. R. (2010). *Design of observational studies.* New York, NY: Springer.

Rosenbaum, P. R., & Rubin, D. B. (1983a). Assessing sensitivity to an unobserved binary covariate in an observational study with binary outcome. *The Journal of the Royal Statistical Society, Series B, 45*(2), 212–218.

Rosenbaum, P. R., & Rubin, D. B. (1983b). The central role of the propensity score in observational studies for causal effects. *Biometrika, 70*(1), 41–55.

Rosenbaum, P. R., & Rubin, D. B. (1984). Reducing bias in observational studies using subclassification on the propensity score. *Journal of the American Statistical Association, 79,* 516–524.

Rosenbaum, P. R., & Rubin, D. B. (1985). Constructing a control group using multivariate matched sampling models that incorporate the propensity score. *American Statistician, 39*(1), 33.

Rousseeuwa, P. J., & Christmann, A. (2003). Robustness against separation and outliers in logistic regression. *Computational Statistics & Data Analysis, 43*(3), 315–332.

Rubin, D. B. (1973). The use of matching and regression adjustment to remove bias in observational studies. *Biometrics, 29,* 185–203.

Rubin, D. B. (1974). Estimating causal effects of treatments in randomized and nonrandomized studies. *Journal of Educational Psychology, 66,* 688–701.

Rubin, D. B. (1986). Comment: Which ifs have causal answers? *Journal of the American Statistical Association, 81,* 961–962.

Rubin, D. B. (1987). *Multiple imputation for nonresponse in surveys.* New York, NY: John Wiley.

Rubin, D. B. (2001). Using propensity scores to help design observational studies: Application to the tobacco litigation. *Health Services and Outcomes Research Methodology, 2,* 169–188.

Rubin, D. B. (2005). Causal inference using potential outcomes: Design, modeling, decisions. *Journal of the American Statistical Association, 100*(469), 322–331.

Rubin, D. B. (2007). The design versus the analysis of observational studies for causal effects: Parallels with the design of randomized trials. *Statistics in Medicine, 26*(1), 20–36.

Rubin, D. B. (2008). For objective causal inference, design trumps analysis. *The Annals of Applied Statistics, 2,* 808–840.

Rubin, D. B. (2010). Reflections stimulated by the comments of Shadish (2010) and West and Thoemmes (2010). *Psychological Methods, 15*(1), 38–46.

Ruddy, S. A., Neiman, S., Hryczaniuk, C. A., Thomas, T. L., & Parmer, R. J. (2010). *2007–08 School Survey on Crime and Safety (SSOCS) survey documentation for public-use data file users* (NCES 2010-307). Washington, DC: National Center for Education Statistics, Institute of Education Science, U.S. Department of Education.

Schafer, J. L., & Kang, J. (2008). Average causal effects from nonrandomized studies: A practical guide and simulated example. *Psychological Methods, 13*(4), 279–313.

Schiller, B. R., & Crewson, P. E. (1997). Entrepreneurial origins: A longitudinal inquiry. *Economic Inquiry, 35,* 523–531.

Schumacker, R. E., & Lomax, R. G. (2010). *A beginner's guide to structural equation modeling* (3rd ed.). Mahwah, NJ: Lawrence Erlbaum.

Seaman, S. R., & White, I. R. (2013). Review of inverse probability weighting for dealing with missing data. *Statistical Methods in Medical Research, 22*(3), 278–295.

Sekhon, J. S. (2011). Multivariate and propensity score matching software with automated balance optimization: The Matching package for R. *Journal of Statistical Software, 42*(7), 1–52.

Sekhon, J. S., & Grieve, R. (2009, June). *A new non-parametric matching method for covariate adjustment with application to economic evaluation.* Paper presented at the Experiments in Political Science Conference. Retrieved from http://ssrn.com/abstract=1301767

Sekhon, J. S., & Grieve, R. D. (2012). A matching method for improving covariate balance in cost-effectiveness analyses. *Health Economics, 21,* 695–714.

Seni, G., & Elder, J. (2010). *Ensemble methods in data mining: Improving accuracy through combining predictions.* Chicago, IL: Morgan & Claypool.

Setoguchi, S., Schneeweiss, S., Brookhart, M. A., Glynn, R. J., & Cook, E. F. (2008). Evaluating uses of data mining techniques in propensity score estimation: A simulation study. *Pharmacoepidemiology and Drug Safety, 17*(6), 546–555.

Shadish, W. R. (2010). Campbell and Rubin: A primer and comparison of their approaches to causal inference in field settings. *Psychological Methods, 15*(1), 3–17.

Shadish, W. R., Cook, T. D., & Campbell, D. T. (2002). *Experimental and quasi-experimental designs for generalized causal inference.* Boston, MA: Houghton Mifflin.

Shen, C., Li, X., Li, L., & Were, M. C. (2011). Sensitivity analysis for causal inference using inverse probability weighting. *Biometrical Journal, 53*(5), 1–16.

Snijders, T. A. B., & Bosker, R. J. (2012). *Multilevel analysis: An introduction to basic and advanced multilevel modeling* (2nd ed.). Thousand Oaks, CA: Sage.

Steiner, P. M., Cook, T. D., & Shadish, W. R. (2011). On the importance of reliable covariate measurement in selection bias adjustments using propensity scores. *Journal of Educational and Behavioral Statistics, 36*(2), 213–236.

Steiner, P. M., Cook, T. D., Shadish, W. R., & Clark, M. H. (2010). The importance of covariate selection in controlling for selection bias in observational studies. *Psychological Methods, 15*(3), 250–267.

Sterba, S. K. (2009). Alternative model-based and design-based frameworks for inference from samples to populations: From polarization to integration. *Multivariate Behavioral Research, 44*(6), 711–740.

Strobl, C., Boulesteix, A.-L., Zeileis, A., & Hothorn, T. (2007). Bias in random forest variable importance measures: Illustrations, sources and a solution. *BMC Bioinformatics, 8*(25), 1–25.

Strobl, C., Malley, J., & Tutz, G. (2009). An introduction to recursive partitioning: Rationale, application, and characteristics of classification and regression trees, bagging, and random forests. *Psychological Methods, 14,* 323–348.

Stuart, E. A. (2010). Matching methods for causal inference: A review and a look forward. *Statistical Science, 25*(1), 1–21.

Stuart, E. A., & Green, K. M. (2008). Using full matching to estimate causal effects in nonexperimental studies: Examining the relationship between adolescent marijuana use and adult outcomes. *Developmental Psychology, 44,* 395–406.

Stuart, E. A., & Rubin, D. B. (2007). Best practices in quasi-experimental designs: Matching methods for causal inference. In J. Osboarne (Ed.), *Best practices in quantitative methods* (pp. 155–176). Thousand Oaks, CA: Sage.

Su, Y.-S., Gelman, A., Hill, J., & Yajima, M. (2011). Multiple imputation with diagnostics (mi) in R: Opening windows into the black box. *Journal of Statistical Software, 45*(2), 1–31.

Takane, Y., & De Leeuw, J. (1987). On the relationship between item response theory and factor analysis of discretized variables. *Psychometrika, 52*(3), 393–408.

Talbot, D., Atherton, J., Rossi, A. M., Bacon, S. L., & Lefebvre, G. (2015). A cautionary note concerning the use of stabilized weights in marginal structural models. *Statistics in Medicine, 34*(5), 812–823.

Thoemmes, F. J., & Kim, E. S. (2011). A systematic review of propensity score methods in the social sciences. *Multivariate Behavioral Research, 46*(1), 90–118.

Thoemmes, F. J., & West, S. G. (2011). The use of propensity scores for nonrandomized designs with clustered data. *Multivariate Behavioral Research, 46*(3), 514–543.

U.S. Bureau of Labor Statistics. (2016). NLS Investigator. Retrieved March 6, 2016, from https://www.nlsinfo.org/investigator/pages/login.jsp

U.S. Department of Education. (2012). *Enhancing teaching and learning through educational data mining and learning analytics: An issue brief.* Washington, DC: Author.

U.S. Department of Education, Institute of Education Sciences, & What Works Clearinghouse. (2013). *What Works Clearinghouse: Procedures and standards handbook (Version 3.0).* Washington, DC: Author.

van Buuren, S. (2012). *Flexible imputation of missing data*. Boca Raton, FL: CRC Press.

van Buuren, S., & Oudshoorn, C. G. M. (2000). *Multivariate imputation by chained equations: MICE V1.0 user's manual*. Leiden: Netherlands Organization for Applied Scientific Research (TNO).

Van der Wal, W. M., & Geskus, R. B. (2011). ipw: An R package for inverse probability weighting. *Journal of Statistical Software, 43*(13), 1–23.

Watkins, S., Jonsson-Funk, M., Brookhart, M. A., Rosenberg, S. A., O'Shea, T. M., & Daniels, J. (2013). An empirical comparison of tree-based methods for propensity score estimation. *Health Services Research, 48*(5), 1798–1817.

West, S. G., & Thoemmes, F. (2010). Campbell's and Rubin's perspectives on causal inference. *Psychological Methods, 15*(1), 18–37.

Westreich, D., Lessler, J., & Funk, M. J. (2010). Propensity score estimation: Neural networks, support vector machines, decision trees (CART), and meta-classifiers as alternatives to logistic regression. *Journal of Clinical Epidemiology, 63*(8), 826–833.

White, I. R., Royston, P., & Wood, A. M. (2011). Multiple imputation using chained equations: Issues and guidance for practice. *Statistics in Medicine, 30*(4), 377–399.

Willis, G. B. (1999). *Cognitive interviewing: A "how to" guide*. Research Triangle Park, NC: Research Triangle Institute.

Wolter, K. M. (2007). *Introduction to variance estimation* (2nd ed.). New York, NY: Springer.

Wu, J.-Y., & Kwok, O.-M. (2012). Using SEM to analyze complex survey data: A comparison between design-based single-level and model-based multilevel approaches. *Structural Equation Modeling: A Multidisciplinary Journal, 19*(1), 16–35.

Yee, T. W. (2010). The VGAM package for categorical data analysis. *Journal of Statistical Software, 32*(10), 1–34.

Zeger, S. L., Liang, K. Y., & Albert, P. S. (1988). Models for longitudinal data: A generalized estimating equation approach. *Biometrics, 44*, 1049–1060.

Zuur, A. F., Ieno, E. N., Walker, N., Saveliev, A. A., & Smith, G. M. (2009). *Mixed effects models and extensions in ecology with R*. New York, NY: Springer.

• Index •

Abadie and Imbens matching
    estimator, 99–101
AdaBoost, 38–41
Amelia package, 28
Analysis stage, 147, 156
arm package, 34
Assumptions, 4
    methods for continuous
        treatments, 133
    methods for multiple
        treatments, 112
    stable unit treatment value,
        4, 112, 178
    strong ignorability of treatment
        assignment, 4, 5, 112,
        133, 178
    weak unconfoundedness,
        112, 133
Average treatment effect (ATE)
        estimation, 3–4
    marginal mean weighting through
        stratification, 80
    multilevel data analysis, 188–189
    multiple treatment effects,
        125–127
    propensity score matching, 93
    propensity score stratification,
        70, 77–79, 84
    propensity score weighting,
        47, 50, 54, 55, 118
    propensity score weighting for
        continuous treatments,
        141–143
    propensity score weighting with
        multilevel data, 184
    See also Treatment effect
        estimation
Average treatment effect on the
    treated (ATT) estimation, 3–4
    marginal mean weighting through
        stratification, 80
    propensity score matching,
        89, 93, 103–104
    propensity score stratification,
        70, 75, 77–79, 84

propensity score weighting, 47, 49,
    50, 54, 56–62
propensity score weighting with
    multilevel data, 184
See also Treatment effect
    estimation
Average treatment effect on the
    untreated (ATC), 3–4

Bagging, 35, 37
Balance of covariate distributions.
    See Covariate balance
    evaluation
base package, 43*t*, 67*t*, 85*t*
Bayesian additive regression trees, 41
Bayesian propensity score
    estimation, 45
Boosting algorithms, 38
Bootstrapped aggregation, 37
Bootstrapping methods, 57, 60
    propensity score matching, 104
    treatment effect estimation for
        multiple treatments, 127

Caliper matching, 9, 41–43, 92
Campbell's framework, 4–5
Causal model, 2–5
Classification trees, 30, 34–37,
    38–39, 40
Clustering effects, 32
    in longitudinal studies, 164
    logistic regression with fixed
        cluster effects, 182–184
    multiple treatment effects,
        126–127
    propensity score matching,
        99, 103, 104
    propensity score weighting, 49
    regression with cluster-robust
        standard errors, 170–172
Code editors, 15
Common support evaluation,
    41–45, 89, 116
Comparative fit index (CFI), 151–152
Complex survey data, 12–13

Comprehensive R Archive Network
    (CRAN), 14
Confirmatory factor analysis (CFA),
    149–152, 161
Continuous treatments, propensity
    score methods for, 131–132
    assumptions, 133
    covariate balance evaluation,
        133–134
    dose response function, 137–139
    example description, 132
    generalized propensity scores,
        131–139, 143
    summary of R packages and
        functions used, 143*t*
    treatment effect estimation,
        141–143
Convergence of propensity score
    estimation, 20, 117
Covariate balance evaluation, 6, 9–10,
    20, 33–34
    for continuous treatments,
        133–134
    for multiple treatments,
        120–121
    inverse probability weighting,
        140–143
    marginal mean weighting through
        stratification, 82–83
    multilevel data analysis, 185–186
    multiple treatments, weights
        from generalized boosted
        modeling, 121–122
    multiple treatments, weights
        from multinomial logistic
        regression, 120–121
    propensity score matching, 96–98
    propensity score stratification,
        76–77, 82–83
    propensity score weighting,
        53–55
    weighting methods for time-
        varying treatments, 169
Covariate balancing propensity score
    method, 45

Covariate measurement reliability, 23
Covariate selection, 21–25
Cross-validation approach,
    22–23

Data mining methods, 34–41, 116
    covariate balance for multiple
        treatments, 121–122
    estimation with multilevel
        data, 184
    generalized boosted modeling,
        30, 35, 38–41, 121–122, 184
    generalized propensity score
        estimation for multiple
        treatment conditions,
        116–118
    propensity score estimation, 30
    recursive partitioning algorithms,
        34–38
    See also specific methods
Data preparation, 7–8, 20*t*
    dealing with missing data, 7–8,
        25–30. *See also* Missing data
Design-based estimation, 12–13
Design stage, 2, 145–146
Discriminant function analysis, 30
Dose response function, 137–139
Doubly robust treatment effect
    estimation, 62–63, 84

Eclipse, 15
Extreme weights, 50–53, 168

Fixed ratio matching, 91
Full matching, 9, 96

geepack package, 173, 174*t*
Generalized boosted modeling (GBM),
    30, 35, 38–41, 116, 121–122, 184
Generalized estimating equations
    (GEEs), 172–174
Generalized Mahalanobis distance
    (GMD), 93–94
Generalized propensity scores, 112
    estimation with data mining
        methods, 116–118
    estimation with multinomial
        logistic regression, 113–116
    for continuous treatments,
        131–139, 143
Genetic matching, 9, 93–95, 101–103,
    154–155

Glass delta, 58
Greedy matching, 9, 48, 90–93

Hidden bias effects. *See* Sensitivity
    analysis
hlr package, 34
Hot-deck imputation, 25

Imputation methods, 25–30
    propensity score weighting, 60–61
Integrated development
    environments, 15
Internal validity, 5
Inverse probability-of-treatment
    weighting (IPTW), 47
    covariate balance evaluation, 169
    for continuous treatments,
        140–143
    for multiple treatments, 118–127
    multilevel data analysis, 184–186
    stabilized weights, 167–169
    time-varying treatments, 163–175
    See also Weighting
ipw package, 166, 174*t*
Item response theory (IRT), 161

Latent confounding variables,
    145–152, 161. *See also* Structural
    equation modeling (SEM),
    propensity score analysis with
lattice package, 41, 73, 115, 128*t*
lavaan package, 150, 159, 160*t*
Listwise deletion, 25
lme4 package, 181, 187, 189*t*
Log binomial model, 129
Logistic regression, propensity score
    estimation, 30–34, 40
    for multilevel data, 179–184
    for multiple treatments, 113–116,
        128–129
    propensity score weighting, 55
LogitBoost, 38
Longitudinal data, 44–45
    clustering effects and, 164
    weighting methods, 163–175
    See also Weighting, methods for
        time-varying treatments

Machine learning, 40
Marginal mean weighting through
    stratification (MMWS), 79–84,
    122–125, 174

Marginal structural models, 164
Marginal treatment effects
    multilevel data analysis, 180, 186
    propensity score stratification,
        70, 85
Matching, 8–9, 87–88, 90–93, 107–108
    analysis with SEM, 153–155
    caliper, 9, 41–43, 92
    clustering effects and, 99, 103, 104
    common support requirements,
        41–43, 89, 116
    covariate balance evaluation, 96–98
    example description, 88
    fixed ratio, 91
    for multiple treatments, 128
    full, 96
    genetic algorithm, 9, 93–95,
        101–103, 154–155
    greedy matching algorithm,
        9, 48, 90–93
    multilevel data analysis, 190
    nearest neighbor, 9, 92
    one-to-one, 91
    optimal, 95, 128
    propensity score estimation,
        88–89
    Rubin's causal model, 3
    sample size after, 87–88
    sensitivity analysis, 105–106
    summary of R packages and
        functions used, 106–107*t*
    treatment effect estimation,
        99–104
    variable-ratio, 91–92
    weighting approach, 48
    weighting versus, 108
    with or without replacement,
        91, 104, 107
Matching package, 15, 93–94,
    97, 100–101, 106–107*t*
MatchIt package, 10, 15, 75, 76,
    85*t*, 92, 95, 97, 102, 106*t*,
    154, 160*t*
Maximum-likelihood estimation,
    12, 31, 159
Measurement error, controlling
    for latent confounding
    variables, 146
Mediation and moderation
    estimation, 162
Mediators, 22
mice package, 15, 28, 43*t*, 60

Missing data
  classification tree algorithms, 37
  data preparation step, 7–8
  dummy indicators for logistic
    regression, 31
  methods for dealing with, 25–30
  recursive partitioning algorithms
    and, 34, 37
  R packages for dealing with, 15, 28
  weighting with multiple imputed
    data sets, 60–61
mitools package, 30, 43*t*, 60–61, 67*t*
Model-based estimation, 12–13
Multilevel data, propensity score
    methods with, 177–179, 189–190
  assumptions, 178
  covariate balance evaluation,
    185–186
  data mining methods, 184
  example description, 179
  individual versus cluster level
    treatment assignment, 178
  logistic regression with fixed
    cluster effects, 182–184
  marginal treatment effects,
    180, 186
  multilevel logistic regression,
    179–182
  propensity score estimation,
    179–184
  propensity score matching, 190
  propensity score weighting,
    184–186
  sampling approaches, 177
  summary of R packages and
    functions used, 189*t*
  treatment effect estimation,
    186–189
Multilevel logistic regression,
    179–182
Multinomial logistic regression,
    113–116, 120–121
Multiple-group structural equation
    models, 149–162. *See also*
    Structural equation modeling
    (SEM), propensity score analysis
    with
Multiple imputation (MI), 25–30
  propensity score weighting,
    60–61
Multiple-indicator and multiple-
    causes models, 158–159

Multiple treatments, propensity
    score methods for, 111–112,
    128–129
  assumptions, 112
  common support
    requirements, 116
  covariate balance evaluation,
    120–122
  example description, 112–113
  generalized propensity score
    estimation using data mining
    methods, 116–118
  generalized propensity score
    estimation using multinomial
    logistic regression,
    113–116
  generalized propensity scores, 112
  log binomial model, 129
  logistic regression, 128–129
  marginal mean weighting through
    stratification, 122–125
  pairwise subgroup matching, 128
  propensity score weighting,
    118–127
  summary of R packages and
    functions used, 128*t*
  treatment effect estimation,
    125–127

Nearest neighbor matching, 9, 92
Network flow theory, 9, 95
Neural networks, 184
nlme package, 187
Non-response weights, 13
Normalizing weights, 13

Observational studies, 1–2
One-to-one matching, 91
Optimal matching, 9, 95, 128
optmatch package, 15
Outcome proxies, 22–23

party package, 35, 37, 43*t*
Poststratification weights,
    13, 79–80
Potential outcomes framework, 2–3
Principal stratification, 4
Probit regression, 30
Propensity score(s), 2, 5–6
  generalized, 112. *See also*
    Generalized propensity
    scores

Propensity score analysis, overview,
    1–2
  assumptions, 4
  Campbell's framework and threats
    to validity, 4–5
  complex survey data, 12–13
  example description, 6
  propensity scores, 5–6
  R packages, 15
  Rubin's causal model, 2–4
  steps, 6–11
Propensity score analysis, with
    structural equation models.
    See Structural equation
    modeling (SEM), propensity
    score analysis with
Propensity score estimation, 8, 45–56
  analysis stage, 147, 156
  analysis with SEM, 152–153
  Bayesian methods, 45
  convergence, 20, 117
  covariate selection, 21–25
  data mining methods, 30, 34–41
  design stage, 2, 145–146
  ensemble methods, 34–35
  evaluation of common support,
    41–45, 89
  example description, 20–21
  generalized boosted modeling,
    38–41
  logistic regression, 30–34, 40, 55
  multilevel data, 179–184
  parametric models, 30
  propensity score matching, 88–89
  propensity score stratification, 71–73
  recursive partitioning algorithms,
    34–38
  steps, 20*t*
  success criteria, 6, 20, 33–34.
    See also Covariate balance
    evaluation
  summary of R packages and
    functions used, 43*t*
  true confounders, 21–22, 31, 45
Propensity score matching. *See*
    Matching
Propensity score stratification.
    See Stratification
Propensity score weighting.
    See Weighting
Pseudo-maximum-likelihood
    estimation, 12, 159

QQ-plots, 10

R
dealing with missing data,
15, 28
packages for propensity score
analysis, 15
resources for learning, 14–15
See also specific packages
Raking weights, 13
Random forest algorithms, 30, 35,
37–38, 40, 116, 184
rbounds package, 105
Recursive partitioning algorithms,
34–38, 116. *See also* Data
mining methods; *specific
algorithms*
Regression imputation, 25
Regression trees, 34–35,
38–39, 116
Reliability of covariate
measurement, 23
Research design validity, 4–5
Root mean square error of
approximation (RMSEA),
151–152
RStudio, 15
Rubin's causal model, 2–4

Sample size
after matching, 87
imputation methods
and, 25
Sampling multilevel data, 177
Sampling weights, 13, 48
covariate balance evaluation, 53
extreme weights, 51
See also Weighting
Sensitivity analysis, 11
propensity score matching,
105–106
propensity score weighting,
63–66
Stabilized weights, 52–53, 167–169
Stable unit treatment value
assumption (SUTVA),
4, 112, 178
Standardized mean differences, 10
stats package, 67*t*, 106*t*,
143*t*, 189*t*
Steps of propensity score analysis,
6–11

Stratification, 9, 69–70, 74–76, 85
common support requirements,
41, 116
covariate balance evaluation,
76–77, 82–83
doubly robust treatment effect
estimation, 84
example description, 70–71
marginal mean weighting through
stratification, 79–84,
122–125, 174
marginal treatment effects, 70, 85
mediation and moderation
estimation, 162
poststratification weights,
13, 79–80
propensity score estimation, 71–73
Rubin's causal model, 3
summary of R packages and
functions used, 85
treatment effect estimation, 77–79,
83–84
weighting approach, 48
Strong ignorability of treatment
assignment assumption, 4, 5
multilevel data analysis, 178
weak unconfoundedness
assumption versus,
112, 133
Structural equation modeling (SEM),
propensity score analysis with,
145–147, 161–162
example description, 147
example latent confounding
variables, 147
multiple-group confirmatory factor
analysis, 149–152, 161
multiple-indicator and multiple-
causes models, 158–159
propensity score estimation,
152–153
propensity score matching,
153–155
propensity score weighting, 155
summary of R packages and
functions used, 160*t*
treatment effect estimation,
156–158
survey package, 15, 30, 32–33,
43*t*, 52, 61, 67*t*, 78, 85*t*, 107*t*,
126, 128*t*, 140, 143*t*, 171,
174*t*, 189*t*

Taylor series linearization, 57, 59–60,
126, 171
Time-varying treatments, weighting
methods for, 163–175. *See also*
Weighting, methods for time-
varying treatments
Tinn-R, 15
Treatment assignment, ignorability
assumption, 4, 5, 112, 133, 178
Treatment assignment, multilevel
data design considerations, 178
Treatment effect estimation, 11
causes of bias, 2
complex survey data and, 12–13
continuous treatments, 131–132.
See also Continuous
treatments, propensity score
methods for
generalized propensity scores
for multiple treatment
conditions, 112–118
marginal mean weighting through
stratification, 83–84, 122–125
multilevel data analysis, 186–189
multiple-group structural equation
models, 156–158
multiple-indicator and multiple-
causes models, 158–159
multiple treatment effects,
111–112, 125–127. *See
also* Multiple treatments,
propensity score methods for
propensity score matching,
99–104
propensity score stratification,
77–79, 83–84
propensity score stratification,
doubly robust estimation, 84
propensity score weighting,
56–60
propensity score weighting, doubly
robust estimation, 62–63
Rubin's causal model, 3
time-varying treatments, 163–164,
170–174. *See also* Weighting,
methods for time-varying
treatments
types of treatment effects, 3–4
weighting for continuous
treatments, 141–143
treatSens package, 64–66, 67*t*
True confounders, 21–22, 31, 45

Tucker-Lewis index (TLI), 151–152
twang package, 10, 15, 38, 39, 43*t*, 53, 85*t*, 116, 118, 120, 121, 128*t*, 155, 160*t*, 169, 174*t*, 189*t*

Validity of research designs, 4–5
Variable-ratio matching, 91–92
Variance ratio, 10
VGAM package, 128*t*

Weak unconfoundedness assumption, 112, 133
Weighted least squares (WLS) estimation, 58
Weighting, 9, 47–48, 67–68
  analysis with SEM, 155
  common support requirements, 41
  complex survey data and, 12–13
  continuous treatment effects, 131–132
  covariate balance evaluation, 53–55
  doubly robust treatment effect estimation, 62–63
  example description, 48–49
  extreme weights, 50–53, 168
  for multiple treatments, 140–143

marginal mean weighting through stratification, 79–84, 122–125, 174
matching and stratification methods and, 48
matching versus, 108
multilevel data analysis, 184–186
multiple imputed data sets, 60–61
normalizing weights, 13
poststratification, 13, 79–80
regression with cluster-robust standard errors, 170–172
Rubin's causal model, 3
sensitivity analysis, 63–66
stabilized weights, 52–53, 167–169
summary of R packages and functions used, 67*t*
treatment effect estimation, 56–60
treatment effect estimation with multiple-indicator and multiple-causes models, 158–159
weight calculation, 49–53
See also Inverse probability-of-treatment weighting

Weighting, for multiple treatments, 118–127
  covariate balance with weights from generalized boosted modeling, 121–122
  covariate balance with weights from multinomial logistic regression, 120–121
Weighting, methods for time-varying treatments, 163–167, 174
  covariate balance evaluation, 169
  example description, 164
  generalized estimating equations, 172–174
  marginal mean weighting through stratification, 174
  regression with cluster-robust standard errors, 170–172
  stabilized weights, 167–169
  summary of R packages and functions used, 174*t*
  treatment effect estimation, 170–174
What Works Clearinghouse, 108
Wilcoxon signed-rank test, 11